THE EDUCATION
OF
PRIVATE URISH

An Infantry Replacement in World War II

Army Serial # 36 909 179
Military Occupation Specialty 604-Light Machine Gunner

EARL L. URISH

For Dorothy
whose unfailing love and quiet courage have made life more radiant for Julie and for me

U & U Publications

4430 Shay Road

Green Valley, IL 61534

Copyright © 2000 by Earl L. Urish

Manufactured in the United States of America

Library of Congress Card Number:

ISBN 0-9715350-0-0

Excerpts from this book have previously been published in *The Voice of the Angels,* the official publication of the 11th Airborne Division Association.

CONTENTS

INTRODUCTION   5

PREAMBLE: ONE BITTER DAY IN SOUTHERN LUZON

I. GREEN VALLEY AND CAMP HOOD   11
II. FT. ORD AND CAMP STONEMAN   37
III. THE PACIFIC   40
IV. LEYTE AND LUZON   46
V. 11th AIRBORNE   51
VI. MT. MACOLOD   60
VII. MALEPUNYO MASSIF   70
VIII. MACOLOD REVISITED   79
IX. TIAONG AND TANAUAN   89
X. LIPA   104
XI. THE REPLACEMENT CONUNDRUM   118
XII. MANILA   124
XIII. REGROUP   140
XIV. OKINAWA AND JAPAN   148
XV. ATSUGI AND YOKOHAMA   164
XVI. SENDAI AND HONSHU   180
XVII. HOKKAIDO AND HOME   202

EPILOGUE   232

REFERENCES AND BIBLIOGRAPHY   235

MAPS
  LUZON TO JAPAN   163
  OCCUPIED NORTHERN JAPAN   182

ACKNOWLEDGMENTS

While the support and encouragement of many individuals helped make this book possible, two people have been essential in getting the project underway and seeing it to completion.

In 1995, following an exchange of letters, Lt. Gen. E.M.Flanagan, Jr.—author of the official history of the 11th Airborne Division and *The Rakkasans;The Combat History of the 187th Airborne*—encouraged me to record my involvement in World War II. The General was kind enough to read my original manuscript and to urge me to publish it.

Dorothy, my wife and partner through many a difficult day, has helped in many ways to see this project through to completion—editing and proofreading, and most of all, understanding when I seemed to be reliving the war years.

Among others who have made major contributions are:

Jim Conover, retired police detective, author and friend, who rendered valuable assistance, offering a number of suggestions that have made this a better book. Carol Kreiling and Bill and June Adams read and commented on an early version.

Norman Petersen, who shared many of the experiences recorded in the book, read and approved my account of those days.

Alan Harkrader, fellow paratrooper in the 11th Airborne Division, veteran of several wars, newspaperman and editor, has ably handled the jacket design and the graphics.

Introduction

From 1936 to 1945 English anthropologist Tom Harrison set up a network of observers to record the views of a cross section of British citizens on a wide range of subjects. The result, the Mass Observation Archive, contains many first hand accounts of events that occurred during the World War II aerial bombardment of Britain by the German Luftwaffe. These accounts were written immediately after the event and can, therefore, be accepted as reasonably accurate. Some thirty years later a number of the surviving mass observers were asked to recount these same wartime experiences. In every case the relationship between the original and the version recalled thirty years later was so remote as to be almost coincidental. Yet, but for the original written evidence, their oral testimony in regard to the incidents would have been accepted as eminently reliable. Assuming that the findings of this study are applicable wherever and whenever men and women attempt to recall events long past, it appears obvious that the reader or listener would do well to be wary of accepting any undocumented recollections as being highly accurate.

With this caveat in mind, I have set about recounting my army experiences during and after World War II. Several chance happenings prompted me to commit these events to paper. One was the Gulf War. A large army of American combat troops was waiting in the desert for the order to attack Saddam Hussein's Iraqi army. My thoughts wandered back some fifty years to the time when so many of us of my generation had been asked to put our lives on the line.

About this time I had been examining the personal effects of my recently deceased father. Among the items in his desk was a box containing the letters I had written home from the far reaches of the Pacific during my nineteen months overseas. Here also were the letters from my older brother who had served at that same time in the Pacific Fleet aboard the cruiser *Pittsburgh*. My curiosity piqued, I looked up my copy of our division's history. *The Angels: A History of the 11th Airborne Division* had been published several years after World War II ended. Reading it carefully for the first time, I noticed an error in the date my replacement group had joined the division.

By coincidence, I had recently read a book narrating the airborne capture of Corregidor during the Philippine Campaign of WW II. The author was Lt. Gen. E.M.Flanagan, Jr (Retired). Here must be the Captain "Fly" Flanagan who had commanded an artillery battery in the 11th Airborne Division during combat in WW II and had written the Division history shortly after the war ended. He was now a retired three-star general, having served his country well through a long and distinguished Army career. I wrote to the General who proved to be both genial and generous as he encouraged me to record my memories of World War II. General Flanagans's history of the 11th Airborne Division has been invaluable in keeping my narrative on track and in verifying my recollection of many events.

Initially, this story was to be an account of one young man's tour of duty during World War II. The personal experiences did not occur in a vacuum, however. To give them meaning, I have attempted, within the limits of my knowledge and ability, to place them in context with the cataclysmic events of those years.

Preamble: One Bitter Day in Southern Luzon

Good Friday, March 30, 1945--Walt Lepley was out of action with a severe case of jungle rot, and Bill Bannon had been evacuated with a bullet wound, so our light machine gun squad was down to four. As part of rifle Company E of the 11th Airborne Division's 187th Parachute and Glider Infantry Regiment, we were deployed in southern Luzon near the recently destroyed city of Lipa. The immediate task of the regiment was to push the Japanese out of artillery range of the Manila-Batangas highway and back into their Mt. Malepunyo mountain fortress. The other battalion of the 187th was on a separate mission so our force consisted of Regimental Headquarters and 2nd Battalion, now down to half strength—less than 350 men---after taking heavy losses during the drive on Manila and in our recent battles in southern Luzon.

When this task force moved out on Good Friday morning, Sergeant Denny Faye, our squad leader, was carrying a carbine and a can of machine gun ammunition; first gunner Petersen was carrying the machine gun tripod, his M1 Garand rifle, and a can of ammo; I was second gunner carrying the machine gun and a can of ammo; and Feling—a young Filipino who had hooked up with the squad as the 11th Airborne Division battled through his hometown on the road to Manila--was at my side carrying my M1 rifle, his own M1, and an extra machine gun barrel.

The regiment was drawn up in a skirmish line facing a large area of open fields with the foothills beginning to rise a mile away and Mt.Malepunyo looming darkly in the distance. The fields to our immediate front--crisscrossed with many small irrigation ditches--lay fallow and dry in this early springtime.

As we moved forward, the squad passed through a plot of soybeans. The beans had matured months earlier but had never been harvested. I was thinking that the plot was not going to yield very much by Illinois Corn Belt standards when my daydreaming was violently interrupted by a high-pitched whining sound followed immediately by an eardrum-bursting explosion. Just up the skirmish line three men disappeared in a cloud of smoke and dust. Reacting automatically, all of the troopers immediately hit the dirt. Incoming Jap artillery shells were exploding all along our skirmish line.

The men near the irrigation ditches jumped in, seeking shelter from the storm of shrapnel that was engulfing the field. About the width of a man, the nearest ditches were filled with several layers of men as the shells kept roaring in. Our squad was in the middle of an open field so we could only hug the ground and pray. An order came down to pull back. A stream bank that offered our best chance for survival was over half-a-mile to the rear. Between explosions we started to run the gauntlet of incoming shells. When a whistle or a roar indicated another incoming round, those men close enough to the irrigation ditches would jump in while the rest of us tried to press ourselves into the ground. In fields that had been leveled for irrigation, there were no low spots to seek for protection. The heavy volume of exploding shells indicated that the Japanese artillerymen were working a large number of guns at maximum speed.

As we hit the ground each time, I held the machine gun in front of me for whatever little protection it might afford. In addition to the fear and terror of the moment, there was the feeling of frustration and helplessness at being unable to strike back at our unseen tormentors.

While the riflemen assisted the wounded, Feling and I stayed a little way behind and gathered their weapons. I could sling these over my shoulder and still carry the machine gun. Through all of this, Feling stuck close by my side. When we finally made it back to the comparative safety of the stream bank, we had the machine gun, six M1 rifles, a carbine, and a Tommy Gun. I had jettisoned my box of machine gun ammo in order to carry more weapons.

While we lay along the steep stream bank catching our breath, I could see the battalion commander, Major Ewing, and his radio operator a few yards away. The major was scanning the lower slopes of Mt. Malepunyo through his field glasses and calmly attempting to give our division artillery batteries the position of the Japanese guns. He was speaking in a loud, clear voice, liberally reinforced with profane and obscene expletives that seemed proper for the occasion. Whether the Japanese artillerymen started receiving counter-battery fire or, perhaps, thought they could still keep their location secret, they ceased firing about the time our men made it back to the shelter of the stream bank.

The 187th had located the massed Japanese artillery batteries the hard way. We had walked directly into their field of fire. Our task force had suffered heavy casualties. Easy Company strength was now probably below the sixty-five men it had fallen to before my replacement group arrived. Potts, one of four of us in Company E who had trained together in the same platoon at Camp Hood, had been killed while running across those rice paddies. Shrapnel had sheared his head from his body.

Feling was still at my side, so we started to check our equipment. Shrapnel had damaged my rifle as Feling ran with it across that bloody field. A jagged three-inch shard of shrapnel had split the hard walnut stock and was still embedded where it had struck. No problem there. We had five more M1s, a carbine, and a Thompson submachine gun, all in working order. The machine gun was undamaged, but at this point we had no ammunition belts. Missing items included the spare gun barrel and the asbestos glove we used to handle the gun when it became hot from continuous firing. Petersen and the tripod were nowhere in sight.

The regiment was in a good defensive position along the steep stream bank in case the Japs had any plans for a counterattack. When it became obvious that they did not, orders came down for the regiment to regroup in a nearby wooded area. Petersen was there and unscathed, still carrying the tripod but no ammo belts. We soon found some ammo, cleaned and oiled the gun, and were back in business as a machine gun squad.

During the shelling, Pete had almost reached the riverbank when he heard the whine of yet another incoming round. Rather than hitting the dirt, he took one more huge running step and dived head first over the edge of the steep bank. The shell exploded just where Pete would have been, had he hit the dirt.

Hoping to take advantage of some enticing shade, we set the machine gun up under a large tropical tree. We quickly discovered that this tree was the home of a vast colony of big red voracious ants that were soon biting us wherever possible. We were forced to move the gun out into the blistering sunlight or risk being eaten alive.

Division Commander General Joe Swing came storming through the area exhorting the troops, "We're going back up there and get those little yellow bastards!" A trooper near me muttered, "You go ahead, Joe. We already been up there." Not loud enough for Joe to hear, though. Joe was right, of course. We would go back up there and get them, but it wouldn't be this day.

As we dug in for the night, a shot rang out a short distance up the perimeter. One of the replacements had shot himself in the foot with a carbine. He was another member of the platoon I had trained with at Camp Hood. My first reaction was one of anger. How dare he wound himself to get out of this Hell? What if we all took this coward's way out? After this first burst of emotion, I reminded myself that he and Potts had been the closest of buddies. To see your best friend's head chopped off by shrapnel and rolling across a dry rice paddy like a bloody basketball could send anyone over the edge. And possibly I was wrong. He could have shot himself in the foot accidentally. "Judge not that ye be not judged."

There was bright moonlight that night. When my turn for sentry duty came, I awoke somewhat bleary-eyed from fatigue and fitful sleep. Upon taking my position behind the machine gun, I immediately looked the field of fire over carefully, this being standard operating procedure. To my surprise, about eighty yards to our front under a large tree, there appeared to be a Japanese soldier bending over what must be a knee mortar. I shook Pete awake and pointed out what I had seen. He thought he saw it, too. We agreed that, on the count of three, we would cut the Jap down with our M1s. One, two, three, Crack! Two rifles fired at the same instant. The smoke cleared. We peered ahead and there was that damned Jap, still bending over. Apparition? Hallucination? Shadows? Who knows what tricks the mind may play? A few hours earlier we had survived another horrendous, mind-shattering day. Being caught in the open by a concentrated artillery bombardment may be the most terrible experience in the whole madness of infantry warfare. When daylight came, I checked the tree the Jap had been crouching under. I found two bullet holes just six inches apart. That was all.

We cleaned and oiled our weapons and equipment that morning, then worked at improving the perimeter defenses. The company sent out reconnaissance patrols in the afternoon—probably as much to keep the troopers occupied as anything, I decided. It would not be good for morale if we had a lot of idle time to think about recent events. But in the dark of the night my mind wandered back over the years our country had been at war with Japan and Germany, and I wondered at the manner in which the Fates had conspired to transport me from the peaceful fields of central Illinois to this killing ground in the Philippines, half a world away.

The following is an account of that uncertain odyssey.

Chapter I Green Valley and Camp Hood

> Beat! beat! drums!—blow! bugles! blow!
> Through the windows—through doors—burst like a ruthless force,
> Into the solemn church, and scatter the congregation,
> Into the school where the scholar is studying;
> Leave not the bridegroom quiet—no happiness must he have now with his bride,
> Nor the peaceful farmer any peace, ploughing his field or gathering his grain,
> So fierce you whirr and pound you drums—so shrill you bugles blow.
>
> ---Walt Whitman, 1861, as the Civil War began.

At 11:15 on the morning of Dec. 8, 1941, Principal John Arthur Jones summoned the eighty students and four faculty members of Green Valley High School to the study hall that also served as the school's assembly room. From a radio at the front of the room, the resonant voice of President Franklin Delano Roosevelt filled the room. It was a voice familiar to the group, heard many times during radio addresses and "fireside chats" as FDR led the people of the United States out of the depths of the Great Depression. But on this momentous occasion the President's voice had an unusually somber tone as he addressed the Congress and the Nation: "I ask that the Congress declare that since the unprovoked and dastardly attack by Japan on Sunday, Dec. 7th, 1941, a state of war has existed between the United States and the Japanese Empire."

The President spoke for only six minutes. In the interest of national security there was much that he could not reveal to his listeners. The previous day, beginning at 7:55 AM Honolulu time, 353 Japanese warplanes had roared over Pearl Harbor and Oahu, bombing, torpedoing, and strafing American ships, aircraft, and military installations. The magnitude of the damage inflicted upon the American armed forces during this sneak attack was shocking.

Before flying the 275 miles back to their waiting carriers, the Japanese airmen had killed 2,403 Americans; sank or crippled 18 ships, 9 of them battleships; and destroyed 347 army and navy aircraft--all for a loss of only 39 Japanese planes.
As they listened to the President, the eighteen members of the Green Valley High Class of 1942 could scarcely dream how the ensuing conflict would alter their lives. When that bloody war ended on Aug. 15, 1945, ten of the thirteen boys in the class had served in the armed forces and two had died in battle. A member of this senior class, I had just turned sixteen on Nov. 28 and continued to make plans to enter the University of Illinois the following fall. That summer I suffered several seizures--one serious enough to require a brief hospital stay. Dr. Allen, the local physician, diagnosed the problem as polio. Fortunately, he was wrong. Being thrown from a horse earlier in the year--an event not reported to my parents--was undoubtedly a factor.

The year following the Japanese attack on Pearl Harbor was marked by reverses for America and her allies. The war news we followed so closely on radio and in the newspapers was far from encouraging. The Japanese ran rampant in the Far East, overrunning Hong Kong, Indo-China, the East Indies, Malaya, Burma, the Philippines, and the islands of the western Pacific. The Imperial Navy destroyed an Allied fleet in the Battle of the Java Sea and sailed uncontested into the Indian Ocean. By midsummer the Japanese reached the apogee of their empire when they occupied Attu and Kiska islands in the Aleutian chain off Alaska, reached India on the Asian continent, penetrated the Solomon Islands in the South Pacific, and crossed the Owen Stanley Mountains of New Guinea.
In May 1942, in the Battle of the Coral Sea, the Allies turned back a Japanese invasion fleet bound for Port Moresby, New Guinea, located only one hundred miles north of the Australian continent. Then, on June 4 at the Battle of Midway, aircraft from the U.S.Navy Carrier Task Force sank four Japanese aircraft carriers, part of a huge Japanese armada sent to conquer Midway Island and threaten the nearby Hawaiian Islands. In one afternoon the gallant U.S.Navy airmen turned the tide in the Pacific war, inflicting irrecoverable losses in carriers and pilots upon the Japanese Imperial Navy. It was the first decisive victory for the Allies.

Despite this encouraging sign that better days would come, the late summer of 1942 was the low point of the war for the Allies. In North Africa, Rommel, after a stunning victory at Tobruk, had driven his Afrika Korps deep into Egypt and was threatening the Suez Canal and the Middle East. In the Soviet Union, Axis forces crossed the Russian steppes, reached Stalingrad on the Volga, and penetrated into the oil fields of the Caucasus. In the Battle of the Atlantic, German submarines operated with impunity to the east coast of the United States and into the Gulf of Mexico, sinking Allied ships faster than they could be replaced.

In late summer MacArthur's forces tenuously grasped the initiative on New Guinea, and on Aug.7 U.S. Marines landed on Guadalcanal and seized an airfield the Japanese were constructing. The marines, the sailors, and the soldiers had set out on the long and bloody course to final victory in the Pacific.

By August of 1942 I had recovered from my baffling illness and, along with two of my high school classmates, Oliver Olivero and Arvin Hilst, I enrolled at the University of Illinois. We rented a room near the campus, and Arvin and I secured meal jobs in the kitchen of a sorority.

Throughout grade school and high school I had been the youngest and smallest boy in my class and, with no discernible talent in either athletics or music, had been fortunate in being able to take the time to indulge my love of reading. This affection for the printed word was not confined to matters relating to the courses in which I was enrolled. The broad smattering of knowledge thus acquired would now provide some benefit; I was able to pass the proficiency exam offered in English Rhetoric I and move directly to Rhetoric II. A few days later I did the same in the required Hygiene I course and became one of the very few among the incoming freshman class to proficiency out of both courses. This gave my self-confidence a needed boost as, at the age of sixteen, I moved from an eighty-student rural high school to a university with an enrollment of 20,000.

During the first week of my college career I walked into what I thought was the university library, looked around, and inquired as to where the books were. I was informed by a smiling co-ed that they were one block west in the university library, definitely not in Smith Music Hall where we were standing.

My roommates and I settled into the routine of a campus where wartime austerity was the order of the day. The armed services were much in evidence. Soldiers and sailors were on campus for training in everything from diesel engineering to cooking and baking. A Navy signal school had been set up at the north end of the campus in the Men's Old Gymnasium and Annex. The sailors trained on Illini Field and the luxurious Illini Union Ballroom served as their mess hall. A Navy V-12 program unit was housed in the women's residence halls. An Army Specialized Training Program (ASTP) was in operation. These high IQ men were in the Army, drew private's pay and allowances, did not wear uniforms, and were studying courses such as engineering and foreign languages. Any of these bright young men who thought that ASTP meant All Safe Till Peace were in for a rude awakening. In the not too distant future, when the Army became hard pressed for manpower, the program was drastically curtailed and a luckless majority of these over-achieving scholars was shunted into the infantry to become replacements overseas. They worked out an equation to explain their fate: ASTP +O (ORDERS)=TS (TOUGH SITUATION?) + APO (ARMY POST OFFICE). APO was the address of all soldiers overseas.

    For male university students, ROTC (Reserve Officers Training Corps) and physical fitness were being stressed. In Physical Education, I enrolled in swimming my first semester and in wrestling the second. These skills were to prove invaluable during the coming years.

    During registration I checked on the branches of the service being offered in ROTC and found that the Cavalry was one of the choices. Upon inquiring further, I was informed that the Army maintained a sizeable stable of horses at the university. We had always kept several purebred American Saddle horses at home for pleasure and for handling livestock, and I fancied myself a pretty fair horseman. So what could be better than an occasional canter about the campus? Many, many things, I soon learned.

    My fellow would-be horse soldiers and I quickly discovered that, as budding cavalrymen, we had four times the equipment to polish and shine as the students enrolled in the other services. And even worse, as my schedule worked out, I had cavalry drill Friday afternoons until 3:00 followed immediately by my English Rhetoric II class. So I would arrive at this class fresh from riding and tramping about in horse manure. The prim young lady who taught the course was something less than delighted. She immediately worked out a seating arrangement that placed me in the far corner of the room next to a window. Late in the semester the Army shipped the horses to Ft. Riley, Kansas. I was not too dismayed. My Rhetoric instructor breathed a sigh of relief.

Adding to the uniqueness of the autumn of 1942, on Sept. 25 the earliest measurable snow in Central Illinois Weather Bureau history fell on Champaign-Urbana. When I emerged from the depths of a chemistry laboratory at 4:00 in the afternoon, the grass and trees were covered with several inches of wet, heavy snow. The dominant foliage color that fall was black.

About midyear the Army came up with a program known as the Enlisted Reserve Corps—a plan designed specifically for men in college. Under this ERC program students signed up for the service of their choice with the implied understanding that they would be allowed to complete the school year. My roommates chose the Army Air Corps. At mid-semester, having signed up practically all of the eligible male students, Uncle Sam beckoned, and they were gone. So much for promises from your recruiting officer. As they packed their bags, there was some debate among the ERC members as to which finger Uncle Sam had used to beckon them.

Too young to join the ERC without parental consent, I continued my studies on a much less populous campus. The wholesale induction of the Enlisted Reserve Corps had seriously depleted the male student population. I arrived at several of my agriculture classes to find that there were only three or four students remaining. The section of an accountancy course in which I was enrolled was closed out. I completed the course by meeting with Professor Broussard once a week in his aerie of an office on the top floor of the Business Administration Building. He would check my completed problems, assign work for the coming week, and then tell me of the problems his wife was having with her home nursery school. Having garnered bonus points for being a sympathetic listener, I received an A in the accountancy course.

The work force at the sorority where I had a meal job was badly depleted. Mrs. Campbell, the cook and general provisioner, had started the school year with four waiters, three dishwashers, and two kitchen helpers. This work force included three Pre-meds, three Aggies, two Liberal Arts scholars, and one Journalism student. We finished the fall semester with a 4.5 scholastic grade average out of a possible 5. The young ladies in the sorority managed to attain a 3.5. When the ERC departed, the work force was reduced from nine down to four. Unable to recruit more help, Mrs. Campbell streamlined the service, and several of us became waiters as well as kitchen help.

As our winter gradually gave way to the spring of 1943, it was apparent from the news that the Allies had wrested the initiative from the Axis powers. The battle for North Africa was reaching its climax in Tunisia. In the cold, fog-shrouded Aleutians off Alaska, infantrymen were digging out the last Japanese on Attu. British and American air forces, in the face of heavy losses in bomber crews and aircraft, were intensifying the bombing of Germany and occupied Europe. Soviet troops, following their pivotal victory at Stalingrad, were locked in a colossal struggle with Hitler's armies. In July the two armies would clash at Kursk where two million men, 6,000 tanks, and 5,000 aircraft would fight the greatest tank battle in history.

The U.S.Navy was engaging the enemy all across the vast Pacific and cooperating with the British Royal Navy to win the Battle of the Atlantic. American submariners were destroying Japanese ships at an ever-increasing rate. Marines, after their hard won victory on Guadalcanal, were preparing to move up the chain of the Solomon Islands and to attack the fortified atolls in the mid-Pacific. American and Australian forces in MacArthur's SouthWest Pacific Theater had won the bloody Buna-Gona-Sanananda battle and were leapfrogging up the coast of New Guinea. The tide had turned, slowly but inexorably. Unfortunately, the heaviest American casualties were yet to come.

U.S. factories, shipyards, farms and mines were producing the tools and goods of war in unprecedented quantities. American arms output increased more than eightfold from 1941 to 1943 bringing the Allied total to three times that of the Axis powers. The United States produced 5800 aircraft in 1939; 13,000 in 1940; 26,000 in 1941; 48,000 in 1942; 88,000 in 1943; and peaked at 96,000 in 1944.

Also on the home front, on June 1, 1942, when wage negotiations broke down 500,000 coal miners went on strike. On Jan. 18, 1943, a ban on the sale of sliced bread went into effect, aimed at reducing bakeries' demand for steel replacement parts.

There was widespread flooding in the Midwest during the spring of 1943. My brother, John, was at home helping with the farming--a livestock and grain operation that required two men. When the Illinois National Guard was activated at the outset of the war, an Illinois State Guard was formed, and John had joined. In April the local guard company was called out to help build up the floodwall at Beardstown, a small, historic city threatened with destruction by the rampaging Illinois River. I convinced Dean Huddleson that I was needed at home to help plant corn and soybeans. He allowed me to leave the university a few days early.

When the river level dropped, John returned from Beardstown and began working for a neighboring farmer, where he would be paid. A few months later he enlisted in the Navy. Our older brother, Wayne, had joined the Navy a year earlier. Wayne had attempted to enlist in the Marine Corps shortly after Pearl Harbor but was underage, and our parents had refused to sign the required papers.

I worked on the farm for the next year. When John received a medical discharge from the Navy and got a job at Caterpillar Tractor Company in nearby East Peoria, I decided that it was my turn to go into the service. Had John not been discharged from the Navy, I undoubtedly would have spent the remainder of the war on the farm--the dutiful son, needed at home. Now I would not be leaving Dad in the lurch as John could help with the farming.

When farm deferment forms came to be filled out and returned to the draft board, I threw them away, much to my father's dismay. After a lengthy, serious, and sometimes heated discussion, he sighed and said, "I'm not going to fight you on this any more if you think you have to go, but, believe me, there are going to be a lot of days when you will wish you had listened to me." Old John N. was a great deal wiser than I gave him credit for at the time.

All things considered, Dad's reluctance to have his three sons go off to war should not have been unexpected. His ancestors had left the Old World hoping to escape the militarism of Europe. Great Great Grandfather George Urish--Georg Uhrig before the name was Americanized--had emigrated from the Odenwald area in the German principality of Hesse-Darmstadt during the summer of 1831. Georg had taken his family and fled from the hodgepodge of German sovereignties of that day so that his sons could not be conscripted or impressed into some princeling's army, to be hired out for the profit of their royal ruler and forced to fight as mercenaries in wars in which they had nothing at stake. This had happened to young Hessians too often.

The land that Georg and Anna Eva Wyhrick Uhrig and their two small children left behind had a long and troubled history. Julius Caesar in his *Commentaries* described the Germanic tribes as barbarous and warlike. Many of these migrated south out of the forests and plains of northern Europe and in the fourth and fifth centuries overran most of the decadent Roman Empire.

By the sixth century the Franks had taken control of most of present day Germany and in 800 Charlemagne was crowned emperor of the Holy Roman Empire. During the centuries that followed there was a gradual erosion of the authority of the pope and the Catholic emperors and the German dukes, their vassals, and the merchant princes gained more and more power.

The religious dissension that had been smoldering within the Church for many years flared up across Europe after 1517. On October 31 of that year Martin Luther, an Augustinian monk and professor of theology, posted 95 theses on the door of the Castle Church in the university town of Wittenberg and thereby challenged many teachings and practices of the Roman church. As the reformation escalated, powerful German princes protected Luther, enabling him to challenge both pope and emperor.

Only after the ruinous Thirty Years War (1618-1648) was a religious settlement reached in Europe. During that war the German states were the battleground across which the armies of Europe waged a war of attrition, year after devastating year. When the war ended, the population of the ravaged German states had been reduced from 20 million to 13 million. The incredible, unmitigated sufferings of the peasantry were remembered for generations.

A map of the German states of the 1700s reveals a crazy quilt of over 300 sovereignties. In many of these states the peasants were little better off than serfs. In order to sustain their courts in regal splendor, the petty princes of many of these states would hire out their soldiers, and England was their major customer. The Hessian soldiers in the ranks fought as mercenaries for the British in the American War for Independence, not because they wanted to, but because they had no choice. They had been impressed into the army to provide income for their royal ruler.

After 1800 Napoleon overran most of Europe. In the conquered German states, men between the ages of 18 and 40 were subject to conscription. German units made up a part of the 500,000-man army Napoleon led into Russia in June of 1812. Only 25,000 of these soldiers would survive to re-cross the border in December.

The descendants of George Urish have wondered what might have prompted him to leave the Odenwald and bring his family to America in the summer of 1831. Evidently it was not for economic reasons, as he was in a family partnership operating a prosperous grist mill. His wife was in the latter stage of pregnancy, expecting a child in July--not an ideal time for a grueling trip across the North Atlantic.

Georg could have visited with some of the Hessians who returned to their homeland after serving the British during the American Revolution. Undoubtedly he heard reports they brought back; stories of open, fertile land, waiting to be settled; of a country where there was no royalty; where no man had to bow to another.

Family tradition indicates that Georg had a pressing problem that probably hastened his decision to emigrate. The story, passed down through the years, suggests that royal officials were looking for Georg, suspecting that he had been poaching game on the local Baron's hunting preserve. There was also a suspicion that he had shot the Baron's game warden during an exchange of gunfire in the Genzbach Forest. Georg may have been seeking refuge, as well as liberty and opportunity, in a far-off land where wild game was plentiful and was not reserved strictly for royalty.

Whatever the motivation, we know that Georg, his pregnant wife, and their two small children left southern Germany and made their way across the Atlantic to America during the summer of 1831. The family arrived in Baltimore in July and spent several weeks there. Anna Eva, twenty-seven at the time, gave birth to their third child during this brief stay in the Maryland city. They journeyed overland to Pittsburgh and then traveled by boat to St.Louis. After a short time they continued up the Illinois River to a boat landing, originally known as Town Site, where Jonathan Tharp, the first white settler, had built a cabin in 1824. The town was laid out in 1829, was named Pekin, eventually grew into a thriving river city, and in time became the county seat of Tazewell County.

The first permanent American white settlers had arrived in 1823 in the area that was to become Tazewell County. When the George Urish family landed in 1831, President Andrew Jackson was in the third year of his first term. In the spring of 1830 a tall, gangly young man of twenty years had accompanied his family as they moved from southern Indiana to central Illinois. Attaining the age of twenty-one in 1831, Abraham Lincoln struck out on his own. After flatboating a cargo to New Orleans, he settled for a time in New Salem, briefly ran a store where he slept in the back room, studied and became a surveyor, and in 1837 moved on to Springfield and immortality.

George Urish and his family moved on to a sparsely settled area near the Mackinaw River and built a log cabin. A few weeks later George walked to Springfield and purchased 60 acres of land for 60 cents an acre. The first and only German immigrants in the area and in the process of learning English, the family had a difficult time the first few years. In 1834, his funds exhausted, George drove his team to Galena. He was able to make some money working with the team around the thriving lead mines in that area. George returned to his family at harvest time and began to prosper in the rapidly developing county.

George was the progenitor of a large, well-known, sometimes prosperous, and occasionally unruly clan. Some of his descendants remained in Tazewell County, and many scattered across the country. In 1831 the county was on the threshold of a period of rapid population increase. Only a few miles south of the Urish homestead, the Delavan Association, formed in Providence, Rhode Island in 1833, staked out 22,000 acres of prime prairie land, and in 1837 the vanguard of a stream of settlers from New England began to arrive. In addition to this influx from the Northeast, emigrants from northern Europe and Britain continued to arrive in increasing numbers. Among these were Alves Meyers from Switzerland in 1834; John Phillips from Lorraine, France, in 1835; James Robison from Aberdeenshire, Scotland, in 1836; William Youle from Yorkshire, England, in 1851; John Hayes and James Ryan from County Limerick, Ireland, in 1851 and 1852.

The migration that began with George Urish and his family soon became a steady stream of immigrants bringing their families from Hessen-Darmstadt to Pekin and central Illinois. Among these were John Heisel in 1841; Nicholas Volk in 1842; Leonard Beck in 1846; John Eidman in 1848; Christopher and George Stoehr in 1850; Frederick Lutz, John Olt, and Adam Heilman in 1852; John Herget in 1853; Nicholas Reuling in 1854; and Jacob Weyrich in 1857.

(During World War II the people of Darmstadt, together with most German citizens, paid a heavy price in blood and property for acquiescing to the monstrous sins of Adolf Hitler and his Nazi thugs. On the night of Sept. 11, 1944, Royal Air Force bombers on a mission in the area were unable to locate their primary target or their secondary target. Through a break in the cloud cover the bomber crews sighted Darmstadt. Before heading home to England, they unloaded their 300,000 incendiary and 700 high-explosive bombs on Darmstadt, igniting a raging firestorm that engulfed the city, killing 12,000 of the city's 100,000 residents and destroying half of the city's buildings, including the historic quarter. The only war-related industry in the area, a chemical plant on the outskirts of the city, was not damaged.)

Nathan Dillon, the first permanent white settler in Tazewell County, arrived in 1823. By the census of 1870, the county's population had reached 27,904. A historical sketch, published in 1870, undoubtedly by some precursor of the chamber of commerce, proclaimed proudly: "Pekin has at the present time a population of about 12,000"--a figure inflated slightly from the 5,696 that the census of 1870 recorded. When the census of 1940 was taken, the population of the county was 58,383.

The John N. Urish and Sons farming operation in the early 1940s was pretty well up-to-date for that time. Some years earlier Dad had bought one of the first combines to be used in the community. Three of our neighbors, however, still harvested their wheat and oat crops the old way. They used a McCormick-Deering binder, which cut the grain, tied it into bundles, and dropped them in rows. The bundles were then set up in shocks where the grain finished drying. Within a few weeks the bundles were pitched onto racks and hauled to a threshing machine, also known as a separator. The bundles were pitched into the machine where they were threshed and the grain separated out. The machine augured the clean grain into wagons and blew the straw and chaff into stacks that most farmers used for livestock bedding or feed. These threshers were large, expensive machines that were owned by a group of farmers or by a custom operator. Tractors or steam engines of a size not usually owned by individual farmers at that time provided power for the threshers by means of a long belt.

After we had finished combining our grain at home and had baled the straw, hauled it to the barns, and stored it for winter use, Dad announced that "we"--meaning son Earl--were going to help the neighbors thresh. This in exchange for some future help they would furnish us. That was Dad--generous to a fault. He didn't mind hard work at all if someone else was doing it.

And so I took a team of horses and a bundle rack and spent part of that hot summer manhandling a pitchfork in one of the last threshing runs in the area. Most of the threshing crews included pitchers--men who threw the bundles up to the man running the rack. The man on the rack would load the bundles, drive the loaded rack to the thresher and pitch the bundles onto the feeder of the machine. In this threshing run, however, the men with bundle racks pitched their own loads. One neighbor never got around to shocking his wheat so we had to pick it up out of the bundle rows.

On the day we finished the run we were at Pete Horn's place. Pete started celebrating a little too soon and was pretty well stewed by the time we were down to unloading the last two loads. He was pitching bundles onto the feeder from one side, I from the other. He was swaying happily but unsteadily as he threw the bundles into the big machine. Ed Goeken, the machine operator, was standing with his hand on the tractor clutch lever, ready to stop the long drive belt that powered the thresher, just in case Pete fell in. I jumped down off my load and went back to the tractor to talk to him. "Hell, Ed, the thresher has enough momentum to take Pete in even if you hit the clutch right away." Ed stopped the machine, and we convinced Pete that some of his cattle had broken down a fence and were likely out on the road somewhere. While Pete was away searching for his wandering livestock, we quickly unloaded the racks.

When I arrived home I unharnessed and fed the horses, then went into the house to check the day's mail. My maternal grandmother had been widowed a few years earlier and was staying with us at the time. Grandma had traveled from Hanover, Germany, to America in 1881 at the age of sixteen. Her ultimate destination was the railroad stop of Bishop Station in Mason County where relatives were to meet her. Someone blundered and she was routed to Bishop Hill, a large Swedish settlement near Galesburg. So little Lena Thies found herself alone at the railway station there, a stranger in a strange land. With the help of some kind-hearted Swedes, Grandma finally made it to Bishop Station, grew up, married a tall young farmer named John Kreiling, reared a fine family, and at this time had five grandsons serving in America's armed forces. She watched as I picked up a letter from Selective Service. I opened it and read aloud: "Greetings: You have been selected . . . ." "You wanted to go, didn't you," Grandma said softly, more a statement than a question, "I pray it works out for you."

That summer Wayne was in the Navy Communications School at Alabama Polytechnic Institute (later Auburn University) in Auburn, Alabama. Mother wanted to visit him before I left for the service. With the summer work on the farm well in hand, I went to Pekin to buy train tickets. As I suspected, there was nothing very direct from central Illinois to east central Alabama. Wartime travel restrictions being what they were, only coach accommodations were available. We were routed through Louisville, Nashville, Birmingham, and Montgomery.

The trains were crowded, and about half of the passengers were servicemen. It was an interesting, though very tiring, trip. Never having traveled in the South before, I had been only vaguely aware of "Jim Crow" segregation from the little I had read on the subject. My earliest recollection of black people was of a group of young Civilian Conservation Corps men who were encamped near Spring Lake in Tazewell County in the 1930s. The CCC was one of the New Deal programs of the Roosevelt Administration. It was designed to get the large number of unemployed young men, white and black, off the streets and into useful conservation work. The Army ran the program, which was successful both in enhancing America's natural resources and in bringing order into the lives of many young men who might otherwise have been getting into trouble, idling about the cities and towns of America. The group at Spring Lake planted trees on thousands of acres of sandy wasteland that was eventually developed into Sand Ridge State Forest. One hot Sunday afternoon during the summer of 1934 Dad loaded my brothers and me into the *Whippet* and took us down to Spring Lake to see the Green Valley baseball team play the black CCC team. It was a friendly game and a good time was had by all.

At the University of Illinois there were quite a number of African-American students on campus plus a few blacks from foreign lands. In the cosmopolitan atmosphere of the large university community, they were treated the same as other students, so far as I could tell from my admittedly superficial observations.

When the train crossed the Mason-Dixon line as we traveled south, the segregation in public facilities was startling to unsophisticated Midwesterners who had never visited this section of the country. In one of the cities we had an hour layover, so Mother and I walked about the station to stretch our cramped and travel-weary muscles. Military Police were ushering a small group of German prisoners of war into the "Whites only" toilet while black American servicemen were forced to use the segregated "Colored only" facilities.

We made a final transfer at Montgomery, Alabama, and traveled the last leg of our journey in a lovely old coach with green velvet upholstered seats. It was a welcome change from the crowded, not too clean cars we had been riding for most of the trip.

Auburn proved to be a quiet, attractive little college town. We arrived in the afternoon while Wayne was in class. We stopped in at the home where he had made arrangements for us to stay, freshened up, and then went downtown to pick up some items at a department store. While we were finishing our shopping, a store attendant locked the doors to one of the two entrances, as it was closing time. A young Negro started to leave the store and discovered the doors were locked. From where he was attempting to leave the store he could not see the open doors or the side aisle where we were finishing our business with the clerk. I had never seen such sheer panic as he exhibited when he thought he had been locked in. The clerk quickly went over and quietly showed him the side exit. From his appearance, I surmised that the young man was a field hand from the farming area around Auburn. I can still remember that look of terror in his eyes.

We spent a pleasant weekend with Wayne, our stay made more enjoyable because of the friendly, hospitable people we encountered in the town. In addition to the sailors studying at Auburn, there were soldiers in town on weekend pass from Ft. Benning, Georgia, which lay about forty miles to the east. Among these soldiers were a few sharply dressed paratroopers wearing jump boots that had been shined until they glowed. Wayne remarked that the sailors left these birds alone. They figured that anyone crazy enough to jump out of an airplane might get violent at any time.

In the dark, cool, pre-dawn hour of Aug. 8, 1944, Dad and I arrived at the imposing old Tazewell County Courthouse in Pekin. My group of inductees had been ordered to report at 5:AM. Mother had chosen to say goodbye at home, her eyes glistening with scarcely withheld tears. As we waited in the Courthouse, Dad pointed out a bronze plaque just inside the entrance. It listed the members of the Tazewell County Board of Supervisors who served at the time the Courthouse was built. On the list was Grandfather Peter Urish.

The inductees were lined up by reporter Paul Ketcham for a picture to be published in the *Pekin Daily Times,* then quickly loaded aboard a bus destined for Ft. Sheridan, located just north of Chicago. No bands. No bugles. No drums. No flags waving. No patriotic speeches. Just another group of young men being hustled away quietly in the pre-dawn darkness as so many others had been during the preceding four years.

In World War II, 4641 men from Tazewell County served in the armed forces, 1305 enlistees and 3336 draftees, drawn from a population that numbered 58,363 in the 1940 census. This would indicate that one of every 6.25 males served at some time during the war. Of the 4641 who served, 293, or approximately one out of sixteen, died while serving as a members of the armed forces. These figures would suggest that, during WW II, one out of every 99 male citizens of Tazewell County died while serving in the armed forces. For the United States, 16.3 million served, drawn from a population of 129 million. When the war ended 407,000 had died, 292,000 in battle, 115,000 from other causes.

Four score years earlier, the people of Tazewell County had sacrificed even more of their sons in the war which preserved the Union. The 1860 census reveals a county with a population of 21,427. The figures are somewhat hazy, but it appears obvious that the county sent over 3,600 men to serve in the Union forces during the Civil War, one of every 3.5 males. Of the men in the services, 520, or one out of seven died during that war. One of every 21 male inhabitants of Tazewell County died while serving in the armed forces during the War Between the States. Disease and pestilence caused a large percentage of these deaths. Many who returned died later from wounds suffered and diseases contracted during their service. North and South combined Civil War deaths totaled 620,000 from a U.S. population that had reached 31 million when the 1860 census was taken.

As our bus rolled toward Chicago, I was pleased to see that the group of inductees included a number of men I knew: Bill Hurley of Pekin; Bill Pflederer of Tremont; Jay Firth, Harlan Runyon, and Alvin Fuller of Delavan; and Midge Parkin of Manito.

At this point in the war it was not possible to enlist in the service of choice after reaching the age of eighteen. A man could only volunteer for the draft. There was an ominous reason for this policy. In what may have been the most serious planning failure of the war, the top commanders had seriously underestimated the battle losses that would occur in infantry divisions, particularly in their rifle companies. Gen. Dwight D. Eisenhower, former Supreme Allied Commander, was to write in 1948:

> In both World Wars, the infantry replacement problem plagued American commanders in the field. Only a small percentage of the manpower in a war theater operates in front of the light artillery line established by the divisions. Yet this small portion absorbs about ninety percent of the casualties.

Combat soldiers—Army infantrymen and Marine riflemen—were the cutting edge of America's war machine. Infantrymen made up only 14 percent of American troops overseas in WW II, yet they suffered 70 percent of the casualties. Their casualty rate was equaled only by Air Force bomber crews, surpassed only by Navy submariners. The number of infantry, armored, and airborne divisions had been kept relatively low, the theory being that they would be maintained at full strength by bringing in replacements as battle casualties occurred. During the invasion of Europe, in the first six weeks after the D-Day landings, infantry divisions had losses of over 100 percent with some rifle companies replaced three times over. By the time these forces closed on the Rhine, men in the divisions which had been in combat since North Africa and Italy would observe: "We have three divisions: one at the front, one in the hospitals, and one in the cemeteries." In Europe, trench foot added to the casualty list. In the Pacific, it was malaria and a variety of tropical diseases. As in World War I, infantrymen were the cannon fodder on which the gods of war fattened.

In the summer of 1944 it was painfully obvious that the number of infantry replacements required to sustain the fighting divisions would continue to be staggering. With this overriding need, practically every man entering the service at this time was assigned to one of the eight Infantry Replacement Training Centers (IRTCs) scattered throughout the southern states. For most of us, it would be fifteen weeks of training, then shipment overseas to the battlefronts.

After a few days spent receiving inoculations, completing mental and psychological tests, and listening to army propaganda, I became part of a troop-train load of new soldiers dispatched to the IRTC at Camp Hood, Texas. This camp, sprawled over several north central Texas counties, was the largest of the IRTCs with 24,000 trainees and a cadre of 844 officers and 4,000 enlisted men. Also, the US Tank Destroyer Training Center was located at the north end of the military reservation.

The training was strenuous and the days long. Activity often extended from 5:30 AM until 7:00 PM. It was a time that separated the men from the boys. Most of the trainees were eighteen, but the Selective Service was also inducting some men over thirty who had not been accepted earlier. With the vigor of youth, the boys of eighteen were still going when the men dropped out. The summer heat in Texas was intense. A green fatigue uniform would start to turn white with salt from perspiration if it had to be worn for several days. Companies would stand retreat immediately upon returning from training in the field. On extremely hot afternoons, we would hear the occasional clatter of a rifle and helmet on the blacktop street as an exhausted trainee passed out.

I was separated from my Tazewell County friends when we arrived at Camp Hood but soon became well acquainted with the men immediately around me in the training platoon. Bunking above me and marching beside me was a man named Underhill, a native of Canada, more recently of Joplin, Missouri. Underhill belied his name by going over the hill half way through the training cycle. The army reclaimed him in due time. Twenty-two months later, just before leaving Japan for home, I saw his name on a set of orders assigning incoming personnel. Underhill had missed the war. A complex and canny character, he may have been playing it that way.

On one side of me in the barracks was a young man from New Mexico, one Tony Turietta, who shortly informed me that he was of Spanish descent. Tony came to Hood from Washington, D.C., where he had been serving as a page in the U.S. Senate, appointed by Sen. Dennis Chavez of his home state. At about 5'5" and 135 pounds,

Tony had to carry the same load as everyone else. Tony was game and always gave it his best shot. We became good friends, going down to Austin together one weekend. I would see Tony on several occasions after we left Camp Hood.

On the other side was a Texas farm boy of Czech extraction whose home was near the camp. Trainees in the platoon held him personally responsible for the lousy Texas weather, the terrain, the mud, the dust, etc. He kept a very low profile, disappearing after duty hours and going home on pass every weekend. He might have invited me to go along had he not wanted to borrow the brown oxfords I had in my footlocker. He figured—correctly—that there was no chance of his borrowing them if he invited me to accompany him. After several weeks, the entire company started receiving passes and I began using the shoes myself on weekends, so Valcik had to go forth in his GI boots.

Bunked on the other side of Tony was a West Virginia coal miner named Guy Trent. I never really got acquainted with Guy. It is difficult to get to know a person who communicates almost exclusively by grunting. Guy was apparently terribly introverted. Tony, to his everlasting credit, befriended and helped him and was the only person Guy would confide in.

After three weeks in camp the trainees were allowed weekend passes. At Hood, weekend passes began after inspection on Saturday and ended at midnight Sunday. Most of the men headed for Temple, the nearest city of any size. When we arrived at the bus station, it was wall to wall with soldiers. Downtown was crowded with thousands and thousands of soldiers milling about. My friend and I wandered around awhile and finally stopped by the U.S.O. Center. About midnight I realized that I needed a place to sleep. I checked with the manager of the U.S.O. to see what might be available. He chuckled and said that everything around town was filled to overflowing, but he still had two pool tables that weren't taken. They would be available at 1:00 AM when he had to turn off the lights and stop the pool shooting. That left me with the unhappy choice of going back to camp, wandering the streets, or trying the pool table. I chose the pool table--unwisely.

When I awoke that morning, I vowed that I would never again visit the fair city of Temple. I would break that vow—unintentionally---thirty years later.

On one corner of the bulletin board at our training company was a list of churches in the area. I noted that there was a Lutheran Church of my particular persuasion near Copperas Cove. The following Sunday morning I caught a bus headed west. Some eight miles later we arrived at the little country town. I was surprised when over twenty other soldiers also hopped off the bus. Waiting at the bus stop was an array of well-used cars and pickup trucks, their drivers ready to transport us to the church, which was located three miles out in the country. The church building was a modest frame structure similar to many rural churches in central Illinois. Take away the western hats and boots and the congregation was also comparable to those in the rural Midwest. The service began and the ancient words were read once more. I could close my eyes and the sounds of the service were identical to those at home.

When the service ended, members of the congregation invited the visiting soldiers to their homes for dinner. Four of us were guests in the home of a rancher and his family. It was a warm, friendly occasion and a welcome interlude to visit with these kind and generous Texans. They were farmers and ranchers of modest means who shared their bread and their love with untold numbers of lonely, homesick youngsters through the long years of war. "We were strangers and they welcomed us; we were hungry and they fed us."

A sergeant and his wife were among the guests. He had seen action in the South Pacific, been wounded, sent home, and then assigned to Camp Hood. He had a few words of advice as we visited in the yard after dinner: "Don't get assigned to a flame-thrower if you can possibly avoid it. Also, replacement infantry officers have an extremely short life expectancy in combat. Officer Candidate School, even if available, might not be a good option."

Our host had saddled a pair of horses and invited me to go for a ride. I eagerly accepted his offer.

I attended the church at Copperas Cove on three occasions. One Sunday afternoon a friend and I decided to go further west to the town of Lampasas. The main attraction there was a fine, large swimming pool. While taking a break from swimming, we visited with some local residents. My friend asked what lay to the west of Lampasas. The reply, after a little consideration, "Well, not much, really." At the next opportunity I checked a map. To the west of Lampasas stretches the Llano Estacado, the staked plains. Lampasas isn't the end of the world, but if you go to the edge of town, look west, and strain your eyes, you can see it from there.

Around the barracks the wrestling knowledge I had gained at the university served me well on several occasions. Despite the rigorous and fatiguing training we were undergoing, there was always a certain amount of scuffling and horsing around among the men, usually all in fun. Among the men in our barracks was a good-natured Native American (an Indian at that time) from Oklahoma named Tenequer. Always addressed as "Chief," he weighed in at 225 pounds and was well over 6 feet tall, was in good condition, but wasn't quite all muscle. The company was restricted to the barracks one weekend, probably for failing to pass Saturday inspection. Some of the men were killing time by engaging in a little impromptu wrestling. Tenequer joined the group watching the wrestlers and immediately announced that he could take anyone in the barracks. I was resting on my bunk nearby, just finishing a few letters home. I rolled out of my bunk, walked over to the group, and suggested that perhaps we should give the Chief an opportunity to prove his claim.

Tenequer had at least a twenty-five pound weight advantage. I was guessing that he was very strong but also rather slow. As we circled one another, I grabbed his right wrist, pulled him toward me, went behind him, and put my arm around his neck. I took him down by kicking behind his left knee with my left foot so that he dropped on my left leg as we went to the floor. From there it was an easy move to go into a "figure four scissors" and a "grapevine." With this hold my legs were wrapped around my opponent so that I could put tremendous pressure on his midsection. My weight was on his right arm and my left arm was under his neck, my left hand holding his left wrist thus immobilizing his left arm. Properly executed, this hold allows a wrestler to quickly render an opponent helpless without causing bodily harm--a little injury to the ego, perhaps, but very little to the body. If the opponent struggles to break free, applying strong pressure to his midsection with the leg scissors will usually quickly subdue him. Tenequer did quite a lot of struggling, squirming, and sweating but was finally forced to admit that he had overestimated his wrestling ability.

This was not quite the end of my Camp Hood wrestling. A few weeks later I found it necessary to give the same lesson to a Chicago boy by the name of Kowalski--all good, clean fun, of course, although undoubtedly more fun for me than for Kowalski. Guided by the maxim that it's best to quit when you're ahead, I carefully avoided this type of activity during the remainder of the training period. Someone who is quicker and stronger will eventually show up if you press your luck too far.

The men in the company had been looking forward to our time on the firing range. At last we would be firing the M1 Garand rifles that we had been carrying, field stripping, cleaning and oiling for weeks. During the time the company was on the range, we were fortunate in having a spell of beautiful fall weather. The trainees would fire their rifles for half a day and then work in the target pits the remainder of the day. Those who failed to qualify the first time around were sent back again and again. The army was not about to lose any warm bodies at this stage just because they couldn't see those damn targets. Trainees in this category were known as "bolos." This is an old army term that seems to have originated during the Philippine Insurrections. The weapon many Filipinos had used in that conflict was a razor sharp machete called a "bolo."

I qualified as marksman with the M1 Garand the first time around. On a descending scale of expert, sharpshooter, marksman, this was adequate but not the sort of shooting that causes one to be known as "Eagle Eye." My recently deceased grandfather was reputedly the best wing shot in Tazewell County in his prime. He would have expected me to do better.

The following week we went back to the range to fire the Browning Automatic Rifle, the B.A.R. Weighing twenty pounds, it was a solid weapon dating back to World War I. When we fired for record, the men in the target pits put me up an excellent score. The man on my right was getting the white flag--"Maggie's drawers" in army lingo. This signified no hits at all on his target. It occurred to me that he had probably fired on my target. I (we) had scored expert. The next time I got down to the Post Exchange, I purchased an "Expert-BAR" medal. I always reflected as I pinned it on that I probably should let the guy who had been next to me on the firing range wear it on alternate weekends.

On the way back to our barracks after one particularly grueling two-day field exercise, the company marched past a compound where German prisoners of war, veterans of Hitler's Afrika Korps, were being held. Having just completed a forty-eight-hour simulated-combat problem, we were exhausted and famished, covered with dust and sweat and mud, our butts practically dragging out our tracks. The very fit, deeply tanned, mostly blonde German POWs were lounging about in shorts and white T-shirts looking fresh, clean, serene, and well fed, apparently well cared for and content in their barbed wire enclosure.

To the infantry replacement trainees, wearily slogging along through the enervating heat of a Texas summer afternoon, it appeared that, at this point, these German POWs were doing much better than we were. They were safely out of the war, well fed, apparently not working very hard, if at all. There was considerable comment from the ranks of the worn out, hungry GIs as we trudged past the POW compound. "Who's winning this damn war, anyway? Those Nazi sonsabitches should be put to work doing all kinds of shitty details." And those were the kindest and most generous of the remarks I heard from my weary compatriots.

Occasionally, while out in the field training, we would see big, silver airplanes in the sky, flying at great altitude. It appeared that they were much larger than the B-17 Flying Fortresses with which we were familiar. A company trainee from southern Kansas told us that Boeing was assembling these huge bombers at a completely new plant in Wichita. He claimed the planes would cover half a football field and had tail assemblies as tall as a two-story building.

As we squinted at those gigantic aircraft, flying so high in the bright blue Texas sky, we had no inkling of the role they would play in the subjugation of the Japanese Empire. We could not know that many of us would survive the war because of the contribution these planes and their courageous crews were to make to final victory.

The B-29 Superfortress had been a tremendous gamble for the Army Air Corps. To build each B-29 required resources that could have produced eleven P-51 fighter planes. Initial development of the B-29 began in 1940 when it was conceived as a hemisphere defense weapon. It was to be used for intervention in Europe, should Britain be conquered--a distinct possibility at that time. In 1941, the Air Force ordered 250 "off the drawing board." The experimental prototype was not flown for the first time until Sept. 1942. The B-29 was bigger, faster, and could fly higher than any bomber in existence at that time. It could carry up to ten tons of bombs to a target 1500-

1800 miles away and return, flying at an altitude over 30,000 feet with a maximum speed of 357 mph. A large number of technological innovations were combined in the B-29, resulting in countless complex engineering problems that had to be solved in a very limited time. At the end of the war there was still a problem with fires breaking out in the super-sized motors. The first planes were ready for their crews in June of 1943. The Air Force now had a weapon that could overcome the vast distances involved in striking the Japanese homeland. Training the crews and deploying the planes came next.

As we watched the planes overhead that summer of 1944, some of the B-29s were already operating from bases in China. On most of their missions the crews were bombing from high altitude, taking heavy losses, and achieving very limited success. The logistical problems involved in flying from bases in China made that entire operation questionable. Not until 1945 would the full potential of the B-29s be realized. It was then that the huge bases in the western Pacific Mariana Islands became fully operational and radically different tactics employed by Bomber Command.

Another project--this one shrouded in the tightest secrecy--had been underway since early in the war. The research and development that would harness the power of the atom for destructive purposes was being pushed forward with all possible speed. The cost of developing the atomic bomb, a figure well publicized after the war, had been two billion dollars. Far less well known was the fact that the development of the B-29 bomber had cost three billion dollars.

"Roosevelt has been re-elected again." This was the news that echoed through our barracks in the pre-dawn hour of Nov.7 as the trainees hurriedly dressed for reveille and prepared for another long day in the field. During the last few months, out in the world beyond Camp Hood, President Roosevelt, his health steadily declining, had been turning back the Presidential campaign challenge of Gov. Thomas E. Dewey of New York.

Busy with a crowded, wearying schedule, the trainees had taken little note of the political campaign. One significant reason for their apparent indifference was the fact that most were legally ineligible to vote. I was among the unenfranchised, far short of the twenty-one years required for voting privileges at that time. Of the infantry replacements in training during the fall of 1944, soldiers who in a few short months would be on the battle lines around the world, about eighty percent were deemed eligible to die for their country but not sufficiently mature to participate in that nation's electoral process --theirs not to reason why, theirs but to do and die, and all that sort of old, bloody crap.

I was quite pleased that FDR would continue to lead the Nation. He was the only president Americans my age had known, the man we remembered for bringing new hope to a despairing nation in the nineteen-thirties. My earliest memories include an image of my family gathered around a battery powered radio in a room illuminated by a kerosene lamp as we listened to the reassuring words of the President explaining his latest proposals to the people of the Nation in a friendly "Fireside Chat." This picture would change dramatically after 1935. That was the year President Roosevelt signed an executive order creating the Rural Electrification Administration. Electricity was soon flowing to farms and ranches all across the nation, vastly reducing the drudgery of country living for Mother and millions of other rural homemakers.

The final two weeks of our training cycle were spent out in the field living in two man pup tents. The early winter weather had turned wet and cold. We ran our training exercises and problems in rainy, muddy, miserable conditions. Between rain and perspiration we were continually wet and cold. The physical discomfort certainly gave us a sample of what might lie ahead. I wondered, however, if men who were wet and cold and uncomfortable to the extreme retained much of what the Army was trying to teach. Borderline hypothermia does not appear to foster good mental function.

With our training completed, we were given a ten-day delay en route on our way to a west coast port of embarkation. Fortunately, this allowed us to be home for the Christmas holiday. This was doubly enjoyable for our family as my Navy brother also made it home for a few days. The ship to which Wayne had been assigned, the cruiser *Pittsburgh*, had just completed a shakedown cruise and was on the way to join the Pacific fleet.

At church on Sunday morning, I saw Bill Hurley for the first time since leaving Ft.Sheridan in August. Bill had also completed infantry replacement training but at a different camp. He had orders to report to a port of embarkation on the east coast. From there, he was sure he would soon be shipped out to Europe. As we visited in the snow covered churchyard that cold, bright Sunday morning, only God knew that Bill would be dead in three months, cut down by German artillery.

A community supper was held between the holidays at Green Valley High School. Along with a marine who was home on medical leave, I was invited to relate my experience in the service. The marine, Clell Luft, had been severely wounded on Guadalcanal. During a Japanese attack a jagged piece of shrapnel had lodged near his jugular vein. Only by the grace of God and an exceptionally proficient corpsman was Clell with us that winter evening. Clell was modest in his recounting of the ordeal on Guadalcanal, but the audience was well aware of the bravery and heroism of the Marines in that pivotal battle. After Clell's talk, my time spent training in the Army seemed hardly worth mentioning. I tried to explain how the Army was attempting to prepare the infantry replacements being thrust into battle on short notice. The audience listened politely.

The day before I was to leave for the west coast I said farewell to a number of friends and kissed a girl friend goodbye. This last without too much conviction. The sometimes girl friend had already kissed two marines and a sailor goodbye as they headed off to war so I wasn't greatly burdened with any illusions of perpetual love.

While I was home on furlough, the Battle of the Bulge was raging in Europe. At great cost American forces blunted, then stopped Hitler's final offensive of the war and began to methodically eliminate the German salient. In Eastern Europe, surging Soviet armies reached Budapest. In the Philippines, the US 6th Army was preparing for the invasion of Luzon. On Leyte, much hard fighting remained, as the 8th Army took over the difficult task of digging out the remainder of the 80,000 troops the Japanese had committed to the defense of that island.

On the home front, beef was rationed once more and new, smaller quotas introduced on most other commodities.

During the Christmas season of 1944 the Urish family gathers for a formal photograph. Seated are John N. Urish and his wife Tillie. Standing at the rear, left to right, are brothers Wayne, John B., and Earl.

Chapter II Ft.Ord and Camp Stoneman

New Year's night, with the temperature hovering around 20 degrees below zero Fahrenheit, my parents took me to Chillicothe and saw me off on the Santa Fe *Scout*. I was bound for Los Angeles and whatever might lie ahead. I found a seat on the crowded train and settled in. My seatmate, a well-dressed, middle-aged gentleman, shortly opened his suitcase and produced two fifths of pre-war Schenley's Whiskey, one of which he presented to me. We drank to the coming year; I stashed the remainder under my seat and went to sleep. When I awoke about midday, we were somewhere in Kansas and the Schenley's was gone. Easy come, easy go.

Arriving in Los Angeles five days later (the *Scout* was no *SuperChief*), we entered a station overflowing with servicemen. Most of them were infantry replacements headed upcoast for Ft.Ord. An announcement over the public address system soon informed us that the *Southern Pacific* was making up a special train destined for Ft.Ord and due to depart in six hours. Half a dozen of us shared a cab out to the famed Hollywood Canteen. It was completely deserted. Not a soul in sight. Maybe it was a sort of Brigadoon, only coming to life at certain times--for movie making purposes. In any case, we didn't have time to wait around to find out.

The train ride to Ft.Ord offered some spectacular views of the Big Sur country where magnificent breakers were crashing against the shore. It was my first look at an ocean. I would see more of this vast Pacific Ocean during the next two years than I actually cared to.

Ft.Ord was a pleasant surprise. Situated in a beautiful area along the Pacific Ocean, it offered accommodations that were "good" by army standards. An attractive Enlisted Men's Club was located on a point above the ocean with the heavy surf pounding on the shore below. At the club, many in the crowd were Italians, former prisoners of war who had been captured in North Africa and Sicily. They were dressed in US Army uniforms and obviously had new status since Italy was now our ally. Looking around the place for a familiar face, I spotted Tony Turietta seated at a table with some of his friends.

We had a few beers, discussed our recent furloughs, and speculated on the future.

At the barracks, members of the permanent cadre were still talking about a group of paratroopers who had passed through a month earlier. They had been billeted on the second floor. When the troops were called out for formations, the paratroopers always lined up and jumped off the second floor fire escapes. Just keeping in trim, they explained.

I discovered that three of my Tazewell County friends, Parkin, Runyon, and Fuller, were also at Ft. Ord. During the next two months, the four of us would stop briefly at two stateside camps, be transported on three ships, and pass through two replacement depots (often disparagingly referred to as repple-depples). While not always in the same unit, we were close enough that we could keep in touch. We would eventually be separated and lose contact when we were assigned to different divisions and shipped out of the Fifth Replacement Depot, then located at Lingayen Gulf in the Philippines.

While at Ft. Ord we were issued some equipment and ordered to send home any non-essential personal effects. Our mail was now censored. Parkin and I secured eight-hour passes and visited the spectacular Monterey Peninsula area. There was some training taking place at Ft. Ord, but apparently we were not expected to be around long enough to participate. I feel that the Army missed many opportunities to further train these infantry replacements. From the time we arrived at Ft. Ord until we were assigned to combat infantry divisions on Luzon, there were hundreds of hours that could and should have been utilized for training and physical conditioning, but instead were spent playing cards, shooting craps, shooting the bull, and just lying around. The fifteen weeks of actual training at the IRTCs was grossly inadequate.

After less than a week at Ft. Ord we were loaded up again and shipped by rail to Camp Stoneman, thirty miles up the bay from San Francisco. This unimpressive appearing camp was located along the bay in an area of rolling hills. For the entire week we were at Camp Stoneman, the fog was extremely thick during the early morning hours. At reveille you could barely see the man in front of you. By ten o'clock the fog would clear, and the rest of the day would be splendid. We had our equipment checked once again, received more inoculations, and were treated to the best food we would eat in eighteen months. Midge Parkin and I managed passes for a day.

We went down to San Francisco, hitchhiked across the Golden Gate Bridge, ate at Fisherman's Wharf (not at DiMaggio's which was closed), looked over the ships being loaded at the Embarcadero, rode the cable cars, ogled the girls on Market Street, and ended up by having a drink at the Top of the Mark. All in all, an enjoyable final day of freedom in the U.S.A.

There was an area at the rear of Camp Stoneman where the chain link fence surrounding the camp could be raised and a man could slip under. It was known around camp as the "Little Burma Road." There were quite a few unauthorized passes taken, utilizing this exit. When I think about that moment in time when we all knew we were within days of boarding a ship which would take us to the battlefield, I am always amazed that there were not more cases of "gangplank fever." That there were not speaks volumes about the patriotism and motivation of these young Americans. Perhaps it is also indicative of their naiveté in regard to what lay ahead for them.

After a week at Camp Stoneman, we were loaded aboard a steamboat for the trip down San Francisco Bay to the Embarcadero. The *Delta Queen* was a stern-wheel excursion steamboat that had been pressed into service for the duration. Prior to the war, the *Delta Queen* had proudly plied the Mississippi carrying tourists and vacationers and would do so again when wartime service ended. The *Delta Queen* visited Peoria on several occasions after the war to race in the Steamboat Days celebration. The handsome old vessel has been designated a National Historic Landmark and continues to carry passengers up and down the "Father of Waters."

Chapter III The Pacific

The *Orizaba*, an armed Navy transport complete with Marine guard, awaited us at the San Francisco docks. We marched off the *Delta Queen*, across the dock, up the gangplank onto the *Orizaba*, then down into the troop compartments. My buddies and I were fortunate in being assigned bunks in a small compartment on the first deck. This would be our home for the next month.

The *Orizaba* got underway as soon as the last soldier was aboard, sailing under the Golden Gate Bridge and out to sea. Leaving New York City, the troops could look back and see the Statue of Liberty. Leaving San Francisco, we looked back and saw Alcatraz. Fortunately, the majestic Golden Gate Bridge and the beautiful San Francisco skyline dominated the view.

The *Orizaba* had an interesting history. On Dec.7, 1941, the ship was part of a huge convoy destined from Halifax, Nova Scotia, to foreign ports. The convoy, composed mainly of U.S. ships, was approaching Cape Town, South Africa, carrying enough British soldiers to populate a small city. Originally destined for North Africa, the convoy was redirected to Singapore. Contrary to popular belief, the U.S.Navy was supporting the British war effort far beyond the north Atlantic prior to the attack on Pearl Harbor.

A member of the *Orizaba*'s crew informed us that, on the most recent return trip from the South Pacific Theater, the transport had carried Japanese prisoners of war. The sailor related that the prisoners were kept locked below deck and their food was lowered to them through the hatches. In accordance with the Geneva Convention, they received the same rations as the crew. The prisoners' food and beverage was poured into G I cans and thoroughly mixed before it was lowered into the hold. From a passenger's point of view, the *Orizaba* was better than any of the army troop transports I was to ship on later. The food was adequate and edible if not always a treat for the taste buds. The crew performed their duties with the efficiency of experienced seamen.

Just off the California coast the ship encountered the gigantic Pacific swells rolling in, and my stomach started rolling with them. I helped feed the fish that evening, skipped the next few meals, and was getting hungry by the following afternoon. Parkin had some candy bars that looked appetizing so I ate several of them. It was a bad idea. They came up quicker than they had gone down. Midge was not affected by motion sickness and had a good laugh at my expense. It was several days before I became accustomed enough to the pitching and rolling of the ship that I could keep food down.

Shipboard routine consisted of roll calls, lifeboat drills, eating and sleeping, with card playing and reading as the principal recreational activities. My Tazewell County buddies usually had a card game going. A Camp Hood friend of Midge Parkin's named Montalbano was a regular in the game. He was a bright, fun loving youngster who did not appear to be over sixteen. A year later I was saddened to learn from a mutual friend that he was one of the many infantry replacements from the *Orizaba* who had been killed in action in the mountains of northern Luzon.

I spent a good bit of my time reading. In 1943 a group of patriotic publishers began issuing special paperbound books to be distributed only to servicemen overseas. These paperbacks were 4 by 5 ½ inches in size with an unusual side stapled horizontal format so that they slipped easily into a pocket. There was an extensive selection of authors ranging from Homer to Dorothy Parker. This is not to say that a serviceman could select any title he desired, or that the books were widely available. Whatever the method of distribution, it must have been extremely erratic, and, so far as an infantry replacement private was concerned, the trickle down system prevailed. Only by constant vigilance and careful scrounging and bartering was I able to have something new on hand to read.

On the Sunday before I left home to be inducted into the Army, the pastor of our congregation called me to the front of the church and read a few words over me. This was a solemn rite that was observed for all of the many young men, and a few not so young, who left the congregation to serve in the armed forces. As part of the ceremony he presented me with a blue Navy New Testament, since he had run out of the brown Army edition. An accomplished scholar and excellent sermonizer, the Reverend Weiss was a bit short on knowledge of the armed forces and didn't feel the cover made any difference. Theologically he was right, of course. Shortly after I arrived at Camp Hood, I acquired a copy of the New Testament issued by the Army. This 3 by 4 ½ inch volume had a brown, imitation leather cover. On the flyleaf was a letter from Franklin D.

Roosevelt "commending the reading of the Bible to all who serve in the armed forces of the United States . . . ." In addition to the New Testament, the little volume contained the Ten Commandments and selected "Hymns, Psalms, and Prayers." During the long days of the voyage, I read the little brown Testament from cover to cover. It was one of a very few personal items I carried that survived until we reached Japan. I lost it there in a fire but quickly acquired a new copy. I still have it.

The ship's officers sounded the call to general quarters on three occasions. In each instance the rumor mill had it that a submarine periscope had been sighted. The passengers had standing orders to stay out of the way until the crew reached their battle stations, then make their way to their quarters in an orderly manner. A big tough-looking veteran Marine Sergeant stood on the upper deck where he could monitor the activity below. A few of the infantry replacements found themselves on paint chipping details immediately after being slow in following instructions.

The chance of encountering a Japanese submarine during the early stages of our journey must have been quite small. As we approached the battle zone, the risk became ever greater. Total blackout precautions were taken immediately upon leaving San Francisco. Also, anyone caught without his life preserver was in some trouble. As we sailed south and west the weather changed from cool to warm to hot and finally to stifling as we neared the equator. At night, with double blackout curtains in place, the holds were suffocatingly hot. Many of us found places to sleep on deck when allowed to do so.

The tropical ocean was particularly beautiful on clear nights with the moonlight reflecting on the waves and the Southern Cross bright in the sky. The luminescence produced by the marine life in the ocean was broken periodically by flying fish spearing along the surface of the water. The ships churning wake sparkled in the moonlight.

With only seawater available for washing, shaving, and bathing, cleaning up and taking a shower was not a very satisfying experience. A few of the passengers came up with the bright idea that they could launder their dirty clothes by tying them to a rope and dragging them alongside in the ocean. I understand that this occurred on every troop transport that crossed the Pacific. The end result was predictable. The soldier would haul in an oily rag that barely resembled clothing--another labor saving idea down the drain.

Early on, a call went out for boxers. Weekly matches were scheduled for the entertainment of the troops and the ships crew. A big, burly member of the Marine guard detachment fought and badly beat an infantry replacement on the first afternoon of boxing. The following week he repeated the performance with another soldier. Apparently feeling very confident after this second victory, he grabbed the microphone and announced that he would beat any damn G.I. infantryman on the ship who had guts enough to fight him the next week. Right away I knew the big Marine had just made a serious mistake. I had gone to a few of the fights that were staged at Camp Hood, and the best boxer I had ever seen there or anywhere was on the Orizaba. I believe his name was Reynolds. He was 25 pounds lighter than the Marine but lean and mean and lightning fast.

Later in the afternoon, I saw Reynolds on deck talking earnestly to a bigger, stockier soldier. I moved within earshot and settled down on the deck. It seems the bigger man was a professional boxer. They were discussing which of them should fight the big Marine. The heavier man finally said, "Well, if you don't think you'll have any trouble with him, go ahead. It'll probably be better if you take him, since you're an amateur."

There was great interest in the fight, caused in no small part by the Marine's braggadocio. Everyone not needed to operate the ship was on deck when fight time rolled around the next week. Climbing into the ring that afternoon, the brawny Marine looked at his smaller opponent and a smile of disdain curled his lips. Goliath must have had that same sort of smirk on his face when he first saw David that long ago day in the Valley of Elath.

The bell rings for round one and the Marine comes charging out, ready to pound this G.I. as he had pounded his opponents the preceding two weeks. Reynolds dances away and around the Marine, boxing like a young Billy Conn. The Marine keeps boring in, but Reynolds keeps dancing away. The Marine yells at Reynolds to come on and fight. Reynolds only smiles. The Marine comes charging in again. Reynolds sidesteps and comes in with a stinging left jab, right on the nose. More dancing, more sharp left jabs. The frustrated Marine can't lay a glove on Reynolds. A boatload of G.I. infantry replacements cheering wildly. Reynolds continues to move and jab, move and jab. The bell rings. End of round one. The Marine's seconds attempt to stanch the blood now flowing copiously from his nose. They apply ice to a face beginning to swell.

The bell rings for round two. The Marine comes out rather hesitantly. Reynolds continues with the boxing lesson. Now the jabs are followed with hard right crosses. The Marine is covering up, backing off, fighting defensively. His face is becoming a swollen, bloody mess. When he attempts to cover his face, Reynolds comes in with body blows.

Round 3. More of the same. I can't decide whether or not Reynolds is carrying the Marine. Given the weight difference, the size of the gloves being used, and the Marine's rugged constitution, perhaps Reynolds cannot put him away. Perhaps.

The bell rings. End of fight. Infantry replacements cheering and shouting wildly. Marine guards and Navy crew very quiet. Referee raises Reynold's arm in traditional victory signal. The Marine, face battered, bloody, and swollen, staggers to his corner and drops on his stool. He makes no attempt to challenge any damn G.I. infantryman on the ship for the coming week.

After this fight any other boxing would be anti-climactic. In early February we crossed the equator for the first time. King Neptune appeared and, with a few of the soldiers as pollywogs, performed the ancient, obligatory, fatuous rituals.

Our route took us far south of the Hawaiian Islands. We sailed for three weeks across what seemed to be an endless, empty ocean with the optical illusion that we were at the bottom of a giant saucer with the horizon forming the edge. The first landfall I witnessed was in the New Hebrides, which lie across the Coral Sea from Australia and New Guinea. The tropical islands seemed to rise slowly out of the quiet sea. It was a reassuring sight.

The *Orizaba* put in at Espiritu Santo, a huge base and supply dump, now in the backwater of the Pacific war. Years later I read that at the time we stopped, a young naval officer stationed there had been busy during his off duty hours. James Michener was at Espiritu Santo, writing *Tales of the South Pacific,* the book that would make him famous. The *Orizaba* had apparently made port here to take on fuel and supplies. We stayed less than twelve hours. No one, other than ship's officers, was allowed to go ashore. The main diversion for the troops was throwing coins into the harbor for a group of native divers to retrieve. The natives were black, muscular, and bushy haired. They were, naturally, referred to as "Fuzzy Wuzzies."

Having arrived in the southwest Pacific at this gigantic army and navy supply base, the *Orizaba's* passengers felt that they must be nearing their destination. Not so. The distance from the dock in the New Hebrides where we were tied up for the morning to Red Beach on Leyte in the Phillipines, where we would disembark from the *Orizaba*, is equivalent to the distance between Miami, Florida, and Juneau, Alaska. It would be ten more days before we left the *Orizaba*.

From Espiritu Santo we sailed west across the Coral Sea. Miles and miles of glassy sea with never a ripple or a breath of air. Shades of the Ancient Mariner. One of the sailors pointed out that Guadalcanal was some 400 miles to starboard. We made landfall near Milne Bay at the eastern tip of New Guinea. Near here the Japanese had established a beachhead on Aug. 25, 1942, in an attempt to outflank Port Moresby. MacArthur had set a trap with Australian veterans of the Mideast fighting. In a fierce battle that lasted ten days the Aussies defeated the Japanese and forced them to evacuate. For the first time a Japanese force was thrown back into the sea after they had established a beachhead.

New Guinea was awesome to behold as our ship moved nearer. The sandy beaches ran back to the blue-green swamps and dark jungles of the rain forest. The Owen Stanley Mountains rose steeply in the background. The landscape shimmered in the intense, humid heat. Tropical rainstorms could be seen dancing in the distance. Observing the forbidding swamps, jungles, and mountains, and feeling the inhospitable climate, I thought it fortunate for this boatload of infantry replacements that the main thrust of the war in the Southwest Pacific had moved forward to the Philippines.

Fierce fighting against by-passed, isolated Japanese forces was still going on in many areas of New Guinea and the adjacent islands. This action principally involved Australian troops. With MacArthur's blessing the Australian government had passed a law in 1943 restricting the use of their conscripts to the area south of the equator. As a result of this legislation, few Australian troops would be available for the Philippine Campaign or the final drive on Japan. They would be involved in the important but, in many ways, thankless task of containing the hundreds of thousands of bypassed Japanese soldiers isolated in the backwaters of the South Pacific.

Chapter IV Leyte and Luzon

The immense anchorage of Humboldt Bay at Hollandia, Dutch New Guinea, was already teeming with ships when the *Orizaba* arrived. A large convoy had been assembled for movement to Leyte in the Philippines. The *Orizaba* was apparently one of the last ships to arrive as we spent only one night at Hollandia.

During the evening, a tropical downpour provided the troops on the *Orizaba* with their first freshwater shower in four weeks. The decks were crowded with soapy, happy soldiers, feeling really clean for the first time on their long boat ride. We were to learn later that it is not a good idea to procrastinate in the shower. Mother Nature could turn off the tropical downpour at any time leaving the bather well lathered but with no rinse water.

After leaving Humboldt Bay the ships in the convoy seemed to cover the sea from horizon to horizon. Destroyer Escorts sped along the fringes of the convoy as the ships plowed through the tropical seas. Navy planes could be seen providing aerial cover as we neared the Philippines. So far as I could see, only a few nuisance raids by Japanese planes marred the trip. We crossed the equator again on Feb.22 and several days later arrived at Red Beach, Leyte, near the city of Tacloban. We climbed over the side, down cargo nets, and into LCVPs (Landing Craft Vehicle, Personnel) that carried us through the surf to the beach. From there we were trucked to the 4th Replacement Depot, which had been set up nearby. During our brief stay, we replacements were used on work details on the beach and in the city of Tacloban where MacArthur had maintained his headquarters before moving on for the recent invasion of Luzon.

At the 4th Replacement Depot the chow lines were the longest I encountered while in the Army, and the food was the most monotonous. Two meals--I use the word loosely--were served each day. After two hours waiting in line each man received one ladle of dehydrated potatoes and one ladle of dehydrated eggs for the morning meal. The afternoon meal was exactly the same except that the eggs were flavored with wieners at the approximate rate of two wieners to a G.I. can (a standard garbage can) of dehydrated eggs.

Well, as Mother always told us, there were a lot of people in the world who would have been overjoyed to have that food. And, of course, she was right. There was surprisingly little complaining among the men, but I do not recall anyone getting back in that line for seconds.

A Jap plane came over nightly. The base personnel informed us that it was just a nuisance flight. The men did not bother to leave their cots when "washing machine Charley" made his nightly flyover.

An incident at the 4th Repple-Depple that sticks in my mind occurred the morning we were mustered with the prescribed uniform consisting only of boots, ponchos, and dogtags. It was the old shortarm routine again. O.K., skin it back, milk it down, turn around, spread your cheeks. All right. Next. The officer in charge of this operation must have been preparing for a postwar career as a standup comedian. He regaled us with a few jokes while we waited in the blazing tropical sun for our turn to expose ourselves. For some unknown reason that causes the human brain to store such valueless debris, I remember his featured story:

An Indian chief called his wife into the tepee and muttered "Squaw, bring drum."
"War drum?"
"No. Condrum. Chief want peace."

Aside from being sexist, racist, and stupid, the captain's stories did add a little levity to the occasion.

Among the great storytellers in the military, Admiral Nimitz, commander of all Naval forces in the Pacific, must have been the most noted. Born and reared in Texas, Nimitz attended Annapolis because no appointments to West Point were available. It was the Navy's lucky day. Nimitz was a brilliant strategist. In the year following Pearl Harbor, he used limited resources to achieve great success. Late in that year, Nimitz went to Brisbane, Australia, to confer with MacArthur on the progress of the war against Japan--a project on which they were cooperating, more or less. At the end of the conference, Nimitz addressed an assembly of army staff members. He referred to the problems he and MacArthur were having in their respective theaters of war. He continued: "The situation reminds me of the story of the two frantically worried men who were pacing the corridor of their hotel. One finally turned to the other and asked 'What are you worried about?' The answer was immediate. 'I am a doctor and I have a patient in my room with a wooden leg. I have that leg apart and can't get it back together again.' The other responded, 'Great guns, I wish that was all that I have to worry about. I have a good looking gal in a room with both legs apart and I can't remember the room number.'" It was reported that there was great applause and even MacArthur laughed heartily. And so it would appear that it wasn't enough that the Navy lived better and ate better than the Army--the sailors were even supplied with a better grade of humor.

At any rate, the shortarm inspection provoked considerable discussion when we returned to our tents. Included in the discussion group were three men from Chicago who had been in the training cycle at Camp Hood. Two of them were genuine wiseacres. They summed up the shortarm situation, "How in hell do they get off calling us privates when even our privates aren't private."

The third Chicagoan was a stocky kid named Valavasquez who had been attending art school when he was drafted. The two wise guys were constantly harassing him in a good-natured manner about his constant inventorying of his equipment, the ukelele he had somehow managed to stow away, and most of all, the sketches he was constantly drawing. I was to see one of the wise guys a year and a half later when we were being separated from the service at Ft. Sheridan. He and the other wise guy had made it through the war. Valavasquez had been killed on Luzon.

On or about March 1 a large group of the replacements boarded an army troop transport that joined a large convoy en route to Lingayen Gulf on Luzon. There was still some Jap air activity so we were forced to spend much of the time in holds where our bunks were tiered six high. When we boarded the ship I hurried to get a top berth, inspired by the possibility of having five seasick soldiers above me if we ran into rough seas. There were several big crap games going in the holds. Over time, most of the gambling money became concentrated into fewer and fewer hands. I saw one roll of the dice for 20,000 pesos, which was 10,000 dollars at a time when a private's pay was 51 dollars a month. Money didn't seem very important at that point as we waited to go ashore at Lingayen Gulf.

Once again we crawled down the cargo nets and were taken ashore on landing craft. Another replacement depot, this time it was the Fifth, awaited us. As we were waiting to be assigned to our tent quarters, I noticed the unusual appearance of a group of soldiers going through a nearby chow line. As we approached these men I was startled to see that some were so emaciated that they looked like walking skeletons. They looked and moved like old men. Some were missing an arm or a leg. Many of these men were survivors of the infamous Bataan Death March. All had been freed from Jap prison camps since the Lingayen landing. They were recuperating here and waiting for transportation home. These abused and emaciated men were living proof of the barbarity of the Japanese Army. If any of the replacements needed a reason to hate the Japs, seeing and talking with these victims of Japanese brutality would surely provide it. For me, it was an unforgettable experience.

I had read the story of the Bataan Death March when it was first verified and reported in the newspapers in 1943. During the months that followed the Japanese sneak attack on Pearl Harbor, American and Filipino troops on Luzon had mounted a gallant resistance to the Japanese invaders. They had made a fighting withdrawal into prepared positions on the Bataan peninsula across the bay from Manila. Unfortunately for these troops, the ammunition, food, and supplies needed to withstand a long siege had not been stockpiled.

General MacArthur, on direct order from President Roosevelt, had reluctantly departed for Australia. General Wainwright, with headquarters on Corregidor in Manila Bay, was placed in command of all American and Filipino forces in the Philippines. Major General Edward P. King was in command on Bataan. By the first week in April his troops were sick, starving, exhausted, and running out of ammunition. On the morning of April 9, 1942, King drove to the Japanese lines under a white flag of truce to ask for terms of surrender. He was taken to Gen. Homma's chief of operations who was adamant in his insistence on unconditional surrender. "Will my men be treated well?" King asked. The offended Japanese general haughtily replied, "We are not barbarians." He lied.

General King unconditionally surrendered 12,000 American and 63,000 Filipino soldiers that day. From Bataan they were marched toward Camp O'Donnell, eighty miles to the north near the town of Cabanatuan. Ten thousand would die on that march. They would die of thirst, starvation, wounds and Japanese brutality. Food, water, and personal possessions were taken from them before the march began. On the march they were denied food and water. Mad with thirst, the men drank from mud holes and buffalo wallows. They were beaten, clubbed, shot, bayoneted, burned, and some were buried alive by their brutal guards. Courageous Filipino civilians, some at the sacrifice of their own lives, stealthily provided them with the little food they received. When they reached Camp O'Donnell 60,000 men were jammed into a bamboo hut camp built for 10,000. Another 2,000 Americans and 25,000 Filipinos would die there during the next three months of their captivity. Now, after three years, the survivors we talked with had been freed and were on their way home.

Chapter V 11th Airborne

After two days at the Lingayen Gulf Depot, a group of the replacements was alerted to be ready to move out the following morning. Runyon and I from the " Tazewell County Four" were informed that we would be in this shipment. Of the other two, I would see Midge Parkin back home after the war but Alvie Fuller would be dead by that time. As usual, we were given no hint as to where we were going or to what unit we might be assigned. But for this group of mostly eighteen-year-old replacements, the die had been cast. Our destiny was now to be the 11th Airborne Division, which, at this time, was battling the Japs south of Manila.

Most of us had heard of the exploits of the airborne divisions in Europe. Premier English historian John Keegan has written of them:

> The 82nd and 101st were the cream of the American Army, trained to a knife-edge and prepared for battle; their eighteen battalions, though scattered [in Normandy] were the equal of a force twice their size.

The 11th Airborne was activated in Feb. of 1943 and first saw action in November of 1944 on Leyte. We had heard little of the 11th Airborne for reasons that we would understand later. Gen. Robert Eichelberger's biographer, James Shortal, has written of the 11th Airborne at the time of their landing on Luzon:

> MacArthur's plan for the landing was daring and dangerous. He was sending one Division to attack Manila from the south at a time when two full corps were getting nowhere from the north. The division MacArthur selected-the 11th Airborne-was the smallest division in the theater. It had one parachute infantry regiment [511th] of three battalions and two glider infantry regiments [187th and 188th] of two battalions each. The unit had almost no vehicles because airborne units were expected to be dropped by airplanes very near their target.

Whatever the Eleventh Airborne Division lacked in quantity, it more than made up for in quality. Eichelberger believed that this was the best division in the army. All its enlisted men were highly motivated volunteers who were willing to jump out of an airplane or ride the dangerous and rickety glider to the battlefield. The officers in this division were also exceptional. Many were regular army officers and there was a large percentage of West Pointers at every echelon of command from platoon through division. This was a division with a great deal of discipline and morale.

I was to discover that the 11th Airborne was, in no small measure, a reflection of the man who had led (and driven) the division since its activation in February of 1943. Joseph M. Swing graduated from the U.S. Military Academy at West Point in the class of 1915. Known later as "the class that the stars fell on," the class included Dwight Eisenhower and Omar Bradley.

After receiving his commission, Lt. Swing was assigned to the force that pursued Pancho Villa into Mexico. He was sent to France in 1917 with the American Expeditionary Force where he served in the field artillery. In 1918 he was made aide-de-camp to Army Chief of Staff Gen. Peyton March. Shortly thereafter Swing married March's daughter, Mary. This union was to last for sixty years. Between the wars, Swing attended the Army War College and the Command and General Staff School. He achieved some fame as the outstanding polo player in the U S Army.

Early in World War II, Swing was sent to the North African Theater to serve as airborne adviser to the commanding general, Dwight Eisenhower. During the Sicily invasion many troop-carrying airplanes were shot down by friendly fire. The paratroopers and glidermen sustained heavy losses. Those who did land safely were scattered far and wide. The future of the airborne divisions was in doubt. Eisenhower recommended to Army Chief of Staff Marshall that the existing airborne divisions be disbanded and that airborne troops be used in units no larger than regiments. Marshall directed that a board be set up to study the problem and make recommendations.

By this time Gen. Swing had returned to the States and was in North Carolina training the 11th Airborne Division. He was appointed head of a second board to study the future of the airborne. At this time, Swing produced a training circular that was to become the "Bible" for subsequent airborne operations.

Secretary of War Stimson, Chief of Staff Marshall, and Chief of Ground Forces MacNair were still in doubt about the proper size and use of airborne units. MacNair ordered maneuvers for Dec 1943, to be carried out by the 11th Airborne Division. Their performance would determine the future of the airborne divisions. After the conclusion of the maneuvers, Gen. MacNair sent a message to Gen. Swing:

> I congratulate you on the performance of your division in the Knollwood maneuver. After the airborne operations in Africa and Sicily, my staff and I had become convinced of the impractibility of handling large airborne units. I was prepared to recommend to the War Department that airborne divisions be abandoned in our scheme of organization and that the airborne effort be restricted to parachute units of battalion size or smaller. The successful performance of your division has convinced me that we were wrong, and I shall recommend that we continue our present schedule of activating, training, and committing airborne divisions.

Tall, white haired, with sharp features, Joe Swing was as physically fit as his paratroopers. When they parachuted, he parachuted. He knew from experience that the harder he trained his men, and the better he conditioned them, the more effective they would be in combat, and the lower the casualty rate would be when they were thrust into battle. When his division was committed to action, Swing could usually be found where the fighting was fiercest.

On Jan.31, 1945, the 187th and 188th Regiments made an amphibious landing 55 miles southwest of Manila at Nasugbu where they encountered light opposition. Racing inland, the airborne troops kept the Japanese defenders confused and off balance. Their rapid advance enabled them to capture vital bridges before the Japs could detonate the demolition charges that they had placed. On Feb. 3, the paratroopers of the division's 511th Regiment dropped onto Tagaytay Ridge and were soon joined by the lead elements of the 188th. That afternoon Eighth Army Commander Lt.Gen.Eichelberger, with MacArthur's approval, directed the division to move out with all possible speed toward Manila. At this point the division had a bridgehead 65 miles long and 1000 yards wide.

Spearheaded by the 511th, the division drove hell-for-leather toward Manila. While the northern outskirts of Manila were not heavily defended, the Japanese had anticipated an attack from the south. On Feb 4 at the south edge of the city the paratroopers slammed into the Genko Line, an in-depth defensive position of 1200 concrete and steel pillboxes, mutually supporting positions, 6,000 feet in depth. The Japs had an abundance of artillery, mortars, and automatic weapons, part of which had been scavenged from ships in the Bay. Anchored on Manila Bay on the west and Laguna de Bay on the east, this formidable defense line had to be breached by frontal assault and destroyed.

Meanwhile, speeding down from the north, a motorized column from the 1st Cavalry Division entered Manila at 6:00 PM on Feb. 3. Meeting only light opposition they pushed on to Santo Tomas University where they freed almost 4,000 internees who had been imprisoned since 1942. The 37th Infantry Division entered northwest Manila the next morning and freed the 500 internees and 800 prisoners of war the Japanese had been holding at Old Bilibid prison.

As the 11th Airborne troopers battled their way through the Genko Line and Ft.McKinley and across Nichols Field, the 37th Infantry and 1st Cavalry began the difficult task of clearing the Japs from the city of Manila, battling block by block, building by building, room by room.

MacArthur's communiqué of Feb. 6 announced: "Our forces are rapidly clearing the enemy from Manila. . . .Our converging columns. . . entered the city and surrounded the Jap defenders. Their complete destruction is imminent." MacArthur's announcement was, as usual, premature. It was not until one month later on March 3 that Corps Commander Griswold could report to 6th Army Commander Krueger that the last large scale resistance in the city had been crushed. As late as July, Japanese holdouts were being rooted out of their hiding places in the rubble of the city.

A narrow gauge railroad ran from Lingayen Gulf down across Luzon's fertile central plain to the city of Manila. Army engineers had repaired the tracks and rebuilt the bridges as the 6th Army drove south. We replacements who had been alerted for movement loaded aboard a train headed south for Manila. Somewhere just north of the city we were transferred to a truck convoy.

We had seen the ravages of war on Leyte, particularly around Tacloban, in the wasted towns around Lingayen Gulf, and down through the central Luzon plain, but we had seen nothing that compared with the destruction that we now viewed. Known in better days as the "Pearl of the Orient," Manila had been a great city with a metropolitan population of 1,000,000. It now lay in ruin, a city made a charnel house by the Japanese. Caught in the crossfire of a battle of annihilation, trapped in the raging inferno of the great fire that engulfed the city, victimized by the horrible atrocities committed by the doomed Japanese, 100,000 of Manila's people had died. Only Warsaw among Allied cities endured more human suffering during this global conflict. The government buildings, which, I was to learn later, had once resembled the structures in Washington,D.C. and our state capitals, were now empty shells surrounded by heaps of dusty rubble. The entire business district, two-thirds of the utilities and factories, and most of the homes had been destroyed. As our truck convoy crossed over the Pasig River on a pontoon bridge and moved on into south Manila, we passed through mile after mile of burned out houses and shell battered buildings. The stench of death and smoldering ruins filled our nostrils.

We rolled out of the city and through the suburb of Paranaque along the highway that leads south to Tagaytay Ridge. Our route took us around beautiful Lake Taal on a breath taking, awe-inspiring road carved in the side of the cliff.

It was late afternoon when the truck convoy ground to a halt and we were ordered to unload. We had stopped in a coconut palm grove near a small barrio (town). Looming above us was a dark, forbidding mountain. This mountain was to figure prominently in the future of these young infantry replacements. For too many, their future would end on its slopes and in its ravines.

The truck convoy had brought us to the command post of the 187th ParaGlider Infantry Regiment. A young paratroop officer greeted us: "Welcome, you are now members of the 187th of the 11th Airborne Division and where in the hell are your weapons?" We had arrived at the front with gas masks but with no weapons. The officer shook his head in disbelief and instructed us to stand by while we were being assigned to companies.

Near where we waited, two Filipino guerrillas had just arrived with a Japanese soldier they had captured. He had been stripped naked to insure that he was not hiding any weapons or grenades on his person. We had just placed our gas masks in a pile, and I stepped aside for a better look. As I watched the Jap gestured and snarled something at his captors. It was to be his last deliberate utterance on this planet. A razor sharp machete flashed in tropic sunlight. One of the Filipinos had amputated the Jap's genitalia.

The terrible wrath the Filipinos exhibited can only be understood in the context of that time and that place. Within a few miles of the spot where we stood, these Filipinos had seen 300 of their friends and relatives forced to work as slave laborers by the Japanese soldiers. They had been compelled to dig caves and build bunkers and other fortifications on this mountain looming above us. When the Filipinos had finished this work, the Japanese soldiers had lined them up along a ravine and cut them down with machine gun fire. The dead and the living wounded were then bulldozed into the ravine and covered with earth. Thus the Japanese made sure that there would be no Filipinos left alive who could reveal the location of the fortifications.

And this was only one of hundreds of instances of barbaric Japanese savagery inflicted upon the people here in southern Luzon and, indeed, throughout the Philippines. The bill of particulars introduced at the 1946 war crimes trial of Gen. Yamashita indicated that here in Batangas Province on Feb. 16-18, 1945, in the city of Lipa more than 2,000 civilians were massacred; on Feb. 19 in Cuenca just a few miles up the road from where we stood, 984 civilians were massacred, a large percentage of the population of the town; on Feb. 20 in San Jose, 500 civilians massacred; on Feb. 28 in Bauang, 500 civilians massacred; from Feb. 16 to Mar. 19 in the Santo Tomas area, 1500 civilians massacred.

Just to the north of us in the Los Banos area, Japanese soldiers had slaughtered 1400 civilians in another frenzy of killing. A task force of paratroopers from the 11th Airborne Division, aided by Filipino guerrillas, had leap-frogged behind the enemy lines. In a classic airborne-amphibious operation they had liberated 2,122 civilian internees from the Los Banos prison camp and evacuated them across Laguna de Bay to safety. In the days that followed, a Japanese force moved into the area, killing any civilians they encountered.

The atrocities the Japanese committed defy belief. Their barbaric behavior during the battle for Manila has been extremely well documented. Filipinos in that city were bayoneted, shot, raped, and burned alive by the tens of thousands. A favorite tactic was to force people into the upper floors of buildings, then start raging fires in the stairways. Babies were thrown in the air and impaled on bayonets in mid-air. Patients were tied to their beds before hospitals were set on fire. This savagery extended across the Philippines as the liberating American forces moved forward. The magnitude of the Japanese carnage is clearly revealed by figures compiled after the war. The census of 1940 pegged the population of the Philippines at 16,356,000. Reparation claims in 1946 indicate that 1,111,938 Filipinos had died at the hands of the Japanese during their conquest and occupation of the archipelago.

By late afternoon the replacements had been assigned and guided to their new companies. I was among those assigned to E Company of the 2nd Battalion, 187th. Because we had no weapons, each replacement was assigned to two of the paratroopers who would share their foxhole with him. The two troopers I joined were lean, weary, and very much on edge. The long period of almost continuous combat since coming ashore at Nasugbu had taken its toll. With a Table of Organization strength of over 180, E Company was down to 63 before we 33 replacements arrived. The troopers who shared their foxhole with me informed me that although the 187th was still officially listed as a glider infantry regiment, its members were qualified paratroopers. Commanding General Joe Swing had made his division capable of using whatever means of transportation might be available for an airborne operation.

The following morning the replacements were interviewed by E Company Commander Brown and assigned to platoons and squads. Along with a big, husky replacement from Oregon, I was assigned to a machine gun squad in the weapons platoon. Norman Petersen and I must have looked like we could carry a heavy load. For the rest of the campaign, Pete was a constant. Members of the squad would come and go with wounds, malaria, jungle fevers, fungus, and other infections, but Pete was always there, carrying his share of the load. The squad theoretically consisted of a squad leader, first and second gunners, and two ammunition bearers. Before we were assigned to the squad, it was down to Squad Leader Sgt. Dennis Faye, First

Gunner Walt Lepley, and an eighteen year old Filipino named Feling who had voluntarily joined the squad as the division battled through his hometown of Paranaque. He could have left at any time but stayed with us through thick and thin and never complained even when things got really hairy. Each of our 11th Airborne rifle companies had a number of these young Filipino volunteers who fought alongside the paratroopers. They were highly motivated and performed admirably. I hope these brave volunteers were adequately rewarded for their service when the war ended. At a time when we were short-handed everywhere, they were a godsend. The guerrilla formations, as well as the Filipino Army units that were activated early in the Luzon Campaign, pleasantly surprised the American commanders by proving to be highly effective in combat.

Sgt. Faye, our squad leader, was a lanky, redheaded Irish-American from Philadelphia whose combat savvy was a big factor in keeping the squad alive through the campaign. Walt Lepley was a Ft. Benning trained paratrooper, intensely motivated and tough as hell. Walt really believed that one paratrooper was worth five regular soldiers and was always willing to personally demonstrate this truth to any unbelievers. Sgt. Faye and Pfc. Lepley gave Pete and me a quick refresher course on the care and operation of a light machine gun that first morning.

Later in the day the replacements were issued weapons. Somewhere, the division had secured a supply of 1903 Model Springfield rifles. Rumor had it that they had been scrounged from the Navy. We spent the rest of the day taking these bolt-action beauties out of the greasy cosmolene in which they were packed. Trained with the M-1 Garand, most of us had never seen a Springfield '03 before. Both time and ammunition for the '03s were in short supply so we had no opportunity to zero in or even fire our new weapons. I wondered how this weapons snafu could occur in the best-supplied army in the world. I suppose the most logical and perhaps most generous explanation might be that many Filipino units had recently been organized and armed, and the demand for rifles had exceeded the supply.

Toward evening, word came down that the battalion would be moving against the Jap defenses on the mountain in the morning.

The 11th Airborne historian sets the stage:

The 187th was preparing for the bloodiest and toughest battle of its military history. In the southeastern corner of Lake Taal, Mt. Macolod climbs sheerly to a magnificent Gibralter-like pinnacle 2,700 feet above the lake. Its north and west slopes rise, nearly vertical, from the water. On the east and south sides, the drop from the peak is vertical for about 1200 feet; then three ridges descend gradually to the bottom of the mountain. . . . In this area the Japanese had constructed a formidable defensive position. They had employed impressed Filipino laborers to construct the underground positions and had slain the laborers when the job was completed to insure secrecy. Only dummy positions were visible from the air, and the mountain bristled with artillery and automatic weapons carefully laid to cover all approaches with interlocking bands of fire.

Chapter VI Mt.Macolod

E Company moved out at the head of a column that included Regimental Headquarters and the 2nd Battalion of the 187th. Spread out along the trail, the column headed onto one of the ridges that gradually lead up Mt. Macolod. Our machine gun squad was positioned half way along the company column as we moved forward at a rapid, steady pace.

Being assigned to a machine gun squad in an infantry rifle company can only be described as a mixed blessing. On the plus side, you know that you will not be the lead scout on the point when the company moves out. On the other hand, the enemy always tries to knock out the automatic weapons first--after the flamethrowers, that is. The fact that only two members of the squad that came ashore on Luzon a month and a half ago are still around would seem to indicate that we are not in an exceptionally safe line of work.

As the column moved up the ridge, the road narrowed to a trail and then to a footpath as we left the coconut palms and moved deeper into the thick tropical vegetation. The jungle growth became denser as we advanced and the narrowing path soon forced the column to move in single file. The overgrowth gradually blotted out the tropical sun, and we were soon moving through the eerie twilight of the dense rain forest.

The battalion commander, a major fresh from the States, moved forward through our squad. I was surprised to see that he was wearing gold oak leaves, the insignia of his rank. From everything that I had read and heard, this was much the same as pinning a target on your chest. A few minutes later we heard the sharp crack of a Japanese sniper's rifle up ahead, then heavier M1 firing as our riflemen cleared out the snipers. Soon, the battalion commander shuffled back down the trail, supported by an aide. A large bloodstained bandage covered his shoulder.

With the snipers cleared out, our column resumed the advance. We had hardly gone another hundred yards when all hell broke loose. Japanese Nambu machine guns opened up on our flank and then to our front. Bullets were snapping and popping all around and above us.

The rapid fire of the Nambus sounded like canvas ripping. We scrambled for cover dragging the wounded with us. Anyone standing up was in mortal danger of being cut down at once by the hail of bullets. With the column pinned down by the heavy crossfire, the Japs started dropping knee mortar rounds in on us. It was painfully obvious that they had the trail completely registered in with their weapons. They were cutting us up from positions so well concealed that we could only guess where to return fire. I was busy hugging the ground, saying a quick prayer, doing exactly what Sgt. Faye ordered and then looking in vain for a target for my 1903 model Springfield rifle.

The battalion's position was becoming more precarious with each second that passed. The Japanese would soon reinforce their advantage with more and heavier mortars and machine guns and possibly an artillery barrage. Attacking the well entrenched and expertly concealed Japanese positions under the existing circumstances would sacrifice the battalion without any reasonable return for that sacrifice. In our present situation, we were sitting ducks. Casualties were mounting as mortar rounds continued to whoosh into our position.

Major Ewing, who had assumed command of the battalion just ten minutes earlier, quickly assessed the situation. As I was to observe on several occasions, Ewing was cool and collected in dire circumstances. In an orderly, fighting withdrawal, he saved most of his command to fight another day. We would get our revenge on these same Japs a month later when the tactical advantage would be on our side. E Company came off the mountain with our eleven wounded, fortunate that we had had no one killed. For the replacements it had been a searing initiation into the world of infantry warfare.

The battalion moved back to the defense perimeter, dug our foxholes a little deeper, and prepared for the Jap attack that was sure to come that night. Banzai attacks still occurred, but most Jap commanders had learned by this time that massed human wave attacks into the jaws of American infantry firepower were a bad idea, unless, of course, you had suicide in mind. They could inflict more casualties on the Americans by staying in their fortified positions and dying there. The Japs persisted, however, in nightly probing attacks, looking for weak spots in our defenses and for opportunities to infiltrate our perimeters.

Our weapons were sited for maximum effectiveness. The machine guns were set up in the most likely hot spots, and the mortars registered in on defilade areas. Nearby artillery, when available, was registered in on areas around the perimeter. Booby traps, grenades, and flares rigged with trip wires were set out to provide warning. We suffered few casualties from the Japs' nightly activities, as at least one-third of our men would be manning their weapons at any time. Some Filipino units in the area, whose men had the idea that tropic nights were made for sleeping, were caught off guard and took heavy casualties on several occasions.

On this night the Japs were especially active. Booby traps exploded on opposite corners of the perimeter simultaneously. Flares lighted the night and tracers streamed steadily from the perimeter as the riflemen opened fire. The automatic weapons gunners held their fire until things got really hot to avoid revealing their positions prematurely. The Japs made one charge, then fell back. None of them got within fifty yards of our lines. They continued to fire into the perimeter from a distance while retrieving their dead and wounded. The firing went on for several hours, dying down for a time, and then growing more intense. Several hours before daylight things quieted down.

When the dawn lighted the area around the perimeter, it revealed the bodies of nine Jap soldiers, one dead horse, and one dead cow. Sgt. Faye remarked that the Japs in the area had carried off their dead and wounded after previous attacks. He guessed that the volume of fire had been too heavy to get these out. The Japs probably drove the unfortunate horse and cow ahead of them to set off our trip-wired booby traps.

Since there was a strong possibility that we would use this perimeter again, the bodies were buried. Pete and I were part of a detail sent to bury the dead horse. New men get these jobs. On our way we stopped to examine the Japs who had been killed. They were short, muscular, bandy-legged, and had apparently been in good health until their recent demise. There was no indication that they were not well fed. Their rations would become much skimpier as we closed in on them during the next two months.

One of the replacements picked up a Jap helmet that he must have thought would make a good souvenir. The sergeant in charge of the detail gave him the same advice Sgt. Faye had given Pete and me earlier. "Throw that away. We travel fast and light in this outfit. Get rid of anything that will slow you down or get in the way. Carrying extra weight or bulk could lose you the seconds that stand between surviving and getting shot."

Travel light? Compared to what? All members of a rifle company were loaded down. In our understrength machine gun squad, the load was even greater. Instead of the carbines that the Army Table of Equipment called for, we carried M1 Garands. After the first attacks on Mt.Macolod, enough M1 Garand rifles were available from the casualties so that we replacements could exchange our Springfields. I doubt that we would have traded our M1s for carbines even if that had been an option. Hit with a carbine bullet, a Jap might not go down; hit with an M1 slug, he was history.

Our machine gun squad varied from three to five members. We carried M1 Garand rifles, several bandoliers of rifle ammunition apiece, the machine gun, the tripod, an extra gun barrel, two or three hand grenades apiece, and individual entrenching tools. We usually tried to start the day with four cans of machine gun ammo. Only in personal gear was there an opportunity to lessen our loads. We carried the essential one or two canteens of water, a waterproof poncho, a spoon, half of a mess kit, a razor and a toothbrush. A blanket would have been appreciated at night, especially on the mountain, but no one was going to carry that extra weight and bulk through the heat of the day.

The division historian summed up our situation:

> Regimental Hqs and the 2nd Bn of the 187th were withdrawn from the battle for Macolod after bloodily attacking to the foot of Brownie Ridge. The battalion commander Loewus was wounded and Ewing assumed command. They were replaced by guerrillas with orders to hold and to prevent the escape of the Japanese defenders. . . .Headquarters and 2nd Bn, 187th were moved east to Lipa and given the mission of attacking to the east, pushing the Japanese out of artillery range of the Lipa highway, and developing the Malepunyo position.

The following morning we were on the move. The destruction of the Mt. Macolod position would apparently have to wait while more pressing problems were addressed. Down in the ranks we were very low on the "need to know" scale. In fact, we replacements were completely off the scale. We knew little of the tactical situation and nothing of the strategy being pursued. We only knew that we would be moving forward, attacking the Jap wherever we were sent, assaulting him in his caves and bunkers. Given the Code of Bushido of the Japanese army, this could only mean that we would pursue him to his death. During the months that I was with Company E in southern Luzon, we took no prisoners. On a number of occasions we had Jap units cornered in positions where they were doomed. They were showered with leaflets instructing them that we would honor these leaflets or a white flag if they would come in and surrender. We were then instructed to stop firing for a specified time to give them an opportunity to comply. There were no takers.

I'm not sure how it would have played out if a number of the Japs had tried to surrender. There was a "take no prisoners" bias among most of the paratroopers. They vowed never to be taken prisoner and never to take a prisoner. In every sense, it was a battle with no quarter given or asked.

Nowhere in the 187th Regiment's area of responsibility could the troopers let their guard down. This need for constant vigilance was tragically demonstrated when, on April 3, the 2nd Bn intelligence officer, the battalion motor officer, and a sergeant were ambushed and killed on the highway near Talisay in an area the regiment had secured weeks earlier. The Japanese then set up a second ambush in order to kill anyone who tried to recover the bodies.

To our south, the city of Lipa had been liberated on March 29. The Japanese made a strong stand there, and American air strikes and artillery barrages had reduced the city to rubble. The important highway from Manila through southwestern Luzon to the port of Batangas on the Sibuyan Sea was now in friendly hands. The army's use of this vital road was being seriously hampered, however, by Japanese artillery in the nearby Malepunyo foothills. Well-concealed howitzers were lobbing shells at any vehicles Jap observers spotted on the road. The Japanese artillerymen would roll their big guns out of caves, fire a few quick rounds, then move them back before our spotters could get a fix on their positions. One of their artillery pieces was a 300 mm howitzer, which was concealed under a skillfully camouflaged sliding roof. When we overran these positions later in the month, we found shell cases for this howitzer that were almost as large as a standard garbage can.

Combat patrols from the 187th spent the next week constantly searching for and then attacking the Japanese wherever we found them. Our patrols were encountering many of the enemy on the move. They were pulling back into the foothills and the Malepunyo mountain fortress. To intercept and destroy as many of the enemy as possible before they could reach these strong defensive positions, we set up ambushes on routes they were most likely to use.

On one of these ambushes the other machine gun from E Company was set up close to ours. Pvt. Theodore R. Theodore, an acquaintance of mine, was their first gunner on this day. I knew Theodore from Camp Hood, the *Orizaba*, and various replacement depots. At roll call at the various replacement stopovers and depots we had been through, there was usually some sergeant in charge who would call out the soldier's last name. The soldier would answer with his first name and middle initial. This apparently worked better than having the soldier respond with "here" or "present" which anyone might call out, especially in the dark at reveille. The sergeant would call out "Theodore" and get a booming "Theodore R" in response. If in a jolly mood, the sergeant would stop to remark, "There's a helluva echo around here."

To avoid being seen or heard by the enemy, we had exercised great caution in moving to this well concealed ambush position. The officer in charge had deployed the machine guns under some extremely tall coconut palm trees. The coconuts, if they are not harvested before maturing, drop from the trees when they have fully ripened. At the moment Theodore Theodore finished loading the machine gun and placed his finger on the trigger, a coconut sixty feet above his head reached full maturity and succumbed to the law of gravity. The big coconut, having achieved considerable velocity as it hurtled toward earth, hit Theodore Theodore's helmet squarely with a big thump, shortening his neck at least an inch. His hand, closing in a reflex action, squeezed the trigger of the machine gun. There was a loud rata-tat-tat--rata-tat-tat as half a dozen bullets whizzed to our front. Audible for miles, the machine gun fire negated the prospect of ambushing any Japs around that area for a considerable period of time. Theodore Theodore had a throbbing headache and a very sore neck.

Several weeks passed before I saw Theodore Theodore again. When I did, he was carrying a flame-thrower. He informed me that, following the ambush incident, he had been selected to go back to division headquarters for a short course in flame-thrower operation.

I could empathize with Theodore Theodore. I had had a somewhat similar experience earlier. The battalion was dug in on a defensive perimeter. It was a cold, pitch-black night made more miserable by intermittent heavy rain. I had just been awakened to take my turn manning the machine gun. The Japs had been coming down from the hills every night to harass and attempt to infiltrate our positions. This was the kind of black, stormy night that suited their purposes. Rifle in hand, I sat behind the machine gun straining my eyes in vain in the stygian darkness. Suddenly there was an eerie swish just above me, and a heavy object hit the back edge of my helmet and brushed down my back. These are the times that try men's sphincter muscles. I swung around to deliver a butt stroke with my rifle. I struck what turned out to be a big palm frond that had dropped from the tree above me. If my finger had been on the trigger of the machine gun, I would undoubtedly have had the same result as Theodore Theodore. The next morning I noted that, as the palm trees grow taller, the lower fronds or large leaves dry up and fall to the ground. After this incident I made it a rule to check overhead before dark whenever we dug in under palm trees.

On one of our defense perimeters there was a defilade area to the front of our machine gun. As usual we set up grenades with trip wires attached to warn of any enemy movement through this area. Late that night while I was on sentry duty one of these booby traps exploded. I started lobbing hand grenades into the defilade area. I was pulling the pin, letting the handle pop, and holding the grenade for an extra count before throwing so that it would explode in midair over the target. That way there was no danger that the Japs would throw them back. As I pulled the pin and let the handle pop on another grenade, there was a loud whisper behind me. "Throw that damned thing." It was Sgt. Faye.

The next morning as we were eating what passed for breakfast, Sgt. Faye read me the riot act, "Hell, the Japs aren't going to have to kill this squad. Urish is going to do it for them by holding on to one those damn grenades too long." He proceeded to explain to me that these grenades weren't all perfect. Once in a while one of them exploded a little sooner than expected.

When Sgt. Faye spoke, I listened. And learned. Never again would I try for air bursts.

While on patrol one afternoon we witnessed the camouflage expertise of Japanese troops from close range. Our patrol had been moving quietly through a rolling, grassy area broken by clumps of brush and tropical growth. When we stopped to rest, the patrol leader moved to the reverse slope of the next hill to reconnoiter our route. Just over the hill, he saw what looked like a number of bushes. As he surveyed the area before bringing up the patrol, these bushes started moving toward a nearby ravine. The patrol leader immediately signaled the patrol to move up on the double from the cover where we were resting. A brief, intense firefight ensued. In this instance the Japs were intent on fleeing and were able to use the ravine as an escape route.

A few days later our machine gun squad was again part of a patrol sent into Jap held territory. This day was unusual only in that we went farther and stayed longer than we had on most reconnaissance patrols. The twelve man group was led by one of our platoon sergeants who seemed to be the only man who knew where we were, what we were looking for, or how in hell we would ever find our way out. As we were taking a rest break in the almost perfect concealment afforded by a bamboo thicket, Pete started musing in muted tones, questioning what might happen if the patrol leader got killed. Following the leader was fine, he thought, unless something happened to the leader. I suggested to Pete that we crumble the crackers in our K rations and leave a trail of crumbs just like in *Hansel and Gretel*. Pete failed to find much humor in this suggestion.

A story that had recently circulated through E Company must have prompted Pete's concern. Several weeks earlier Sgt. Gagliano, a squad leader in the company, had led a patrol deep into Japanese held territory. Much deeper than he had been instructed to go, in fact, and it was generally suspected that he had gotten lost. When the patrol finally returned, the sergeant, aided by friendly Filipinos in the patrol area, had gathered a great deal of valuable information on enemy dispositions. For this exceptional foray, above and beyond the call of duty, Sgt. Gagliano was awarded a medal.

E Company took more casualties as we continued to patrol and to attack Japanese bunkers and outposts in the area leading to the Malepunyo hill mass. It was the kind of grinding, day after day fighting in which we would wipe out one well dug in Jap position, only to encounter another over the next hill. At this time Walt Lepley was temporarily out of action with a severe fungal infection. He was replaced in our machine gun squad by Bill Bannon, a jovial little Philadelphian of Irish extraction. Bill had just returned from a hospital after a bout with malaria or one of the other tropical diseases. He took over as first gunner with Pete as assistant gunner.

Shortly after Bill joined the squad we were in position one afternoon firing into a bunker. It was a fairly routine operation until a Japanese machine gun, which we had not detected, opened fire in our direction. Perfectly concealed in the jungle growth, invisible until the Japs opened fire, the machine gun had been placed to cover the bunker. Because of the Jap's position to our left and above us, our squad was completely exposed. As the Jap gunner continued his rapid fire, the bullets were kicking up dust in a pattern moving relentlessly toward us. He was traversing horizontally in a methodical manner, no doubt just as he had been trained. Feling and I were to the left of our gun where the bullets would arrive first. We were returning the fire just as fast as we could push clips of ammo through our rifles. Sgt. Faye had immediately grabbed the handle of our machine gun, released the traversing mechanism with the same motion, and turned the gun on the Jap position. Between our rifle fire and Faye's quick action, we silenced the Jap machine gun. Not, however, before a bullet had creased Bill Bannon's left buttock. Quick thinking, quick acting Denny Faye may just have saved his squad that afternoon.

As soon as we had the bunker knocked out, we checked Bill Bannon's wound. There had been some bleeding, but the damage did not appear to be very serious. Sgt. Faye suggested that Bill go back to the aid station and get the wound treated. Bannon objected:
"If I go back to the aid station, they're gonna give me a Purple Heart. Everyone in Philly will hear about it. I get home they'll all ask, 'Bill, where were you hit? Let's see the scar.' What am I gonna do then? Besides that, they'll send a telegram home, and it'll worry the hell out of my mother." Sgt. Faye did not insist.

By the following morning Bill's rear end was sore and swollen and obviously severely infected. This time he did not object when

Sgt. Faye ordered him to get his sorry ass back to the aid station. Bill Bannon, intrepid paratrooper, explaining to his buddies back in Philadelphia how he got shot in the rear while attacking a Jap bunker would have been a tale worth hearing. Bill's mother was a widow and I'm certain that the part about not wanting to worry her was genuine.

Chapter VII Malepunyo Massif

On Good Friday, March 30, 1945, the regiment was hit by heavy artillery fire while advancing toward the Malepunyo mountain fortress. The division historian summed up our situation:

> Meanwhile, the 187th (less the 1st Battallion) moved eastward from Lipa toward Mt. Malepunyo and the village of Sulac at its base. As they crossed the first low ridge east of the city of Lipa, they were hit by a prolonged artillery concentration and heavy mortar and automatic weapons fire. Here were the Japanese that weren't in front of the 188th. The 187th was weary from its fierce battles on Brownie Ridge during the preceding week and they needed reinforcements. So the 3rd Bn of the 511th, fresh after resting for twelve hours as division reserve at Rosario, moved in on the right of the 187th, and was attached to them.

April 1, 1945--Easter Sunday, two days after being hit by Japanese artillery in front of Mt. Malepunyo, the battalion rests in place. The Chaplain comes by early in the morning and conducts services in the perimeter. Pete and I attend. Word comes down that we are to have a hot meal at noon. First warm food in a week other than part of the 10-in-1 field rations we sometimes cooked in cans or in Walt Lepley's helmet. We march three miles to a place where a field kitchen has been set up. As we go through the chow line it occurs to me that this is not only Easter Sunday; it is also April Fool's Day. The meal is steak, dehydrated vegetables, and dehydrated potatoes with watery gravy--all served very cool. The whole mess just barely edible if one is extremely hungry. Toughest steak I had ever encountered anywhere, any time, anyhow. Had division supply found some old carabao (water buffalo) that had been killed in an artillery barrage, or were our cooks capable of so completely destroying decent steaks? And we had dragged our weary butts six miles for this? Garbage like this makes field rations look good.

As we wait to march back to our perimeter, someone slaps me on the back. It is Ron Svoboda, a good friend from Camp Hood days.

When we came to the 11th Airborne, he was assigned to the 1st Battalion, 187th. We discuss recent events. Ron tells me that during the previous week his battalion had attacked Japanese fortifications at Bukel Hill on the approaches to Mt. Macolod. As the troopers moved forward to assault the enemy positions, Jap soldiers came up out of the ground all around and behind them. The Japs had concealed themselves in "spider holes," perfectly hidden and camouflaged. Svoboda's unit had carried the day but only after taking heavy casualties. Good Catholic Svoboda tells me that he has practically worn out his Rosary since joining the 11th Airborne.

As we move down a long hill on the route march back to the perimeter, I look up and back at our battalion, strung out along the road. The 2nd Bn. looks to me to be about the size of a regular company. I figure that if we continue to lose men at the current rate, with the attacks on Mt. Macolod and the losses in the Malepunyo artillery barrage, E Company will be all gone in about two weeks.

A steady rain begins to pelt us as we march along down the road. Why not? Too bad Bill Bannon got hit. Bill was always good for morale. While the division was in New Guinea, a few lucky men were selected to go down to Australia on Rest and Rehab furloughs. Bill was one of the fortunate few. However chosen, he was an excellent selection as he entertained the company for months with tales of his adventures among the Aussies. We had a great need for a little humor on this first day of April.

Late in the afternoon, we received news that army and marine divisions had landed on an island less than 400 miles from the Japanese homeland. Early reports indicated that there was only light opposition from the Japanese. It sounded too good to be true. It was. During the next eighty-one days the troops there, along with a large part of the Pacific Fleet, would be mired in that special hell that was the battle for Okinawa.

Back in the States, we had been told of triumphant American forces, splendidly equipped with the finest arms, well supplied and powerfully supported, moving relentlessly forward against crumbling Japanese defenses. Since our replacement group arrived, things had not been happening quite that way for Company E, 2nd Bn, 187th.

The reason why was never clear to me until I studied the Philippine Campaign, long after the war ended. There was one far-reaching decision that made the reduction of Luzon such a difficult, prolonged struggle for the troops fighting there. After the fall of Manila, MacArthur decided to pull out part of the troops then engaged on Luzon and use them to liberate the central and southern Philippine Islands. The Japanese in those areas were continuing their savage and murderous assaults on American prisoners and Filipino civilians. The primary purpose of the campaign was apparently the rescue of the people in the southern Philippines as most authorities agree that the strategic value of that area was questionable at this stage of the war. The debate continues to this day regarding the wisdom of sending the 8th Army south rather than employing the troops to speed up the clearing of Luzon, a rugged island the size of England. The fact that MacArthur started the southern Philippines operation before the Joint Chiefs in Washington approved it has added to the controversy.

To accomplish the liberation of the southern Philippines, MacArthur transferred the equivalent of three of Gen. Krueger's 6th Army divisions to Gen. Eichelberger's 8th Army. This left Krueger seriously short of troops and firepower to complete the destruction of the Japanese armies on Luzon. On Gen. Yamashita's orders, these enemy forces had pulled back into well-prepared positions in jungle-covered mountains where the terrain varied from rugged to well nigh impenetrable. The Japanese strategy at this stage of the Luzon campaign was to prolong the fighting and to make the battle as costly in American blood as possible.

In a realignment of fighting units the 11th Airborne was transferred from 8th Army to Gen. Griswold's XIV Corps of the 6th Army along with the 1st Cavalry Division and the 158th Regimental Combat Team. The airborne troops and the cavalrymen had just been through the long, difficult battle for Manila. (My replacement group arrived on Luzon at this time.) MacArthur sent the three units, some of his best, into southern Luzon with the immediate task of clearing the area, securing the shoreline, and seizing the port of Batangas. Securing the shoreline would open up a much shorter sea-lane from Leyte to Luzon. Opening the port of Batangas would supplement the overtaxed facilities at Manila and Lingayen. Later, a hospital center and a landing craft assembly plant were to be established at Batangas in preparation for the invasion of the Japanese home islands.

At this time Gen. Swing commented in a personal letter that 6th Army, in assigning areas of responsibility, must have used two maps with widely differing scales. His division, with just half as many men, had been given more territory to clear than either the 37th Inf. Div. or the 1st Cavalry. "In a way it's a compliment but the men can't keep it up endlessly," he concluded.

In a letter to his elderly father-in-law, retired Gen. Payton March, Swing wrote:

> Not once has any member of Army staff gone to my front lines- [they] fly in to a jeep strip by my headquarters and always have too much important work back at Army headquarters to bounce out in a jeep 20 or 30 miles to the nearest scrap where they know it will be a 45 minute climb up the mountainside.
>
> Just to make things a little worse, one third of my transportation is jacked up for lack of tires... Perhaps if some of Doug MacArthur's critics could see our shortages, they would realize what handicaps he had had. Have a tank company attached. 12 out of 16 tanks laid up for lack of parts. Hope before we start after Japan proper that a few supplies are diverted from P.O.A. [Pacific Ocean Areas, Nimitz' command] and E.T.O. [European Theater of Operations]

While we heard that the 511th and 188th were making steady progress, the 187th had been hitting heavy concentrations of well-entrenched, fanatical Japs. Now, as April wore on, the 187th had a welcome turn-around in fortune. While we were making the March attacks on the Mt. Macolod defenses and subsequently on the Malepunyo foothills, there seemed to me to be little effective support for the infantry units of the 187th. The highest priority of the division at that time was the drive of the 188th to the east coast of Luzon. This move would cut off the Bicol and isolate the Japanese forces in that rugged peninsula. Until that objective was attained, I assumed that the artillery, armor, and air support was focused in that area.

The Japanese in the 187th. area far outnumbered us. Had they been able to concentrate their forces for a counterattack, we would have faced a very difficult situation. There was no well-defined battle line in our sector. The Japs were scattered about in pockets, entrenched in fortified positions on the hills and mountains, in some of the barrios, and at other strategic points they were trying to hold. Japanese survivors of recent battles were moving through the area, attempting to join the defenders of the strongly fortified positions on Mt.Macolod and Mt.Malepunyo. Others were fleeing toward Mt. Banahao, well to the east. During the day we would attack the Jap positions, set ambushes, and patrol aggressively. At night the Japs would come out in varying numbers to attack and attempt to infiltrate our defensive perimeters. The situation was quite fluid.

In this situation, the Division was fully committed at all times. Gen. Swing never had the luxury of a division reserve with the exception of the twelve hours that the 3rd Bn, 511th spent at Rosario. There was never a reserve to send in if an objective proved to be too well fortified for the probing force. We could only attempt to keep our casualties down, hoard our resources, and hit them again later under more favorable conditions.

Gen. Swing wrote of the campaign in southern Luzon:

> Down here we bit off a 'chunk' at a time. By the very nature of his defense the Jap has lost his mobility and the ability to counter attack in force. Subordinate echelons are tied to their particular piece of real estate. It is possible to reduce a group of fortifications-mutually supporting-ignore the groups on either side and get no reaction from them while they wait their turn.

So we had been chewing them up, bit by bit. But, until now, some of the bites in the 187th area had been too large to chew. That had just changed. With the 3rd Bn of the 511th on our right flank, we were no longer outnumbered in our immediate area. Also, while the Japanese artillery batteries were raining death and destruction on us on March 30, Major Ewing's call for support by friendly artillery had gotten results. A spotter plane headed for the area and the long duration of the Japanese barrage allowed the artillery spotter to pick up muzzle flashes and pinpoint their location. He radioed the map coordinates to all of our artillery batteries in the area. Their counter-battery fire eventually knocked out all of the Japanese guns.

From this time on we would have strong artillery, armor, and air support, we would have more veterans returning from hospitals, we would receive more new replacements, and the 187th would go on to victory after victory.

The 187th and the 3rd Bn, 511th probed the Japanese positions in the Malepunyo foothills and in a coordinated attack on April 6 captured the barrios of Sulac, Sapac, and Talisay. Company E was engaged in heavy fighting in and around Sulac. At one point in the drive on Sulac our machine gun squad was supporting an E Company rifle platoon as we attempted to knock out a Jap bunker. This bunker was similar in construction to most of the others in southern Luzon and throughout the South Pacific. It was dug in about six feet and was built up to extend three feet above ground level. Multiple layers of coconut logs formed the sides and top and these were then covered with earth so that only the firing ports were vulnerable. Finally, the bunker was camouflaged so that it was almost invisible from the ground or from the air. The bunker we were attacking was part of a series of defensive positions protecting a nearby motor pool. Earlier in the day the bunker had survived an air strike and artillery shelling that left the motor pool a shambles.

A big gun blasting directly into the firing ports could have made short work of the bunker. Unfortunately, no tanks, tank destroyers, or flat trajectory guns were immediately available. Nor were any flame-throwers or bazookas. The attack was going forward on our flanks. We would have to assault and take the bunker in order to keep pace. Three of the replacements I knew were in the assault team: Smith, Short, Woerz. As we kept a steady stream of covering fire pouring into the firing ports of the bunker, they charged in from the flanks and threw fragmentation and white phosphorus grenades through the openings. The maneuver worked just as it had in training at Camp Hood except that here the air was filled with flying lead. It struck me that a man could only do this assault thing for a limited time before the law of averages caught up with him. It caught up with Short and Woerz before another month ended. Both were killed in action.

But today we were lucky. We silenced the machine guns in the bunker and then threw in more grenades to make sure the gunners were dead. Our platoon leader had us pull the four recently deceased Japs out of the bunker to check for any papers or maps that might be of use to our regimental intelligence officer. I helped search the noncom who must have been in charge of the bunker. Among his possessions was a packet of photographs. One photograph was a family portrait. In the photo this Jap, now a scorched and bloody lump lying at our feet, was wearing a black dress uniform bedecked with medals. His wife was seated beside him, dressed in a fancy kimono. Two pretty little girls in white stood next to them.

We turned the papers we had found over to the lieutenant. The only intelligence I had garnered: Here had been another human being who wanted to live and to return to his family, just as we did. But we had to kill him or he would have killed us. Sherman had it right.

Only for a fleeting moment could I feel anything resembling compassion for this burnt and bloody pile of flesh at our feet. Then, like a sudden, icy blast, the remembrance of all the atrocities these sons of Nippon had committed swept away any such emotion. How could supposedly civilized men perpetrate the inhuman cruelties that Japanese soldiers had inflicted on the Filipinos, on the men captured on Bataan, on all the peoples they had overrun during their years of military conquest? I was left only an awareness of the reality that our only option at this time and place was to kill these barbarous little bastards. As Stonewall Jackson said at Fredericksburg, "Kill 'em! Kill 'em all!"

My feelings in this regard were reinforced only a few hours later. In a ravine outside the barrio of Sulac, we found the mutilated remains of over a hundred Filipinos. The Japs had murdered these defenseless civilians and thrown their bodies into the ravine and left them to rot. This was not a singular incident. Similar massacres occurred throughout southern Luzon.

The morning after we took Sulac, a line of trucks pulled up on the road outside the town. The 2nd Bn. was strung out along the highway, waiting. Behind us, the Malepunyo hill mass loomed, dark and forbidding. Nearby the barrio of Sulac still smoldered from the previous days battle. The hulks of burned out Japanese vehicles lay scattered about the captured motor pool. To the south, sporadic rifle fire could be heard coming from Malaraya Hill. That jungle and bamboo covered wilderness proved to be the key to the entire Japanese defense network in the Malepunyo mountain fortress. In a brilliant attack, the 3rd Bn. of the 511th had seized the hill the previous day. The paratroopers had held the position in the face of repeated desperate Japanese counterattacks.

With our recent victories in the foothills and at Sulac, morale in the 2nd Bn. had risen with each successful attack. Company strength was up with veterans trickling back from hospitals and fresh replacements arriving. We continued to take casualties but at a reduced rate due in no small part to the strong support we were now getting. Before the final attack on Sulac a heavy artillery barrage had been laid down, an air strike had gone in, and a company of tanks had blasted away in support of the infantry. And so it was with a feeling of renewed self-assurance and confidence in ourselves and in our regiment that we loaded our equipment and clambered aboard the trucks that had arrived to take us to some unknown destination. The question on the minds of all we "little picture" people: "What now?" A trooper on our truck announced that he had some great news. He had this news on good authority from a runner who had talked to a corporal working at division headquarters. This knowledgeable corporal had confided in the runner, who then passed the wonderful news to our trooper, who now announced to this truckload of skeptical listeners that the entire 11th Airborne Division was being sent back to Hawaii for Rest and Rehabilitation leave. We were probably even now being trucked to some port to begin our trip to hula-hula land. OK! All Right! If you're going to circulate a rumor, why not make it a good one.

At the outskirts of the city of Lipa, the truck convoy ground to a halt. An officer jumped off the truck just ahead of us. It was Lt. Kenney, a former E Company First Sergeant who had received a battlefield commission during the assault on the Genko Line. Three soldiers were standing along the highway looking at our truck column. Kenney grabbed one of them by the scruff of the neck and the seat of the pants and hoisted him onto a truck. I commented to my fellow truck riders that I knew we were badly in need of replacements. I wondered, though, if it was permissible under current army regulations to shanghai people standing along the highway.

As we rumbled along the road, one of the "old men" enlightened me. An "old man" was anyone who had been with the division since it was activated in 1943. Most of the "old men" were twenty or perhaps a few years older while the replacements were eighteen or nineteen. Anyway, he explained that the man Kenney had just unceremoniously hoisted aboard a truck was Pfc. Joe Devitis, a longtime E Company member. Joe had sustained a flesh wound in the fight for Nichols Field on the outskirts of Manila. When wounds of this type had healed sufficiently, the field hospitals would release the recovered soldier who would then make his way back to his unit on his own. In many cases, this returning to the unit took considerable time.

There was a story about a rifleman I had known at Camp Hood who was assigned to one of the infantry divisions on Luzon. He had a large, prominent birthmark on his back, right where his pack rubbed. Why this problem was not taken care of at Camp Hood, I know not. On Luzon the birthmark was soon worn raw and inevitably became infected by the dirt and the unsanitary conditions of the tropical battlefield. The rifleman was sent back to a base hospital on Biak, an island a thousand miles to the rear near New Guinea. Surgeons solved his problem by removing the birthmark. It took this straggling convalescent the rest of the war to get back to his division.

It is not difficult to understand why many of the men took their time returning to the fighting. Why not take a few days Rest and Rehab in Manila or wherever among these friendly people? What can the authorities do if I'm a few days late? I'm already in a front line infantry company, subject to being blown away at any time. Loyalty to their buddies and to their units, the fear that they were letting their friends down, these more than any other considerations usually caused the men to return after a day or so of free time. When I was hospitalized briefly with a fever at a later date, it never occurred to me to do anything except return immediately to the company. We were not on the line at the time.

The trooper continued to tell me about Joe Devitis. Joe had been something of a goldbrick all through training and hadn't improved much since coming overseas. On one occasion when his squad was on patrol, Joe spotted a Jap moving silently through the jungle. Joe called to the other members of the squad, "Jap! Jap! Shoot 'im! Shoot 'im!"-- which they did. Asked by the patrol leader why he hadn't shot the Jap, Joe replied sheepishly, "I just cleaned my rifle. I didn't want to have to clean it again for just one Jap."

Chapter VIII Macolod Revisited

As our truck column moved up the road, Mt.Macolod loomed larger and larger to our front. Someone at the rear of the truck shouted up at the trooper who had passed on the wonderful rumor that the division was going to Hawaii for Rest and Rehabilitation, "Hey, Mac, we must be getting close to Honolulu. That mountain up there looks like Diamond Head."

General Flanagan has spelled out the situation in the division history:

> On 12 April, the remainder of the 511th . . . relieved the Regimental Headquarters and the 2nd Bn. in front of Malepunyo. The orders for the 187th? Easy. Back to Mt.Macolod and wipe it out. . . It was painfully obvious that it would take more than a battalion to destroy the tenacious defenders of Mt.Macolod. For a short period it was possible to take care of first things first, so it was decided to order the 511th to probe the Malepunyo position for an all out attack later in April and to order the 187th, with all the support we could muster, to attack and destroy the Mt.Macolod position first.

If there was a glimmer of doubt in anyone's mind that Mt.Macolod was our next objective, that doubt was dispelled when the truck column ground to a halt near the barrio of Dita at the foot of the mountain. Looking up at the mountain, we could see that certain changes had taken place. The ridge where we had originally attacked was now bare. Where previously lush tropical growth had covered the lower slopes, there was now only scorched earth and blackened stumps. A number of parachute fragmentation bombs that had failed to detonate lay scattered about the area.

This time the assault on Mt.Macolod would be quite different from our attacks of a month earlier. We would not be attacking blindly without support. Our patrolling and the probing attacks, along with aerial surveillance, would pinpoint the Japanese positions. The partial denuding of the mountain made all this less difficult.

To take this mountain Joe Swing had assembled all of the firepower he could possibly muster. Marshalled in our support were two battalions of 155 mm. howitzers, two battalions of 105 mm. howitzers, a company of 4.2-inch chemical mortars, a company of medium tanks, and a company of tank destroyers. For several days the infantry companies would aggressively probe the Macolod defenses while the artillery and mortars continued to pound the Japanese positions. Walt Lepley had returned from the hospital so our machine gun squad had our loads lightened slightly as we went out on patrol.

The Japanese commander for Southern Luzon, Gen. Fujishige, was made a prisoner of war when Japan surrendered in August of 1945. During interrogation by American intelligence officers he made these comments about the Mt.Macolod position:

> I personally made a seven-day reconnaissance of the area and planned and organized the defense myself. My positions were so placed and camouflaged that they could not be seen by ground or air observations. This was the best position in southern Luzon. My subordinates prepared the other ones and they were not as good. Some of my best troops were on Mt.Macolod. I actually cried when the commander was killed. The person who attacked this position did a good job and should be awarded the highest honor your army could give.

Fujishige neglected to mention the three hundred Filipinos who were forced at gunpoint to prepare the fortifications and were murdered when they finished the work. That matter did come up during his war crimes trial. Fujishige was found guilty of murder and was hanged by the neck until dead.

The 2nd Bn. developed a defensive perimeter in a coconut grove near the base of the mountain. The 4.2-inch chemical mortar company, which was supporting the operation, shared our perimeter. The big mortar tubes were set up, ready to drop high explosive rounds on the mountain.

The Filipino guerrilla unit that had been guarding the approaches to the mountain during the last month was dug in about a mile away. These Filipino volunteers did an excellent job containing the Japanese while the 187th (less the 1st Bn.) was occupied with the Malepunyo mission. Our perimeter was relatively quiet, but the Filipinos could be heard firing fitfully through the night. As one would expect, the fire discipline of these relatively untrained volunteers was not of the highest order. They did a considerable amount of firing whether there were any Japs about or not. If the Filipinos were skittish, they had ample reason. They had recently been hit hard by furious Japanese night attacks and had suffered a substantial number of casualties.

Shortly after sunrise on the morning of April 13, our machine gun squad troopers were sitting on the edge of our foxholes breakfasting poorly on field rations. One of the members of the squad had traded with a Filipino--a can of Spam for a bunch of monkey bananas--so we were supplementing our diet with fruit. He had attempted to trade a can of pork sausage but the locals had become too savvy to make that deal. The pork sausage in 10-in-1 rations was 99% lard. Bill Bannon had remarked earlier that the only thing worse was the Australian mutton stew that had been issued in New Guinea. We would occasionally substitute juice from the ubiquitous coconuts for the concentrated lemonade or coffee that made up a part of the field rations. Since coconut juice tended to be laxative, this was a dubious move for men who were constantly on the verge of diarrhea.

As we ate, the weapons platoon sergeant, a hard-nosed Kentuckian named Rone, stopped by to discuss the coming days operation with Sgt. Faye. The company radio operator walked up. He had just received word that President Roosevelt had died. Sgt. Rone shrugged, "Hell, there've been a lot of good men die around here lately. A helluva lot younger than Roosevelt, too." From his further comments, I gathered that Rone did not share my great admiration for our late Commander-in-Chief.

A sudden commotion on the far side of the perimeter interrupted our discussion. A sergeant in one of the rifle platoons had been sitting on the edge of his foxhole drinking coffee and talking to the men in his squad. He suddenly pitched forward, his body convulsed several times, and he lay still. The members of the squad immediately rushed to his aid. A trickle of blood was oozing from a small hole at the base of his skull. The call for a medic was in vain. The sergeant had died in seconds when a bullet ripped into his medulla oblongata. Death calls us in countless ways.

The troopers on the perimeter were instantly on double alert. The sudden early morning activity came as a surprise for it had been a relatively quiet night in our immediate area. Any Japanese infiltrators normally cleared out of the vicinity of our positions long before daylight. There were several possibilities as to the origin of the bullet that killed the sergeant. It could have been a random bullet from the firing going on in the distance. Or it might have been a Jap sniper with some kind of silencer on his weapon. A patrol was sent out to comb the nearby area. If a Jap sniper had killed the sergeant, he had vanished into the nearby jungle. The patrol found nothing. It was an ill-omened start for Friday, the 13th of April 1945.

At the base of Mt.Macolod there is a deep ravine along the highway that runs through the barrios of Dita and Cuenca. A few days before the final assault on the mountain, E Company was moving out on patrol. We halted briefly along the road below the bare face of the mountain. Nearby, division engineers were putting the finishing touches on a deep fill that would make it possible to move tanks across the ravine and on to the mountain. Along the road stood a group of officers scanning the mountainside with field glasses. Next to Gen. Swing was the officer who was his immediate superior, Corps Commander Lt. Gen. Griswold. A junior officer crossed the road and instructed our machine gun squad to report to the generals. Griswold spoke to our squad leader, "Sgt, see that dark object by the shell hole about 500 yards up the mountain. Through these field glasses it looks like it might be a Jap observer. Would you put a few rounds in there for me?"

We knew from experience of Sgt. Faye's skill as a leader in combat. Now we would see just how good he was as a marksman. We quickly changed cartridges in a belt so that every second round was a tracer. If that proved to be a Jap observer out there, only the first burst of fire would count. After that, he would be safe in his cave if we missed. By this time there was a good-sized audience along the ravine. Most activity in the immediate area ceased as E Company and the rest of the troops along the ravine realized what was happening. At this point I was wondering how accurate our Browning light machine gun would be. I had been carrying the gun, off and on, for the last month. Caught in the artillery barrage in front of Mt.Malepunyo, I had held the gun in front of me for protection as I hit the ground when Jap shells came roaring in. At night on a number of occasions we had fired until the barrel glowed cherry red in the darkness.

    Sgt. Faye checked for breeze, adjusted the sights, and instructed Walt Lepley to steady two legs of the machine gun tripod. Satisfied, he squeezed the trigger and the gun barked into action. The tracers arced toward the mountain and hit the left side of the target. Holding the trigger back, Faye traversed slightly to the right, then back left. The dust in the target area cleared. The dark object looked exactly as it had before the burst. The sergeant, in a dazzling display of marksmanship, had just put a dozen rounds into a blackened stump. As we cleared the machine gun, Gen. Swing moved over to our position. "Fine shooting, Sergeant." Praise from Caesar.

    In the early morning of April 19, the members of E Company were cleaning and checking weapons and equipment in preparation for the coming day. Up the perimeter line, G Company was getting ready to move out on what we presumed would be another combat patrol, probing the Jap positions. Lt. Durfee, our weapons platoon leader, came over to the area where Sgt.Faye was supervising our preparations for the day's work. "Sergeant, Capt. Miley is taking his G Company and Lt.Brooks' rifle platoon from E Company up the mountain today. They need another machine gun squad, and it's your turn, so you're it."

    We hurriedly loaded up and moved out with G Company on what we thought would be a half-day patrol. We headed up the steep southwestern side of Macolod, which we considered the backside of the mountain. The patrol encountered no Japs and by mid-afternoon we were well above and behind the main Japanese fortifications. We moved to an area near the top of the mountain with the peak not far to our rear. To our front the sheer face of the mountain fell away, honeycombed with Jap infested caves.

    The patrol leader deployed the men into a defensive position, and we rested from the long, difficult climb. I had developed diarrhea a few days earlier and was feeling pretty well wrung out. As soon as we had the machine gun positioned and set up, I stretched out on the ground and quickly dropped off into a fitful sleep. I was awakened shortly by something on my bare arm. Still half asleep, I gazed at the arm I had extended forward on the ground as I slept. I remained very still as a colorful tropical snake slithered over my arm and continued on its way.

Captain Miley radioed down the mountain for instructions. He got them: "Dig in. You're holding where you are for tonight. We'll send water, rations, and more ammo up." By this time it was late afternoon and most of us realized that there was no way a supply party was going to make it up to our position before dark. We shared what little water we had left, dug in deep, and waited.

The thought occurred to me that we might be on top of the mountain to bait the Japs into coming out of their caves for an attack on our perimeter. The easiest way to dispose of a lot of the Japs holding the mountain would be to cut them down when they made a banzai attack. This is assuming that we had enough firepower to prevent their overrunning our perimeter. This night the Japs chose not to attack. Their commander had apparently decided that they could sell their lives more dearly by waiting for us to attack them in their well-prepared caves and bunkers.

At the foot of the mountain, tank destroyers had been parked on the highway near Dita and 155 mm. howitzers had been sited where they could fire directly into some of the caves just below our position. Through the night the artillery and tank destroyer gunners fired intermittently at the caves to keep the Japs occupied. Our perimeter was located on a hogback ridge above and just back of the Jap caves and fortifications on the face of the mountain. Several times the gunners launched long rounds that roared over our position and exploded against the mountain peak, 200 yards behind us. Given our position and the trajectory of the shells, we were in no danger from these rounds. Still, it was not a grand night for sleeping.

My diarrhea precipitated an extremely urgent call of nature just before daylight. This presented me with a rather difficult personal problem. If I left the foxhole, there were several equally discouraging possibilities. If a Jap sniper had our perimeter under observation, he would probably shoot me. If this didn't happen, I might be cut down by friendly fire, as there was an understanding that anything moving about at night was considered enemy. Having no desire whatsoever to die with my boots on and my pants down, I dug a deep hole in the corner of our foxhole, made use of it, and then covered it. This was known as a cathole, to be used only in a foxhole you were leaving the next morning.

At daybreak, Miley sent a patrol down the mountain to the level where coconut palms grew. We brought back enough green coconuts for everyone to have a drink. Not a good prescription for curing diarrhea but better than going thirsty. The supply party from the base of the mountain arrived shortly, accompanied by demolition experts from Division Engineers. With them were forty Filipinos carrying an abundant supply of explosives to use in blowing the Jap caves.

The water and supplies were quickly distributed as we prepared for the attack down the mountain. Our reinforced company was drawn up in a skirmish line along the hogback ridge where we had spent the night. When they deployed to move out, the troopers were only a few feet apart. As we attacked down the mountainside, the interval would steadily increase as we fanned out to cover all of the ravines and ridges. As we moved out in our attack, the other units of the 187th assaulted the Jap fortifications from the lower slopes, forming the other jaw of a pincer movement.

Our machine gun squad moved down a ridge so that we could cover a ravine on our right and another on our left. It was difficult for the troopers to maintain an even front in the broken terrain. SCR radios and walkie-talkies were used continually to keep the attacking troopers on line. This was essential in order to keep the Japs from getting in the rear of any of our advancing squads. This was one place where we definitely did not want to bypass any of them. The engineers moved forward with our line and dynamited the caves shut as we advanced. The forty Filipinos carrying the explosives seemed to be enjoying their work that day.

A number of incidents that occurred during that long day come back to me with special poignancy. In softening up the Jap fortifications, the Air Force had used parachute fragmentation bombs. With these, the pilot could come in low and bomb accurately without being caught in the blast from his own bomb. Many of these para-frag bombs had not exploded and lay scattered about the battlefield.

About seven hundred yards to our left front and below us a Jap in a deep foxhole had placed two of these bombs in a V in front of him. A rifle squad from G Company was moving up on the Jap. The bombs had been hit repeatedly by rifle fire but had not exploded. As we watched, the squad moved closer, using good fire and maneuver tactics. Then a tremendous explosion obscured the area. Somehow, the Jap had managed to detonate the bombs. He took four good American paratroopers with him as he joined his ancestors.

At one cave entrance a rifleman had climbed into a spot that allowed him to pitch grenades into the cave without being hit by small arms fire from any of the Jap positions. He threw in several fragmentation grenades without any apparent result. The Japs in many cases had deep, small diameter holes into which they would try to roll grenades before they exploded. The squad members started tossing white phosphorus grenades up to the trooper and he kept heaving them into the cave. It must have gotten awfully warm in there. Twelve Japs in full battle gear, gas masks in place, bayonets at the ready, came charging out in single file running at top speed. The Browning Automatic rifleman from the squad had been providing covering fire. He was crouched on one knee near the cave entrance, waiting. As their momentum carried them forward, he made one great big heap of those sons of the rising sun.

It was not unusual for Japs to flee from their caves that day. As we moved forward and were above and near enough to a cave entrance, the engineers would place their charges and blow the cave shut. The Japs undoubtedly had connecting tunnels underground but as we moved down the mountain many of them deserted their caves and took up other defensive positions. The paratroop commanders kept the machine guns and BAR men on the ridges. When a group of Japs decided to leave their cave rather than risk being buried alive, we would attempt—usually successfully--to cut them down before they could take up new defensive positions.

By mid-afternoon the regiment had considerably compressed the area of the mountain held by the Japs. We had continually moved the machine gun forward as the day wore on and were once again set up on a ridge where we could give supporting fire to the rifle squads just below us. Observing that we would not need to move the machine gun for a while, Sgt. Faye sent Pete and me down to help carry out the wounded. Casualties were waiting because the stretcher-bearers were having a difficult time getting the wounded back to the aid station through the intense fire and over the treacherous terrain.

As Pete and I loped down a rocky ravine carrying a stretcher, a nearby rifleman shouted over the din of battle, "Run like hell through that draw up ahead. A sniper just killed the last two men who tried to get across." Pete and I ran across that draw as though our lives depended on it--which they did, of course.

We made it across the draw and joined a rifle squad from E Company. The squad leader was examining his helmet. A Jap bullet had just pierced it. The bullet and fragments from his helmet liner had taken some hair off the side of his head and had seared but not broken the skin just above his ear. "Dammit, that really stings," he cursed as he gingerly placed the damaged helmet on the side of his head and continued to direct his squad. He pointed to a sheltered ravine nearby where several wounded men were waiting to be evacuated.

As we moved along in the shelter of a rocky outcrop, we passed a medic trying to calm a replacement who had arrived a few days earlier. Blubbering and crying, the young soldier had obviously snapped. The medic gave him an injection to quiet him, sat him down in a protected spot, and hurried on to catch up with the fighting.

On down the ravine we found the wounded trooper we were looking for. He was an E Company rifleman who had taken a bullet in the thigh. The medic had given him a shot of morphine to control the pain and prevent shock and had placed a tight compression bandage over the wound to stop the bleeding. The wounded trooper was cool and calm as we placed him on the stretcher. Probably cooler and calmer than Pete and I after our race through that draw. He remarked that he had a ticket out for a while. Not a "winner," though. By infantry definition a "winner" was a wound serious enough to get you out of combat permanently without leaving you crippled for life. Most of the troopers doubted that there was such a thing in this theater of war. Shortly before the war ended E Company had a man return from the hospital who could not walk very well, let alone run. He swore that he would never go back into combat in that condition. Fortunately, the war ended soon thereafter, and he was sent home.

Pete and I found a safer route out of the area and delivered our man to an aid station. He would be stabilized there and then taken out to a field hospital. We returned to the machine gun in time to help move to a new position on down the mountain. Late afternoon came and we were still clearing out Japs and blowing in caves. We could look down and see a line of trucks far away on the road at the foot of the mountain. Rumor had it that they were waiting to carry us back to a rest area where our first warm food in a long time was being prepared. If the rumor was true, the food went to waste. Just as darkness settled on the mountain, we hastily dug in for the night.

It seemed strangely quiet as dawn broke on the mountain the following morning. It did not remain that way for long. We covered the engineers as they blew in the remaining caves. By noon that task was completed, and we were ready to move down off the mountain. The mountainside was a grim sight, littered with the bodies of dead

Japanese soldiers, already beginning to bloat and stink in the tropical sun. How many more were buried in the caves, no one could tell.

As the regiment moved off the mountain, E Company marched past a Sherman tank. The gunner, lounging in the sun on the tank's turret, called down to one of the worn out troopers, "How many Japs did you kill up there?" Without looking up the tired paratrooper wearily replied, "All of them." Watching from a nearby vantage point was Corps Commander Griswold, come to see the 187th chop off "this bitter thorn of southern Luzon."

The three hundred Filipinos the Japanese had murdered after forcing them to prepare the fortifications on Mt.Macolod had been avenged. We also had our revenge for that day in March when these same Japs had ambushed the 2nd Bn. as we moved against Brownie Ridge on the lower slopes.

We had Mt.Macolod, but we had paid a price. Among the dead was Woerz, killed when a Jap bullet pierced his chest. He was the last of my Camp Hood training platoon mates who had been assigned to E Company. Another man killed coming down the mountain was Private Campbell, the last of three brothers killed in combat in World War II. Among the wounded, Pfc. Archie Miller received his fifth Purple Heart since landing on Luzon.

During the months that we remained in the Philippines, nothing would secure the immediate undivided attention of a group of 187th troopers so quickly as walking up and announcing that a large Japanese force had moved back onto Mt. Macolod, and the 187th had orders to retake the mountain pronto. A sobering thought, indeed. The kind that spawns bad dreams. And not entirely beyond the realm of possibility, considering the number of Japanese still surviving in southern Luzon. After fleeing from Mt. Malepunyo, Gen. Fujishige directed all of his remaining troops in southern Luzon to assemble on the upper slopes of Mt. Banahao. He had about two thousand men in that wilderness area when the war ended, and in northern Luzon Gen. Yamashita surrendered 50,000 Japanese soldiers who were making a desperate last stand in the Cordillera and Sierra Madre mountains.

Chapter IX Tiaong and Tanauan

"The 187th Infantry, weary from its hard won battle of Macolod, was dispatched to Tiaong to relieve the 188th and to prevent the retreat of Japanese out of Malepunyo to the east." So states the 11th Airborne Division historian. He has frequently referred to the 187th as being weary during March and April: weary from the fierce battles on Brownie Ridge; weary after being hit by prolonged artillery fire in front of Mt.Malepunyo; weary from the hard won victory on Mt.Macolod. But many would never be weary again. Better weary than dead.

Bone weary we were as we came off Mt. Macolod. Days of constant danger, friends killed and wounded, nights spent sleeping fitfully in holes in the ground, food consisting almost entirely of field rations, living with dirt and dust and mud and filth, plagued by fevers and tropical diseases, all these grind an infantryman down. Even superbly trained, highly conditioned airborne units eventually wear down. Perhaps because I was a replacement, I was worn down a bit more than average. My weight had dropped from 190 to less than 160 pounds since arriving in the Philippines. I had diarrhea, a low-grade tropical fever, and the fungal disease we called jungle rot on my face, feet, and ankles.

The day we came off Mt. Macolod, the 2nd Bn. moved to the town of Tanauan. There we set up a temporary base from which we would be operating during the coming weeks. The 187th Regiment had a large area to cover in carrying out its mission of destroying Japanese troops moving east toward the mountain stronghold of Mt. Banahao. E Company was engaged in extensive combat patrols, manning outposts, and guarding bridges. We followed up on all reports by the Filipino civilians in the area who were constantly on the lookout for the hated Japs. The 187th was able to intercept many of these enemy soldiers in numbers ranging from individual stragglers to well-organized groups of several hundred.

During a rest break at Tanauan, Philippines in April of 1945. Clockwise from the lower left are: Martin, Yoder, Earl Urish, Raybon, Norm Peterson, Denny Faye, and Feling.

On April 30, one of our patrols discovered a Japanese squad hiding in a ravine near Tiaong. In the firefight that ensued, the Japs fought to the death, as usual. They were searched for maps and papers that might contain useful information. Upon examining the papers, the Regimental Intelligence Section found that one of the Japs had been keeping a diary. It was translated and the daily entries give a vivid picture of the final struggle for southern Luzon as experienced by one Japanese soldier:

14 April 45. My suffering surpasses even that of death. I finally arrived at Mt. Malepunyo. I have just one ball of rice to eat. The enemy air and artillery bombardment is fierce.

15 April 45. The enemy has concentrated great numbers of troops in Tanauan, San Pablo, and Lipa, and is approaching our front—the enemy artillery bombardment is terrific. We, who are ready to die, are preparing for the enemy attack. My great crisis is approaching. This morning the enemy approached to within 100 meters in front of us. Their rifle and artillery fire is increasing.

Day after day the enemy drop propaganda leaflets which request us to surrender. To hell with them, I'll never surrender even if I must die. No food and no water, only grass and wood. The suffering is great, and there is no communication with Headquarters. Perhaps death is finally upon me.

16 April 45. I'm hungry! I want to eat rice, fish, and vegetables. I want to eat everything. My bowels are growling. If I go down the mountain, I will be able to drink sweet coconut juice, but there are many troops.

Why don't friendly troops come quickly from Manila? There are no friendly planes. Day after day, there are only enemy airplanes. I want to take a bath.

Today again I survived. I wonder when they will attack again. The friends, who promised to die together, have died, but I am still wandering around the fighting zone. At present only seven men under Sergeant Okamura are left from the squad.

17 April 45. I'm still alive! This morning another hopeless day has come. I finally started to eat grass. Enemy aerial bombardment is fierce. Corporal Sugihie and two others went to Headquarters for a message. I pray that they got through safely and will accomplish their mission. My hope is

that friendly troops will come from Manila and help us. Mt. Malepunyo is cold in the morning and night. Every night I'm thinking of home.

18 April 45. Hunger woke me! About 1500 hours the enemy approached our rear. The crisis is great now. Artillery shells drop like drops of rain. The end has come. I'm going to die bravely. I pray for the country's everlasting good fortune. I'm completely surrounded. I am going to attempt to cross the enemy lines under cover of darkness. I anticipate going towards Manila. Passing through mountains and ravines I penetrated the enemy front lines.

19 April 45. Manila is still far away. Today I was assigned as a supply man.

20 April 45. The enemy is all around. 3 men killed and 3 wounded. The annihilation of the unit is imminent.

21 April 45. Danger is approaching this ravine. Last night an enemy patrol entered the ravine, but we repulsed them. Enemy bombardment comes closer and closer.

24 April 45. Another day and no food. At 0800 I started to penetrate the enemy lines with seven other men as a raiding unit. By 1830 I accomplished my mission.

25 April 45. I'm still alive, the danger is increasing. I heard that Headquarters is fighting fiercely, despite being surrounded by the enemy. The enemy seems to have stopped our supplies. Today three men came under my command.

26 April 45. The enemy is fierce, but the morale of my men is high. Three messages from Headquarters came through the enemy `lines.

27 April 45. Preparation to move was completed by 0400, and at 0800 we departed towards Mt. Banahao via Tiaong. I wonder if we can get through safely—the enemy line is dangerous.

29 April 45. Arrived east of Mt. Malepunyo. I sent out a patrol. Arrived near Tiaong and hid in the ravine.

30 April 45. Day has come and because of the enemy we cannot talk. No food. I hope the enemy will not find us.

Sometime later in the day after the Japanese diarist made that final entry, our patrol sent him to join his ancestors. This Japanese soldier evidently survived the earlier battles in southern Luzon and made his way to the Malepunyo mountain fortress. Then, shortly before our 511th Regiment overran that stronghold, he slipped out and headed for Mt. Banahao. On the way there, his luck finally ran out. He had to be quite a survivor to last as long as he did. He didn't choose to stick around Malepunyo and fight it out to the bloody end. Why not slip away and try to escape to the east? This Jap was ready to die for emperor and country, but not just yet if he could avoid it.

Manila had been liberated and the Japanese forces there destroyed months earlier. The Japanese commanders had to know this but apparently did not pass the information on to their troops. Obviously, that news would have been bad for morale.

The Japanese soldier writes of heading toward Manila on April 18 but on April 27 he and his squad managed to slip away from Mt. Malepunyo and head toward Mt. Banahao via Tiaong. This was a far more logical destination even though they failed to get through.

Living conditions for E Company improved immeasurably during the interludes when we were at Tanauan. A battalion mess had been set up and we were able to have warm meals when in camp. My diarrhea abated in a few days. During our first morning at Tanauan, Sgt. Faye gave me some very explicit instructions: "Urish, I'm tired of looking at your cruddy face. Get the hell down to the medics and see if they can't do something for that damn jungle rot." So, for the first time since entering the army, I went on sick call. The medics had something new--penicillin. It worked wonders. Within a week the jungle rot sores on my face were gone.

A Filipino barber set up shop at the edge of camp and quickly improved the appearance of the troopers. With warm food, a chance to bathe and clean up, and, most important of all, several nights of uninterrupted sleep, all combined with the resilience of young men in their prime years so that the troopers were soon ready to go again.

The first week in May our machine gun squad was sent out on bridge guard. We were to secure a Bailey bridge ten miles north of our Tanauan base camp. These steel Bailey bridges were giant Erector Set structures, designed by a British engineer, Sir Donald Bailey, and refined by the U.S.Army during the Lend-Lease period. The pieces of the bridge could be trucked in and quickly coupled together on site. The completed bridge could span up to 180 feet and support the weight of a tank. The Baileys proved invaluable worldwide. On tropical Luzon, with its many deep river gorges, they were used extensively. Only in unusual instances did the retreating Japs fail to destroy the bridges, some of which had been built during the 300 years the Spanish ruled the islands.

The squad dug in next to the bridge so that the position could be defended against attack from any direction. With a good supply of ammunition on hand, we felt that we could hold the bridge against any number of Japs likely to wander in. If they had mortar tubes, that would definitely complicate the situation.

Sgt. Faye divided the squad so that two troopers could scout the area during the day. The scouts contacted the Filipinos in the area for they were our best early warning system. In addition, the scouts traded for or purchased fruit to supplement our rations.

At the bridge, our only problem the first few days had been an occasional carabao that decided it didn't want to cross the stream on this scary new iron thing. These water buffalo were the main source of power and transportation in the rural areas of Southeast Asia and the Philippines. Large animals ranging in weight up to a ton, they can be stubborn as any mule. Now that most of the Japs had been pushed back into the mountains, the Filipino farmers were starting to do their spring work. The river that our bridge spanned had cut a deep ravine. The banks were too steep to allow the carabao drivers to ford the stream so they had little choice except to coax, cajole, or push the big animals across the bridge. After helping to push several obstinate beasts over the bridge, we found that a little urging with a bayonet sometimes helped.

We had been at the bridge about five days when Feling decided he should visit his family up at Paranaque. He had not had any contact with them since joining the 11th Airborne during the battle for Manila and was quite concerned about their welfare. He asked Sgt. Faye if it would be all right if he left for a few days. Sgt. Faye agreed, of course. Then Feling asked if I could go along. Now that request put the Sergeant in a bind. We were all beholden to Feling. He had stuck with us during some really hairy times when he could have headed for home and safety. On the other hand, if I were to go with Feling, it would leave the sergeant seriously shorthanded on the bridge. If anything went wrong, he would have his neck out. The sergeant thought a moment and then said, "You can go if you think you can be back by tomorrow evening. It will probably be better if the two of you go. Some rear echelon G.I. officer might decide that since Feling doesn't have any papers, he shouldn't have that uniform or the rifle."

We flagged down the next truck, and Feling and I were off toward Manila. When we reached the Manila-Batangas highway, traffic was substantial. We rode a tank destroyer for a distance, then thumbed a fast jeep ride most of the way. It was mid-afternoon when we reached Paranaque.

Feling's mother was overjoyed to see him. The men in the family were fighting in various units on Luzon, but Feling had a happy reunion with the rest of the family. In their excitement, they would switch from English to Tagalog and back as they discussed the events of the last few months. The family had been fortunate in one respect. Their home was far enough off the highway into Manila that it had not been damaged. It was fairly large compared to most working-class homes in the barrios. It was typical in that it was built up about four feet above the ground, had bamboo sides and floors, and a roof that was partly thatched and partly covered with corrugated metal. Several rooms had plank floors laid over the bamboo.

Feling and his family visited far into the night. So many things had happened in the last four months: father and brothers out somewhere on Luzon fighting the hated Japs; friends and relatives in Manila killed or missing; so many of their homes and businesses destroyed. After a time I took the opportunity to catch up on some sleep I had been missing.

About mid-morning of the next day Feling and I said our good-byes and started back for our bridge. We were lucky once again in getting good rides. I imagine the two of us, standing along the road with our M1 rifles slung over our shoulders, wearing dusty battle-worn clothes, boots, and helmets, must have looked like we really needed a lift. When we were asked what unit we were with and we briskly replied, "The 11th Airborne Division," there were usually no further questions. We had no passes or papers of any kind to explain what we were doing on the Manila–Batangas highway but no one asked.

An officer who gave us our first ride out of Paranaque informed us that the war in Europe had just ended. Good for those lucky guys over there, I thought. My second thought was that now we'll soon be getting more of everything over here so that we can finish off the Japs sooner.

It was late in the day when we arrived at the bridge. A truck was parked next to the gun position and Pete and Walt were loading the machine gun aboard. We were being relieved by another squad. As we pulled up, Sgt. Faye smiled and remarked, "I was just wondering how I was going to explain two missing men to the company commander."

The 511th was closing in on the Mt.Malepunyo mountain fortress at this time, and the number of Japanese fleeing eastward toward Mt,Banahao was increasing. In reducing the thirty-five square mile Malepunyo fortress, the paratroopers found that it contained a headquarters, a hospital, huge supply dumps, and many artillery positions, almost all located in caves and tunnels. The hills and lower mountain slopes were covered with bamboo thickets and almost impenetrable rain forest. Only jungle trails led into the area.

With more Japs slipping away from Malepunyo each day, things were heating up for the bridge guards. The division intelligence section received word that a large number of the enemy was between Malepunyo and the bridges. They hurriedly reinforced the guard at three adjacent river crossings, deploying a machine gun section (two guns) at each. Shortly after midnight the gunners spotted troops moving toward the bridges. They also sighted some strange looking objects that they could not identify in the dim light. The Japs began moving over all three of the bridges. On signal, all of the machine gunners opened fire, supported by the rifles of fifty Filipino guerrillas.

Over a hundred Japanese soldiers were killed or wounded, including several high-ranking officers. When questioned, a wounded Jap prisoner told his interrogators that the ambush had nearly netted General Fujishige. He explained that the strange looking objects our troops had been unable to identify the previous night were sedan chairs. The top Japanese officers had been retreating in style. Bugging out with flair. After the war, interrogation of captured Japanese officers indicated that Fujishige and two hundred of his men had slipped away from Malepunyo a week earlier, escaped the 187th dragnet, and moved east to the Mt.Banahao wilderness. Fujishige would vehemently deny ever having used a sedan chair for transportation.

Mt. Banahao soars above southern Luzon, reaching a height of 7,149 feet. The size and ruggedness of this mountain jungle wilderness made operations there extremely difficult. The 1st Cavalry Division, which had responsibility for the area, divided the mountain into pie shaped sectors, hoping that no part would be missed by reconnaissance patrols. After extensive and exhausting searching, the patrols reported that there were no large Japanese elements remaining in the area.

When he surrendered after the war, Gen. Fujishige indicated when questioned that he had issued orders for all of his surviving troops in southern Luzon to assemble on the upper slopes of Mt. Banahao. Two thousand Japanese soldiers were subsisting in that forlorn mountain hideout when the war ended. The troops had planted gardens immediately upon arriving on the mountain and were expecting their first harvest in October. Fujishige told his interrogators that his troops were ready to hold out for ten to twenty years if necessary.

Returning to Tanauan, we found that E Company had received more replacements. In addition, many of the troopers who had been wounded earlier had returned from hospitals. We were looking more like a company. Harry Martin rejoined our squad. One of the "old men," Harry had been wounded in the assault on Nichols Field at the south edge of Manila. Introduced to Pete and me, he looked us over and remarked, "Well, it's nice to have a few new recruits around." Sgt.Faye bristled and fixed him with a scathing glare, "Recruits, Hell! Martin, these guys have seen more of this damned war than you have."

A large stack of mail had arrived while we were out on bridge guard. It was mid-May and for many of us a part of this mail had been following us through camps and replacement depots since January, never quite catching up. The first letter I opened was from my friend and former college roommate, Oliver Olivero. When he left the university with the Enlisted Reserve Corps in the spring of 1943, Ollie had high hopes of going into pilot training. The Air Corps discovered that he had a slight vision problem so he was sent to gunnery school. The letter I received came from Italy. Ollie was serving with the 15th Air Force as a tail gunner on a B-17 Flying Fortress. In the letter he sympathized with me for being in the infantry in the Pacific, wished me well, and commented that the 15th Air Force had been mighty busy.

The next letter I opened was from Mother. With it was a newspaper clipping reporting that Ollie's plane had failed to return from a mission over Germany. The crew was listed as missing in action. In a letter written later, Mother reported that it was now assumed that the crew had perished.

Ollie was an only child. His mother and father ran the restaurant back home in Green Valley. It was the gathering place and meeting point for several generations of young people growing up in the area. Minnie and Louie had moved to Green Valley from the mining area of southern Illinois during the Great Depression. Louie worked in a coal mine near Peoria, and Minnie started a restaurant in a rented building. The Oliveros were industrious, thrifty, friendly people. The restaurant thrived, they were able to erect a new building, and eventually Louie could retire from mining. Minnie was a second mother to practically every youngster who went to school in Green Valley during that time—a kind and generous and lovely person. My heart hurt that day when I learned that Ollie was gone: for Ollie; for Minnie and Louie; for me.

When they were not patrolling aggressively, setting up ambushes, or guarding bridges, the troopers were put to work building a base camp in a coconut palm grove near the ruins of the city of Lipa. Pyramidal tents with the sides stretched out on bamboo frames provided better housing than the troopers had enjoyed in many months. In these six-man tents, army cots with mosquito nets added to our comfort. A screened tent was provided for the field kitchen. Warm food, provided during the days we were in camp, was much appreciated after the austerity and monotony of field rations. We would be in and out of this camp for the next three months.

The entire 11th Airborne Division would soon be encamped in the Lipa area with Mt.Macolod to the west and the Malepunyo massif to the east. During their occupation of the Philippines, the Japanese had built a concrete airstrip near Lipa. The availability of this all-weather airfield had been a prime factor in the decision to encamp the 11th Airborne in the area.

In preparation for setting up the pyramidal tents, a detail was sent out to cut bamboo poles for the tent frames. We found a fine stand of bamboo near the campsite and started to cut the poles we needed. We had just begun when two older Filipinos appeared on the scene, razor sharp machetes in hand, obviously very upset with what we were doing. Their English was limited, but they managed to convey the message that the bamboo we were cutting was their property, and they wanted us to quit. Sgt.McCliment attempted to assure them that the U.S. Government would pay them for the bamboo. It soon became quite apparent that they preferred to keep their bamboo rather than accept any promise the sergeant might make in regard to future payment, so we moved on up the road to a different bamboo thicket. No need to have a confrontation with any members of a local population that had been so helpful during the recent fighting, McCliment wisely observed as we moved up the trail.

The two Filipinos who confronted us were old enough to remember back forty-five years to January of 1900 when American soldiers came to southern Luzon and Batangas Province, not as liberators, but as enemy invaders.

In the years prior to the Spanish-American War, the Filipinos had rebelled against their Spanish rulers. In 1896, following the execution of patriot-author Jose Rizal by the Spaniards, the revolt spread throughout the Philippines. Led by Emilio Aguinaldo, the revolutionaries made significant progress. A makeshift peace agreement was reached, and Aguinaldo was exiled. Both sides ignored the treaty. When the Spanish-American War broke out in April of 1898, the ever-smoldering Filipino revolt burst into flame.

Commodore George Dewey led a U.S. Navy squadron into Manila Bay and destroyed the antiquated Spanish Fleet on May 1, 1898. He brought Aguinaldo home from exile, supplied the Filipinos with arms, and urged them to attack the Spaniards. By the time American troops arrived, the Filipino rebels had captured most of Luzon outside Manila and had issued a Declaration of Independence. On Jan. 23, 1899, a new republican government was inaugurated with Aguinaldo as president.

The fate of the Filipinos was being determined, however, on the far side of the world. In Paris, on Dec. 10, 1898, in the treaty ending the Spanish-American War, Spain had ceded the Philippines to the United States. In Washington, D.C., President McKinley had hesitantly moved toward annexation. In reaching a decision he determined that the Filipinos "were unfit for self-rule and would soon have anarchy and misrule." His only choice, therefore, was to take the archipelago and "to educate the Filipinos, and uplift and Christianize them."

Immediately after Dewey's victory in Manila Bay, McKinley had ordered that an expeditionary force be sent to the Philippines. This force began to arrive in May and take up positions next to the Filipinos who were besieging Manila. Relations between the two forces were poor and deteriorating. The Spanish in Manila agreed to surrender to the Americans if a sham battle could be staged to preserve the Spaniards' honor. The deal required that the Americans keep Aguinaldo's men out of the city. The phony battle was staged on Aug. 13, 1898. The Americans occupied Manila and, as promised, prevented Aguinaldo's Filipino rebels from entering the city.

The United States was now on a collision course with the new Filipino republic. On Feb. 4, 1899, two days before the U.S. Senate ratified the treaty to acquire the islands, the American and Filipino forces outside Manila clashed. Aguinaldo and the Filipinos were once again in rebellion, this time against the United States. In battle after battle the Americans defeated the poorly armed and poorly organized Filipinos in the area of Luzon north of Manila. Aguinaldo finally realized he could never win in conventional battle. In mid-November he ordered the troops under his immediate command to retire to the mountains and carry on guerrilla warfare.

The Americans then turned their attention to southern Luzon, where, in Batangas Province the Filipino commander, Miguel Malavar, awaited with an undermanned, ill equipped force of rebels. The next two years would be an excruciating time for the people of southern Luzon. It would also be a time of maddening frustration for the volunteer soldiers of the American force. Malavar had not learned from Aguinaldo's defeat in the north. He was defeated time after time in battles that involved perhaps a thousand men on each side and usually lasted only a few hours. The Filipinos in southern Luzon soon reverted to guerrilla tactics. The ambushes and hit-and-run tactics of the guerrillas infuriated the Americans. It was impossible to distinguish guerrilla fighters from non-combatants. A group of farmers working in a field would wave and shout "Amigo" as an American patrol passed, then drop their hoes, pick up rifles, take a shortcut across country and ambush the patrol a few miles up the trail. Atrocities by both sides became more and more frequent.

The guerrilla war in southern Luzon dragged on and on until January of 1902 when the U.S. Military Command sent 4,000 soldiers into Batangas. The inhabitants of the province were herded into fenced, guarded camps. Anyone outside the camps after curfew was considered a guerrilla and was subject to execution. The U.S. Military referred to these areas as "reconcentration zones." Outside these zones the army operated with minimum restraints, killing or capturing anyone in the area, devastating the countryside, burning buildings, destroying stores of food, and killing livestock.

On April 16, 1902, Malavar marched into American army headquarters in Lipa and surrendered. The other guerrilla leaders followed during the next two weeks. Civilians were released from the reconcentration zones and returned to their homes by the end of April. The battle for southern Luzon was over.

The end of the fighting did not end the suffering of the Filipinos. The food crisis continued. Disease was rampant. A continuing malaria epidemic and a cholrea outbreak, aggravated by the reconcentration program, continued to plague the hapless Filipinos. Many young workingmen had been killed in the fighting. Ninety percent of the carabao, so vital for rice production, had been killed or had died of rinderpest during the years of war. From 1896 to 1902 the population of Batangas Province fell from 332,456 to 241,721. In March of 1903 a census taken by the U.S. recorded a total of 257,715, which was 55,000 fewer people than in the last Spanish census taken in 1877.

On July 4, 1902, President Theodore Roosevelt formally declared the end of the "great insurrection against the lawful sovereignty of the United States." For that time, it had not been an inexpensive operation. On the American side, 4,234 had been killed, 2,818 wounded. Thousands more had contracted tropical diseases that would kill them after they returned home. For the Filipinos, the cost was much greater. Over 20,000 Filipino soldiers had been killed, an unknown number wounded. At least 200,000 civilians had died as a direct result of the war. Large areas of the archipelago had been devastated.

Regrettably, the "splendid little war" against Spain had led to a vicious little war against the Filipinos. But even as the war still raged in southern Luzon, Americans began an effort to make amends for the destructiveness of the conflict. As early as August, 1901, a ship arrived in Manila Bay with five hundred young men and women aboard, all teachers, many of them recent college graduates, the vanguard of many Americans to come, all zealous to bring learning and enlightenment to the Filipinos. William Howard Taft, appointed Governor of the Philippines by President McKinley at an earlier date, had been instructed to promote "happiness, peace, and prosperity" for the Filipinos "in conformity with their customs, their habits, and even their prejudices." In reply, Taft stated, "We hold the Philippines for the benefit of the Filipinos." Matching deeds soon followed these high-sounding words. Land reform was accomplished early. The U.S. purchased and resold the widespread holdings of the Catholic friars, eliminating a primal cause of the early revolts against Spanish rule. Americans built roads, bridges, railways, port facilities, and irrigation systems. The population, which had trended downward during the years of rebellion, doubled between 1900 and 1920, due in no small part to the public health and sanitation measures instituted by a benevolent administration. By fits and starts the U.S. government--its attitude varying according to the political party in power at a particular time--moved toward self-government for the Filipinos.

During the Japanese occupation of the islands, more and more of the Filipinos joined in guerrilla action against the invaders, spurred by the cruelty and brutality of the Japanese occupation force. When the Americans returned, over 200,000 Filipinos were engaged in guerrilla activities. When the troopers of the 11th Airborne Division stormed across the beach at Nasugbu and parachuted onto Tagatay ridge, the people of southern Luzon greeted them with open arms, eager to assist in any way possible. Gen. Swing was moved to write on March 4, 1945:

> The only thing which keeps my lines open [during the drive to Manila] and allows me to spread so thin is the fact that we have organized 5,000 guerrillas and have attached them to all the infantry, artillery and engineer units. We let them wear the 11th A/B shoulder patch over their left breast, they are proud as punch and really fight. Put artillery forward observers with them, give them all the captured Jap machine guns and mortars and they keep pushing.

On March 23, Gen. Swing writes again:

> Am so darn proud of my guerrillas . . . attached a battalion to each one of my infantry battalions and they are doing most of the mopping up for us. They have killed 1898 Japs to date. Finally persuaded Army to give me uniforms for them. With

their big straw hats and white shirts they were easy meat for a Jap m.g. [machine gun]-since receiving the uniform and watching our men work they can now take a cave as neatly as anybody.

If a few members of the older generation of Filipinos harbored bitter memories of the 1900-1902 battle for southern Luzon, they were a minuscule minority by 1945.

Chapter X Lipa

In the Lipa area of Batangas Province the coconut palms grow tall and stately, nourished by the rich volcanic soil and the abundant rainfall. There is a barrio nearby that, in the Tagalog dialect of the region, is called Mataasnakahoy, which translates to "tall tree." The coconut palm groves, planted many years earlier, made excellent campsites in 1945, the evenly spaced trees ideal for laying out company streets and for tying ropes to anchor pyramidal tents.

The third week of May found almost all of the troopers of E Company at their base camp in this area. Most patrols and bridge guards had been called in, and the troopers were informed that there would be reveille with a company formation the next morning--the first such occasion since my replacement group joined the division.

Early the following morning, the peaceful atmosphere was shattered by the shrill notes from a whistle being blown by First Sgt. Tolpi, followed by his bellow for the company to "fall out." One of the "old men" of the weapons platoon peered out of a tent to see if any company officers were present. Seeing none, he yelled, "Go to hell, Tolpi. Stick that whistle up your ass."

Almost all of the troopers had responded to the First Sgt's call when a company officer arrived, inspiring the tardy to scurry into formation. The officer received the standard "All present and accounted for" report from the First Sgt., then launched into a short lecture on the importance of taking the anti-malaria drug, atabrine. The little yellow tablets were then distributed. On command, each trooper either tossed the pill into his mouth or flipped it over his shoulder.

Atabrine had a bad reputation, largely undeserved. The drug was produced in a rush program after the Japanese seized Java and most of the other areas that produced quinine, the pre-war treatment for malaria. Atabrine would produce immunity to malaria when taken regularly for several weeks. This treatment had to take place before the anopheline mosquitoes injected a man with the sporozoan parasites that cause malaria. The treatment would have to continue as long as the soldier was in the tropics. Unfortunately, atabrine turned the skin a yellowish color that some soldiers thought might be permanent. The story that atabrine would end a man's sex life was also patently untrue, but many of the troopers weren't taking any chances. And there were undoubtedly a few who figured that there could be worse things in their future than going to the rear with malaria.

During the early campaigns in the South and Southwest Pacific theaters, malaria had reached epidemic proportion, with practically every man in many units infected with the disease. The Army had reacted with mosquito control programs, requiring the troops to use mosquito nets when possible, supplying insect repellant, and insisting on the use of atabrine. Manila and other areas where large numbers of troops were stationed were regularly sprayed from the air with the insecticide, DDT. The entire program was highly effective for base personnel but only marginally successful for the infantrymen digging Japs out of the fetid, insect infested, jungle covered mountains.

With the atabrine tablets duly disposed of, the First Sgt. announced that all replacements who had joined the company after February should remain in place when the company was dismissed. Oh, Great! I thought--another crappy work detail of some kind, just for the replacements.

The company officer gave us "At ease, rest," and had us gather around. He informed us that the 11th Airborne was opening a parachute school at the Lipa airstrip. The men who had been assigned to the division after February could take paratroop training and stay with the 11th Airborne or be sent to a replacement depot and from there be assigned to a straight infantry division. That, I surmised, would probably be one of the understrength, exhausted divisions still battling their way through the jungle covered mountains of northern Luzon, digging out Yamashita's remaining 70,000 Jap diehards.

I glanced around at the group. Less than half of the thirty-three of us who had been assigned to the 11th Airborne in March were still with the company. This included six who had returned from hospital after recovering from wounds. A few more would return during the next two months. They were far leaner and more serious than when they left San Francisco back in January. Also in the group were over twenty other replacements who had been assigned to the company later. All had seen some combat.

When he had completed his presentation-cum-sales-talk, the officer asked if there were any questions. A big, stocky lad from my replacement group, who was wearing eyeglasses with lenses like the bottom of a coke bottle, raised his hand and was recognized. "I want to stay with the division but I don't know whether I can pass the physical to become a paratrooper." A trace of a smile flickered across the officer's face. "Wilson, you've survived all kinds of hell the last few months. Physically and mentally you have done fine. You look all right to me. I may give you the physical myself. We'll look in your left ear and if there's no daylight coming through, you're in."

The entire group volunteered for paratroop training. For those of us who had been through the battles of the last several months, it was an easy decision. When we went into combat once again, as we surely would, we wanted to be with the men we had been fighting alongside. When your life is on the line, the most important thing in the world is to know that every man around you will steadfastly do his duty. No one ever doubted the courage and tenacity of these paratroopers. Throughout the 11th Airborne there was a will to excel, a desire to be the best of fighting units, and the fierce pride of being airborne.

As the officer expressed his satisfaction that we were all volunteering to become paratroopers, I was thinking of a news report I had read shortly after the D-day invasion of France. Gen. Eisenhower visited the paratroopers of the 101st Airborne Division just before they boarded the planes from which they would parachute into Normandy. The General inquired of a young paratrooper, "Do you like to jump out of airplanes?" "Oh, hell no, sir, but when there's going to be fighting, I like to be with men who like to jump out of airplanes."

Parachute school, Lipa airstrip style, was all business and no monkeying around--just the essentials. Physical training consisted of extended calisthenics and enough running to insure that the trainees had the necessary physical capabilities. The Japanese control tower at Lipa Airfield was converted to a forty-foot jump tower. Cables were attached to one side for descent training. Nearby, mock doors, harness frames, and tumbling pits were set up. The instructors were old pros, having trained volunteers at two previous 11th Airborne parachute schools, first at Camp Polk in Louisiana and then at Dobodura on New Guinea. At Lipa, they trained over a thousand volunteers before closing up shop.

After a week spent jumping out mock doors, manipulating parachute lines from suspended harnesses, jumping off the tower, and learning how to land painlessly in the tumbling pits, we were more or less ready for the real thing.

The morning of our first jump I was not really very hungry. It seemed that my fellow would-be paratroopers were also preoccupied as we went through the chow line, nibbled at the food, and then rode the trucks down to the airstrip. As we moved about the hangar, selecting parachutes and strapping them on, the jump instructors moved among us, helping to adjust the harnesses and offering a few final words of advice: "Get those straps straight and those buckles tight. Tuck those family jewels in carefully. When you're coming down, if it looks like you'll land in a tree, cross your legs tightly. There's no place in the 11th Airborne for a soprano."

A line of C-46 transport planes, their motors idling, was waiting on the apron of the airstrip, ready to take us up. These Curtiss Commandoes and the C-47 Douglas Skytrains were the workhorses of the Pacific air forces. They delivered paratroopers, transported troops, towed gliders, and hauled cargo, many times under difficult and hazardous conditions. The C-46 that we boarded could carry forty fully equipped paratroopers at a maximum speed of 195 mph with a range of 1170 miles. The C-47, a military version of Lockheed's highly successful DC-3 civilian airliner, was one of the most important of Allied aircraft, contributing to Allied successes all over the globe. The C-47 could carry twenty-seven paratroopers at a top speed of 230 mph with a range of 1600 miles. The Japanese built a copy of the DC-3, which they used in the Pacific war. This resulted in serious recognition problems in a number of instances when planes thought to be friendly started spewing out Jap paratroopers. Troopers of the 11th Airborne had this experience on Leyte.

Because the trainees were making this first jump without any extra equipment, we settled into the bucket seats on each side of the C-46, and then another stick was seated on the floor down the middle of the plane. A stick is a group of paratroopers, for example, a rifle squad, who go out the door as a unit, one following another in rapid succession. With the roar of the motors and the wind rushing by the open doors, conversation was difficult, if not impossible. Not that it mattered much for each man was immersed in his individual thoughts as the plane took off and gained altitude on the flight to the drop zone. For many, this was not only their first jump from a plane; it was also their first ride in an airplane.

Landing on Luzon

As the plane neared the drop zone, the pilot turned on a red warning light in the cabin. The jumpmaster immediately shouts over the roar of the engines: "Get ready." Seconds later the command rings out: "Stand up and hook up." The troopers seated in the middle of the plane spring to their feet and hook their static lines to a steel cable running the length of the plane and anchored at each end.

While the men hook up, the jumpmaster commands: "Check equipment." Each trooper examines the parachute and gear of the man in front of him. The next to last man in the stick turns and checks the end man.

"Sound off for equipment check," the jumpmaster yells. "Sixteen O.K." "Fifteen O.K." and on down the line from the front of the plane comes the response.

"Close up and stand in the door." The first man in the stick moves up into the door and gets into position to jump. The rest of the troopers move up behind him as closely as possible.

The light turns from red to green and a bell rings indicating that the pilot thinks that we have reached the drop zone. At about the same instant, the jumpmaster, who has been watching the terrain, yells "GO," and the lead man, who has been crouched with his hands on the edge of the doorway, propels himself out of the plane. The rest of the men in the stick shuffle (to prevent any tripping) quickly to the door and follow him out. It is important for the stick to get out of the plane speedily so that the men will be as close together as possible when they land. A sixteen-man stick should be out the door in ten seconds or less.

The paratrooper should look at the horizon as he leaves the plane. Looking down tends to cause a man to dive. The fetal position with the body vertical is the preferred position after clearing the door. As the trooper leaves the plane, the slipstream, a combination of the propeller wash plus the wind from the plane's forward motion, hits him. Fifteen feet of the static line he had hooked up in the plane plays out from the parachute pack on his back and then rips the cover off the pack tray revealing the parachute canopy. The canopy is pulled from the tray by a small cord attached to its apex. The trooper is leaving the slipstream, pulled downward by gravity.

Opening canopy and falling body work against each other at this point. As the canopy catches the air of the slipstream and pops open with a boom, the jumper receives the full impact, known as the "opening shock," which exerts a force up to 5 Gs on his body.

The jumper has decelerated from 115 mph to near 0 in an instant. The paratrooper can be injured and his weapon and equipment lost if the harness and straps are not well adjusted and tightly fastened.

Only three seconds have elapsed since the trooper cleared the door of the plane. He has shouted, "One thousand, two thousand, three thousand." If, at the count of three thousand, he has not had his teeth rattled by the opening shock, he pulls the handle of his reserve chute. I never figured out how to work "Geronimo" into this routine.

The jumper should now look up to see if there are blown panels in his parachute canopy. If there are many of these, he must quickly decide whether to ride down a little faster or employ his reserve chute. There is some danger here as the reserve could streamer or wrap around the main chute.

Now it is time to look down to see if there are any trees, rocks, gullies, or other hazards directly below. It is possible, to a limited extent, to maneuver by pulling on the parachute lines. This is tricky as an unanticipated breeze can change your landing spot.

To reduce the impact of landing at twenty feet per second, the trooper attempts to execute a forward roll as he hits the ground. The impact is similar to jumping off a two story barracks. Thirty to sixty seconds have elapsed since the jumper left the plane, depending on whether he jumped at 600 or 1200 feet or somewhere in between. There is a feeling of relief and elation after a successful landing. This is particularly true after that first jump. Hey, look, here I am, alive and in one piece!

My training group made five jumps in five days with only a few serious injuries but with numerous sprains, contusions, and so forth. Harlan Runyon, the other Tazewell County replacement assigned to the 11th Airborne, had made it through combat with only minor wounds. Unfortunately, at jump school his luck seemed to run out. In ground training a mishap that occurred as he was going off the jump tower required a number of stitches to re-anchor an ear. Harlan was determined to finish jump school but bad luck continued to plague him. On his first jump from a plane, he broke a leg when he hit the ground. Some time after recovering from this injury, Harlan was struck down by one of the tropical diseases and was evacuated to a base hospital on Guam. He was never able to return to the division.

My only mishap was an exceptionally hard landing caused by a strong ground wind that rocked me as I was coming down on my fourth jump. A ground wind can cause a parachutist to swing like a pendulum from his chute. I came in on the backswing and landed hard on my tail. The powerful wind then filled the parachute and dragged me across the drop zone. The jolt when I hit the ground had temporarily paralyzed me from the waist down. I took hold of the lower lines intending to spill the air out of the parachute so as to collapse the canopy. Just then a young Filipino who was passing by ran in ahead of me and grabbed the lines in an attempt to help me. He was small so the parachute dragged both of us over the ground until we hit some rocks. I was beginning to recover the use of my legs by this time. With a little assistance from the helpful young Filipino, I rolled up the parachute and limped back to the assembly area.

I didn't mention my sore back to anyone that evening. The following morning, June 1, we E Company trainees made our fifth and qualifying jump. That evening I wrote my parents and my Navy brother that I was now a full-fledged paratrooper. This news was not received with unqualified joy at home. With my brother and I both in harm's way on the far side of the world, Mother was terribly worried about us. I'm sure Dad was also deeply concerned but he managed to keep his feelings to himself.

Wayne's ship, the cruiser *Pittsburgh*, was now with the Third and Fifth Fleet. This awesome armada (14 fast attack carriers with over 1,000 aircraft, 6 fast battleships, 15 cruisers, and 58 destroyers) was designated Third Fleet when it was commanded by Adm. Halsey and as Fifth Fleet when it was commanded by Adm. Spruance. While Halsey and his staff were with the fleet executing a mission, Spruance and his subordinates were ashore planning the next operation and vice versa. The ships stayed at sea. Halsey explained: "Instead of the stagecoach system of keeping the drivers and changing the horses, we changed the drivers and kept the horses. It was hard on the horses but it was effective."

Spruance had commanded in brilliant fashion during the pivotal victory at Midway. He was in command at the time only because Halsey was ill. Halsey commanded in the Carolines, the Palaus, and at Leyte Gulf, Spruance during the conquest of the Marianas and at Okinawa. On many of these operations the fleet was at sea for extended periods of time. Adm. Mark Mitscher commanded Task Force 38/58 including the fast carriers of the fleet. He observed at the time of the Leyte Gulf battle: "About 10,000 men never set foot on shore during a period of ten months. No other force in the world has been subjected to such a period of constant operation without rest or rehabilitation." Halsey was right. The system was hard on the sailors and airmen.

The fast carrier task forces were able to remain at sea for long periods of time as a result of the development of what was actually a floating base. Made up of an immense fleet of oilers and supply, ammunition, and repair ships, these floating bases made possible the long range strikes Admiral Nimitz' forces made in the vast expanse of the Pacific.

Brother Wayne's cruiser was now a part of Task Force 58. On March 15, 1945, Task Force 58 sortied from the anchorage at Ulithi toward the Japanese home islands with fourteen fast carriers and their escort. On March 18, Task Force 58 aircraft struck airfields on Kyushu, the southern island, with the objective of reducing Japanese air capability before the imminent invasion of Okinawa. The task force had three carriers damaged by bomb and kamikaze hits.

The following day the aircraft of Task Force 58 hit the Japanese fleet anchorage at Kure on the Inland Sea, striking at the very heart of Japan. The Japanese struck back with effective kamikaze attacks badly damaging the carriers *Wasp* and *Franklin*. The *Franklin* was further damaged by internal explosions and was burning furiously. The great ship was dead in the water and drifting toward the Japanese shore. The *Pittsburgh* took the flaming carrier in tow and pulled it to safety. The *Franklin* lost 832 men, the heaviest loss of life ever suffered on any US ship of war.

A series of events now occurred that would return Wayne home before the war ended. Task Force 58 bombarded Okinawa and her aircraft bombed Kyushu in late March. On April 1 the task force supported the army and marine landings on Okinawa. The next eighty-one days were a trying period for the fleet. Relentless kamikaze attacks kept the ship's crews on constant alert. In addition to the 7600 soldiers and marines who died taking Okinawa, nearly 5,000 sailors and naval aviators lost their lives in the struggle for the island--15% of all US Navy losses in World War II. The ferocious Japanese attacks sank 36 ships and damaged 368 in less than three months.

As May ended, Halsey replaced Spruance as fleet commander and on June 5 drove the fleet into one of the worst typhoons in recorded history. This was the second time that Halsey had taken the fleet into a typhoon, suffering almost as much damage and loss of life as in a major battle. Several smaller ships were severely damaged in the mountainous seas. Most of the ships suffered some degree of damage.

The typhoon ripped off 104 feet of the *Pittsburgh's* bow. The storm was the wildest, most daunting experience of his war, Wayne related later when Navy censors allowed him to write home describing the typhoon. He feared more for his own and his shipmates' lives during the typhoon than during the worst of the kamikaze attacks off Japan and Okinawa. There were times when it seemed that the big ship would capsize as it rolled on its side but it always righted itself. In the radio shack where Wayne was on duty, everything was tightly secured. The radio operators strapped themselves to their seats to keep from being thrown about. There was scarcely a man on board who did not suffer from motion sickness. The *Pittsburgh* escaped without loss of life only because the ship's captain had cleared the forward compartments and sealed them off.

In a similar incident on Dec. 18, 1944, Halsey had ignored the approach of a typhoon in Philippine waters and failed to consult his task group admirals for information on the storm's track. He attempted to refuel but had to give up in the face of mounting seas, leaving three destroyers dangerously unballasted. Among the ships damaged by that violent typhoon were three fast fleet carriers, four escort carriers, and eleven destroyers. The three destroyers with nearly empty fuel tanks turned turtle and sank. On the *Hull*, the *Spence*, and the *Monaghan*, 605 men went down with their ships. Only 92 survived. A court of inquiry found Halsey culpable in both incidents in which he allowed the fleet to be caught in a typhoon. Any other officer would probably have been relieved of command.

During the Battle of Leyte Gulf, Halsey left the landing beaches uncovered while he pursued a Japanese decoy fleet far to the north. This move could have been disastrous for the landing forces. With Halsey speeding away with the entire Third Fleet, the Japanese naval force in the central Philippines reversed course and suddenly appeared, moving out of the San Bernardino Strait with four battleships, six heavy cruisers, and ten destroyers. The only American naval element standing between this powerful Japanese fleet and the ships unloading soldiers and cargoes at the beachhead was the landing support force consisting of thin-skinned escort carriers and destroyers. Their mission was to support the landing rather than to engage in a sea battle.

When the escort carrier group sighted the Japanese fleet, a wild mêlée ensued, the American destroyers attacking with torpedoes and 5-inch guns, pitted against Japanese battleships with the largest naval guns in the world, ranging up to 18.1 inches. American pilots, their aircraft armed for close support of the landing troops, attacked with whatever ordinance they had available. By their heroic effort against terrible odds, the sailors and airmen were able to damage and delay the Japanese fleet. The valor of the American Navy has never shown more brightly than on that day at Leyte Gulf.

The Japanese commander had victory within reach, but, for reasons still unclear, turned his fleet away and headed out to sea. An American sailor, standing on the deck of a battered destroyer, watched the powerful Japanese fleet receding in the distance and shouted, "Goddammit, they're getting away." Halsey at last sent fast battleships to the rescue, but they arrived after the Japanese had gone.

There was talk in Washington of retiring Halsey after the Leyte Gulf battle, but he was such a popular hero in the States that nothing was done. And to give him his due, Halsey had earned that admiration and respect during the dark days that followed the Japanese attack on Pearl Harbor. He was a fighter, a colorful risk taker who led the early carrier attack on Tokyo and the subsequent attacks on Japanese island bases in the mid-Pacific. Nimitz then sent Halsey to take over the Solomon Islands campaign when the issue on Guadalcanal was in some doubt. As theater commander, Halsey led the marine and naval forces to a pivotal victory. Nimitz remembered those days well and would never censure Halsey.

When Halsey successfully completed the Solomons campaign, he had not commanded a fleet for two years. It seems there had been technical and tactical advances during that time which had passed him by. It was at this time that the Third/Fifth Fleet rotation was instituted. America's most popular admiral could not be put on the shelf. It has been reported that most fleet officers preferred the quiet, methodical, unflappable Spruance to the impulsive, aggressive Halsey. Spruance's orders were always well-considered and clear and he never made mistakes when he was in command of the fleet. Spruance lacked Halsey's flair for publicity and self-promotion, however, and never became a popular hero, either with the sailors or the general public.

Wonder of wonders, Halsey and MacArthur, each with a gigantic ego, liked one another, had worked well together when their

South Pacific and SouthWest Pacific Theaters needed coordinating. At his headquarters, MacArthur would brook no criticism of Halsey, even after the Leyte Gulf near-disaster.

After the typhoon of June 5 had roared through the Third Fleet, the battered *Pittsburgh*, now bow-less and 104 feet shorter, limped back to Guam where a stubby bow was jury rigged for the trip back to the States. The *Pittsburgh* arrived in Bremerton, Washington, on July 15. At the Puget Sound Naval Yard a new bow had been prefabricated and was ready for attachment.

When he arrived back in the States, Wayne wrote telling the entire story of the typhoon.

Half a century later, as I looked at the letters Wayne and I had written home, letters that Mother had carefully preserved, I marveled at how we had glossed over the deadly events in which we were involved. Censorship of letters contributed greatly to this, but a desire to spare our parents as much worry as possible was an equally important factor. The letters my brother and I wrote to each other gave a far more realistic picture of our situations.

My replacement buddies and I received some good news shortly after we qualified as parachutists. We had been promoted to Privates First Class and had been awarded the Combat Infantryman's Badge and the Good Conduct Medal. Someone quickly figured that with paratrooper pay, combat infantry pay, and overseas pay, we were now making the munificent sum of $125 a month. Much better than the $35 a month we had collected at Camp Hood after insurance and laundry were deducted there.

The replacements who had joined the company in March were now well accepted by the "old men"—the men who had been with the division since its activation in 1943. We had seen a great deal of hard fighting in the time we had been with the division, and our non-commissioned officers had quickly taught us that, to operate effectively in combat, the men in the squads and platoons must function as a close-knit team. Survival depended on working together closely and being able to rely on one another without reservation.

To bring the company up to strength, more replacements were arriving, and the "old men" were now in the minority. In June, as the mop-up continued in southern Luzon, the new men the 11th Airborne

United States Navy photo

A dramatic survivor of a Pacific typhoon in June of 1945, the USS Pittsburgh returns to dry dock after losing 104 feet off her bow.

had recently been assigned were sent out into the mountains under seasoned veterans, so that these replacements could get some combat experience. One of the veterans who drew this duty was Pfc. Joe R. Siedenburg of F Company, 187th. His squad, as part of a larger assault force, attacked Japanese positions on Mt. Batulao, an area that had been by-passed during the earlier fighting. The first day on the mountain, they destroyed the Japanese fortifications on the lower slopes, killing twenty-seven of the enemy in the attack.

The following day, as the assault force moved higher on the mountain, Siedenburg's squad was hit by extremely heavy machine gun and rifle fire coming from concealed bunkers. One of the replacements was in the open and was seriously wounded by the first burst of fire. Siedenburg immediately left his cover and started across the open area to rescue the wounded man. He was hit by a fusillade from the Japanese positions but continued on, gathered the wounded man in his arms, and carried him to safety. Hit twice again while bringing the replacement to cover, Siedenburg collapsed and died as he laid the wounded man down. Greater love than this hath no man . . . .

For this selfless act of heroism, Pfc. Joe R. Siedenburg was awarded the Distinguished Service Cross—posthumously. And for his grieving mother: a broken heart, a folded flag, a gold star, and "the solemn pride that must be yours, to have laid so costly a sacrifice upon the altar of Freedom." During the occupation of Japan, the post where the 187th was stationed near Sapporo on Hokkaido was named Camp Siedenburg in honor of this brave, self-sacrificing trooper.

With the end of organized resistance in southern Luzon, there was some thought that the troopers would be taking it easy for a time. It didn't really work out that way. In addition to the combat patrols, the men were kept busy with a variety of activities. Weapons training and equipment maintenance took up part of our time. There was even close order drill in the program. Whenever the other activities were not physically demanding, we did calisthenics and ran a few miles. Joe Swing was making sure that his 11th Airborne would have that razor edge whenever and wherever the division was needed.

Soon after my group finished parachute school, the 187th was on the way to a new assignment. We had been attached to the Provost Marshal in Manila.

Chapter XI The Replacement Conundrum

Replacement. No doubt there could have been a more inspiring title than this for the hundreds of thousands of men who answered to that designation at one time or another during WW II. Replacement is not a word with the power to stir men's blood. Mention the word replacement and it is doubtful that you would bring to mind the image of an American infantryman, rifle and bayonet poised, charging a Japanese machine gun position. But the word does describe, perhaps more precisely than any other, the function of these men.

Replacement is defined as one that replaces another, especially in a job or function. To replace implies a filling of a place once occupied by something lost, destroyed, or no longer usable or adequate. For example: We need a replacement for that broken carburetor. Or: We need replacements for those dead, wounded, and sick infantrymen. Late in the war, the Army considered changing the designation from "replacement" to "reinforcement." This would not have improved the situation, would in fact have been a misrepresentation. When a company was assigned six green newcomers to take the place of ten dead or wounded veterans, that company had not been strengthened. The problem was not with titles but with the system responsible for the men from the time they left their training camps until they reached the battlefront--the ill-fated, star-crossed Replacement System.

The Replacement System was the U.S. Army's most consequential operational failure in World War II. The difficulties that emanated from this flawed system increasingly haunted Army leaders as American involvement in the ground war escalated and casualties mounted. In planning for World War II ground combat, Army Chief of Staff Marshall and his assistants decided to keep the number of infantry and armored divisions relatively low. To keep these divisions on the battle line, as men were killed, wounded, or became ill, the Army would feed in more soldiers through the Replacement System. Thus, at any time, unit numbers would be maintained, and full strength divisions could be kept in combat indefinitely. Blooded veterans would lead the way for the green replacements.

Secretary of War Stimson disagreed with Marshall, believing that more divisions would be necessary in order to give the Army greater flexibility and to provide a reserve in case of emergency. A crucial element in this discussion was the fact that 8.3 million men was estimated to be the maximum strength that the Army would be able to muster as its share of the available U.S. manpower pool. The problem, then, was how best to utilize these men. In most armies at that time, 35% of the soldiers were combat troops. Marshall contended that logistics were so crucial in this far-ranging global effort that barely 20% of the U.S. Army could be combat troops.

Unable to agree, Marshall and Stimson took the matter up with President Roosevelt who concurred with the Army Chief of Staff. There would come a day when Marshall would complain that he was sick and tired of one replacement crisis after another—though in all likelihood not nearly so sick and tired as the combat soldiers in the critically understrength rifle and armored companies being pushed forward against well-entrenched German and Japanese forces.

Tragically for many replacements, the army planners had far underestimated the number of casualties that would be suffered, especially in infantry rifle companies, once the battle had been joined around the world. During the fierce fighting in Normandy, there were rifle companies that sustained 400% casualties in just six weeks. The pressure to get more replacements to the front intensified. The combat readiness of the replacements, never too high a priority, became less important.

One embittered infantry replacement, having survived the war, expressed a desire to attend a war crimes trial for the men responsible for the Replacement System--and then see them shot. The survivors from the hundreds of thousands of men who passed through replacement depots on their way to the battlefront would understand his outrage.

After an infantry replacement was sent out from a replacement depot, he became subject to conditions transcending his wildest nightmares. Simply put, there is no training, no mental conditioning, no psychological manipulation that can fully prepare a man for the terror of the battlefield. When a green replacement arrived at the combat squad to which he had been assigned, he was like a castaway abandoned among strangers. Except in rare instances, he has long since been separated from the men with whom he trained. The rifle he carries had been issued to him a day or two earlier, covered with sticky cosmolene. He has fired it only a few times, if at all. The men in his new squad, men on whom his life will now depend, are total strangers. Friendless and forlorn, he and his fellow replacements will now likely face the most traumatic days they will ever know in this life.

The tough and the smart, if they are lucky, may survive. The rest will soon become casualties, many within the first few days. The survivors will learn the skills they need to stay alive. They will find that luck is always a factor. Even the most careful, battle-wise veterans are subject to the law of averages and the vicissitudes of fate. How the veterans in his new outfit will receive the replacement will vary from unit to unit, but of one thing he can be certain; he will be low man on the totem pole. He will learn that he and the other new replacements will get the dirtiest jobs and the most exposed positions.

If a replacement was fortunate enough to join his new outfit when it was in a quiet area or behind the lines, he at least had a chance to become acquainted with his sergeant and the members of his squad. When replacements joined their new units under the chaotic conditions of severe combat, their chances for survival lessened. Too often the latter condition prevailed.

Replacements killed or wounded during their first week in action, because they were inadequately trained and haphazardly thrown into battle, had little opportunity to contribute to their unit's success or to final Allied victory. It was inevitable that many young Americans would have to sacrifice their lives. None of those lives should have been wasted. In the Replacement System, the Army was at fault in failing to care for it's most vital element, the combat soldiers. It was a grievous fault and grievously did many young Americans answer for it.

The shortage of replacements became so critical in Europe in 1944 and 1945 that men were winnowed out of service and quartermaster units, given a short period of infantry training, and funneled through the replacement depots to the battlefield. Back in the States the Army Specialized Training Program was cut to 30,000, releasing 120,000 of those bright young men for combat training. The Air Force had been hoarding some of the most promising enlistees for pilot training and Gen. Arnold was persuaded to release 71,000 surplus aviation cadets for ground duty. With air superiority achieved in most war zones, many Anti-Aircraft Artillery units were deactivated making 65,000 men available for other combat duty. These measures, combined with a shortening of the training period for incoming draftees, kept more warm bodies flowing into that pipeline known as the Replacement System. Even then, the plan to keep the combat divisions up to strength failed miserably. A principal reason for this failure was the awful fact that many of the ill-prepared replacements were being killed or wounded during their first few days in combat. No one has documented this sad chapter in our history more poignantly than Stephen Ambrose in his book on the American Army in Europe, *Citizen Soldiers*.

The most disgraceful dereliction of duty in all of this was the failure of the Army to make any significant improvements, even after it became painfully obvious that the system was badly flawed. Stephen Ambrose lays the blame for the replacement debacle in Europe on Eisenhower, Bradley, et al. They were the men in command. They should have known what was happening and moved to correct the situation. Ambrose feels that the commanders had no clear conception of life on the front line. They failed to listen to the men in the foxholes. Stephen Ambrose's conclusions are not off the cuff. They were reached after years of research and study. All Americans would do well to ponder them.

Gen. Marshall, for all of his wisdom and brilliance as a leader in World War II, must also share some responsibility for the wasteful replacement system. Perhaps it is significant that neither Marshall nor Eisenhower had ever served as a junior officer in a combat situation. Marshall distinguished himself in World War I as a staff officer at Pershing's headquarters. Eisenhower spent that war in the States training troops.

In the SouthWest Pacific Theater, after heavy losses at bloody Buna, MacArthur's leap-frogging, "hit 'em where they aint," strategy did, with a few notable exceptions, keep casualties relatively low. Malaria, dengue fever, dysentery, jaundice, hepatitis, jungle rot, and various other tropical afflictions sidelined many men for a period of time, but practically all of them were able to return to their units. The campaign, hopscotching up the New Guinea littoral, was mainly a series of short, sharp battles followed by interludes during which the divisions would regroup and prepare for their next attack. When the divisions were committed to the prolonged, bitter campaigns on Leyte and Luzon, the need for replacements increased dramatically.

Once in MacArthur's theater of war, a man's only way out alive was to lose an eye or a limb. Early in 1944 a rotation program was to be instituted with one percent of the men in hardship areas to be rotated to the States each month. With the New Guinea campaign escalating, MacArthur discontinued the policy "until further notice."

The tour of duty of my replacement group paralleled that of most infantry replacements of the time. Although I have read of no other replacements spending their first night in the foxholes without rifles, I would guess that there were some. There are, however, many other appalling stories concerning replacements. One story tells of the sergeant who sent back this message: "Don't send up any more replacements. We don't have time to bury them."

From an island in the South Pacific came the story of a rifle company holding a defensive position. Jap snipers would infiltrate through the jungle during the night and conceal themselves in trees near the perimeter. The first Americans to crawl out of their foxholes in the morning would be the targets of these snipers. Newly arrived replacements were not informed of this danger. The Japanese snipers, when they fired on the early risers, could be spotted and eliminated.

A Ranger veteran related an incident that occurred at the bloody Anzio beachhead in Italy. His platoon had been ordered to make a probing attack--a foolish and well-nigh suicidal move under the prevailing circumstances. The platoon had recently been assigned eight new replacements. They were sent out on the point of the attack. When the action ended the following day, the eight replacements were dead, but all of the old members of the platoon had survived.

William Manchester writes of six young marine replacements arriving during the battle for Okinawa. He describes them as looking "pallid, mottled, and puffy"; seventeen-year-old boys sent directly from boot camp; children he hesitated to brief when they first reported to him.

E.B. Sledge, a replacement himself at an earlier date, writes of replacements assigned to his company of the 1st Marine Division during extremely stressful battle conditions. He relates that they were insufficiently trained and in some cases cracked almost immediately when sent into battle. Many did not survive long enough to get their names entered on the company roster.

In the jungles of Burma, replacements assigned to Merrill's Marauders during the battle for Myitkyina were traumatized to the point of ineffectiveness by the horrendous sights that greeted them. On April 21, when the 187th came off Mt. Macolod after the final assault, only twelve of us from the original thirty-three replacements were with E Company. At least twelve were in hospitals and most of these would eventually return to the company. Four of us who trained together in the Third Platoon of Company A, 150th Training Battalion at Camp Hood had been assigned to E Company in March: Potts, Rokich, Urish, Woerz. Potts had died when shrapnel sheared his head from his body in front of the Malepunyo foothills. Rokich was in the hospital with a shattered foot. Woerz was killed when a Japanese sniper's bullet pierced his heart during the final day of the assault on Mt. Macolod.

Chapter XII Manila

By mid-June Manila had changed dramatically since that afternoon in March when our replacement group had passed through the smoldering, reeking ruins on our way to southern Luzon. Now those of us who had survived the fighting and tropical afflictions of the campaign returned as part of the 187th of the 11th Airborne to briefly garrison the city. As our truck column moved through the streets, it was apparent that some progress had been made in cleaning up the wreckage. Civilian and military traffic was heavy on the streets and avenues. Vehicles were backed up for blocks at the Bailey bridges that now spanned the Pasig River.

Manila Bay, thirty miles long and thirty-five miles wide, the best natural harbor in the orient and one of the finest in the world, had been cleared sufficiently for use by all kinds of ships. Quartermaster and other service troops had activated a supply depot designated Base X. From April on, this base received a monthly average of 380,000 long tons of supplies, a record that no other Southwest Pacific base had ever equaled. The big build-up for the coming invasion of Japan was underway.

Navy ships were calling at the port and thousands of sailors were taking liberty (or liberties?) in the city. Supply ships were disgorging their cargoes in a steady stream. Quartermaster, transportation and other service troops of every description continued to move in to handle the deluge of supplies arriving daily. Even a few combat troops fighting in central and southern Luzon were getting passes for a couple of days in Manila.

It was the first opportunity in months, even years, for many of the servicemen to visit what had been a modern city. After the dreary jungles of New Guinea and the other South Pacific islands, the soldiers were back in a civilized country where the friendly inhabitants spoke their language. Recently, liberty time for sailors in the Western Pacific had consisted of going ashore on isolated, uninhabited atolls with names like Mogmog and Ulithi. Enterprising Filipinos set up a variety of businesses to service the needs and desires of this influx of wealthy American servicemen. Fruit stands,

United States Navy photo by Victor Jorgensen

A sailor on liberty in May 1945 visits a fruit stand in Manila.

barbershops, souvenir stands, dance halls, nightclubs, breweries, distilleries, and brothels sprang up like mushrooms in the ruins of the city—not necessarily in that order.

Into this boomtown atmosphere rode the paratroopers of the 187th--riding on two and one-half ton army trucks, that is. Maintaining order in this wide open city was to be our primary mission for the next month. There was trouble enough but the combat hardened paratroopers quickly convinced soldiers, sailors, and civilians alike that law and order would prevail. Traffic control was a large responsibility, and there were vital areas to be guarded. In addition to these duties, Jap stragglers were still hiding out in the ruins of the city, and they had to be tracked down and dealt with.

Urban services were being reestablished, but the utter destruction of much of the city made this a slow and laborious process. The police force had not yet been reorganized. Electric service was limited. The water supply from the mountains above Manila had been insufficient until American and Filipino troops wrested Ipo Dam from the Japanese in late May. Many of the city's people still had to walk long distances to secure potable water.

The 2nd Battalion, 187th, set up camp in Malcanang Park, directly across the Pasig River from Malcanang Palace, the traditional home of Philippine rulers. We erected pup tents, which we raised about three feet above the ground on stakes. The tents served as a roof over two cots and allowed any breeze to circulate freely. Raising the pup tents on stakes also made it possible to use mosquito nets over the bunks.

After we had finished setting up the tents, Sgt. Faye spotted an older Filipino in a rowboat near the riverbank. Faye called him over to shore and proceeded to make a deal. The Filipino agreed to take the squad across the river to Malcanang Palace. We discovered that it had escaped the destruction that had engulfed most of Manila. Its location away from the main battle had saved the palace. Bullet holes in the walls indicated that small arms fighting had taken place in the area. Most of the furnishings had been removed from the sections of the palace that we visited, and everything seemed to be in a general state of disrepair. It was apparent that the palace had once been a beautiful structure and undoubtedly would be again sometime in the future. Soldiers working in the area told us that Philippine President Osmena had moved into a section of the palace.

Malcanang Park in Manila, June 1945, where the 187th was set up in pup tents across from the Malcanang Palace. From the left are: Emil Piontek, Earl Urish, and Norm Petersen.

Our Filipino ferryboat operator was waiting patiently to take us back across the river when we finished sightseeing. We richly rewarded him with food, candy, and cigarettes, the most precious commodities in the city.

The profusion of soldiers and sailors at work in the Manila area was a startling reminder of the number of support troops necessary to keep one man on the battle line. Because we were at the end of one of the longest supply lines in the world, each man at the front was supported by nineteen other members of the armed forces ranging from truck drivers delivering supplies to the front lines all the way back to clerks working in the Pentagon. These men and women, though they may have been away from their homes and families, were subject to military discipline and regimentation, underwent some discomfort, and were sometimes in danger, did not know the terror of combat experienced along that thin red line where men are exchanging small arms fire with the enemy. While we realized that these people were serving their country and were performing work necessary for the conduct of the war, it was difficult not to be envious of the fact that they lived and ate far better than the combat troops.

Along with most frontline troops, the paratroopers felt that they were at the far end of a long supply line from which much of the cream had been skimmed before the supplies reached the fighting men. We read of some events in Europe that tend to confirm these suspicions. From Italy, Bill Mauldin reported that for months rear echelon personnel in Naples and other cities were wearing the new style combat boots and improved field jackets while frontline soldiers shivered in their foxholes in the mountains, wearing water soaked leggings and flimsy jackets.

Stephen Ambrose writes that combat troops fought the Battle of the Bulge in leather boots that soaked up water during the day and then froze at night in the zero weather. There were good insulated winter boots, shoepacs with leather above and rubber below, available in the theater. Quartermaster and rear echelon troops back in Paris and the rear areas were wearing them by mid-December. It was late January before the men at the front, the men who so desperately needed them, were issued these new winter boots.

And so it was not entirely paranoia when the troopers perceived that the service and supply people sometimes became so busy taking care of themselves and one another that they forgot the frontline troops. Nothing we saw in Manila contradicted this perception. The old members of the 11th remembered the hungry days in the mountains of Leyte. Who among the replacements would ever forget that first night on the battle line without weapons?

One of the most egregious examples of support troops living very well while combat troops were given the dregs occurred in India in mid-1944. The 5307th Composite Unit (Special), known unofficially as Merrill's Marauders, was an all-volunteer group that had been organized to carry out long-range penetration missions behind the Japanese lines in Burma. It has been estimated that among the volunteers in the unit were the misfits and renegades of half the infantry divisions in the army. In spite of this, or perhaps because of it, the Marauders were among the toughest, most effective fighting units fielded during World War II.

The Marauders were the only American combat troops that Gen. Stilwell had under his command in the China-Burma-India Theater, and the only unit on which he could depend completely. He used them to spearhead his attacks and to operate for long periods behind enemy lines. He wore them out and used them up. He sent them back into battle long after most of the men had become physically and mentally unfit for combat. The Marauders fought five major and thirty minor engagements in the fetid jungles and mountains of Burma, their efforts culminating in the brilliant capture of Myitkyina Airfield.

At long last the surviving Marauders were pulled out of the fighting and sent to India to what was supposed to be a rest camp. They were hauled to a field vacant save for some huts that looked like livestock shelters. They had been told that their rest camp would have showers. A truck pulled up. Some pipes and rusty oil drums were thrown off. The Marauders were informed that these were their showers. Coming up the road to their "rest camp," the Marauders had noticed that all of the British and American rear echelon troops, men who had never been within a hundred miles of a battlefield, were living in comfortable quarters with screened mess halls and concrete shower stalls.

When those oil drums and pipes rolled off the truck, it was the last straw. The long-suffering Marauders went berserk, individually and collectively. They destroyed Red Cross Canteens where they had been told that there were no supplies for them. They were told that the supplies were for the troops already in the area. After the war a

Marauder veteran told me that he had asked for a toothbrush and had been refused, even though the canteen had a good supply on hand. After hearing about their rest camp, Marauders in a nearby hospital started to take the place apart. Finally, the Marauders burned the huts that were supposed to be their quarters. Then most of them went AWOL. (Absent Without Official Leave).

The Marauders were completely out of control. It was dangerous to give an order, impossible to enforce one. There was only one thing left to do. One of the toughest fighting forces the US has ever fielded was disbanded.

Some ancient sage once philosophized that taking the coat off another man's back will not make one's back any warmer. I would respectfully suggest that this is not always true. When the 187th arrived in Manila, those of us who had completed our parachute training at the Lipa Jump School were still shod in our G I combat boots. Though an improvement over the G I shoes and leggings we had worn in infantry training, these combat boots presented problems for a paratrooper; they did not provide enough ankle support for the hard landings that often occurred when a paratrooper came down carrying from seventy to a hundred and twenty pounds of arms, ammunition, and equipment. Where the heels of combat boots were squared off, the heels of paratroop boots were angled off at 45 degrees to prevent tangling in lines and gear. Worst of all were the two big buckles on each combat boot that could catch on the lines as men jumped from a plane.

In Manila we soon discovered that there were people with no connection whatever to the airborne who were walking around wearing paratrooper boots. At the same time there were many of us in the 187th who would soon be parachuting into battle wearing unsatisfactory, potentially dangerous footwear. Recognizing the idiocy of this state of affairs, the troopers of the 187th, led by their non-commissioned officers, immediately began to take corrective action.

One of the few buildings not completely destroyed in what had been the modern downtown section of Manila was the Post Office. It had recently been cleaned out and converted into a Red Cross Center. Coffee and doughnuts were served. Reading rooms were provided, stocked with magazines, paperback books, and stationery. A large bulletin board provided a possibility of contacting friends who might come through the Center. Most servicemen visiting Manila or stationed in the area would stop by. A majority were service troops, now flooding into the area to handle the huge quantity of war materiel being unloaded at the docks and stockpiled at Base X. On most days the Center throbbed with activity as thousands of men passed through. The 187th, on orders from the Provost Marshal, mounted a four-man guard to maintain order.

Our resourceful sergeants set up an "interview room" in the Center and stocked it with G I boots and shoes of various sizes. Any non-airborne soldier who entered the building wearing paratrooper boots was ushered into this room. The sergeant in charge of the guard detail would begin with an explanation that went something like this:

> The 11th Airborne Division has a little problem that you can help us with. Due to poor resupply, theft of supplies, and so forth, many of our paratroopers do not have proper boots. This could result in injury when they make their next jump. Now, so far as I can see, you are not in any outfit that is going to be jumping out of airplanes. In the interest of the war effort, wouldn't you like to exchange your paratroop boots for some of these other nice shoes or boots we have here?

The sergeant would give the soldier a minute to consider this proposition. Then, if he heard no affirmative response, he would continue: "You are going to trade boots with us. You have a choice. You can do it yourself, the easy way, or I can do it for you, the hard way." Only a few poor, misguided souls chose to do it the hard way, usually much to their regret. The end result was always the same-- one more 187th paratrooper properly outfitted in jump boots.

My fellow squad member, Walt Lepley, and I were walking down the street in Manila a few days after our arrival in the city. Suddenly, Walt stopped in his tracks with a big, "Whoa! Just look at that across the street." What had attracted Walt's attention was a strapping young Filipino wearing a brand new uniform, cap and everything. But best of all, he had on a shiny pair of paratroop boots that looked like they might be my size. Charging across the street, Walt confronted him with, "Buddy, where did you get those boots?" "Colonel Hardy gave them to me," came back the self-assured reply. Now if this young man intended to impress or intimidate someone by dropping a colonel's name, he had surely picked the wrong audience.

"It's best not to speak to paratroopers about saluting. They always ask where you got your jump boots."

Pfc. Walt Lepley, scion of generations of Pennsylvania coal miners, graduate cum laude of Ft. Benning Parachute School, and veteran of two bloody campaigns, was not, at twenty years of age, a man easily impressed. Walt figured that some rear echelon officer had hired this young man as an orderly, that is, as his personal servant. In garrison, enlisted men were assigned these duties, something most of the egalitarian-minded G.I.s hated with a passion. "Dog robbers," as these orderlies were derisively known, were held in especially low esteem by the enlisted combat troops. Months later, in Japan, a new replacement announced to our squad that he had applied for and been assigned duty as an orderly. After big, burly Bienkowski had been appropriately dressed down, the squad threw his clothes and equipment into the barracks hallway and forced him to stay there until he moved to his new quarters the following day.

Walt proceeded to explain to our Filipino friend that it would be necessary to exchange boots so that we could get on with the war. Soon, without violence or bloodshed, but with some lamentation, he sat down on the curb and we traded boots. The husky young Filipino didn't look quite so sharp in my old battle-worn combat boots, so Walt tried to cheer him up by assuring him that we were going to let him keep that fine, shiny new uniform, which, by the way, was considerably better than those we were wearing. My new paratrooper boots were well broken in, but they served me well on a battalion jump we made a few weeks later, and until we reached Japan. When the 187th returned to southern Luzon in early July, almost all of the troopers were properly outfitted in jump boots.

One afternoon when we were off duty, Pete and I were looking around and came to Quezon City. Located on the northeastern outskirts of Manila, this area had not suffered as much damage as most of the city. We saw a large, splendid church with people entering and leaving and decided to go in. The church was filled with people weeping and moaning, mourning for loved ones they had lost. The scene made me realize, more than ever before, that the 100,000 Filipinos killed in the battle for Manila were not just numbers. They were the beloved husbands and wives, sons and daughters, mothers and fathers, brothers and sisters, of these grieving people.

With little seniority in E Company, I usually ended up with the less desirable guard posts around the city. The spookiest assignment I drew was on the north shore of Manila Bay. Another trooper and I were sent to guard a Japanese ship tied up in this remote area. The ship had escaped destruction during the battle for Manila only because it was in this out of the way location. The Sergeant of the Guard, on assigning us the post, informed us that reports indicated Japanese soldiers or sailors were still hiding out in the area. This was not unusual as the 187th was frequently sending out patrols whenever Filipino civilians reported sighting Japanese survivors hiding in the Manila area.

A jeep driver dropped us off at the boat late in the afternoon with just enough daylight left to search the vessel thoroughly. I had an eerie feeling that we were being watched but could not see anyone in the area. The other guard and I decided that our best bet would be to take up a position on the flying bridge so that we could observe the entire area around the boat. No one could sneak up on us if we stayed on the bridge. We spent the long night back to back on full alert. The early morning light, revealing the wreckage in the bay and the ruins of the city, brought a sigh of relief from my companion. It had been another of those nights that we were only too happy to see end.

During the battle for Manila, the Japanese destroyed the bridges over the Pasig River in a futile effort to stop the advancing American troops. Army engineers had first placed the pontoon bridge that my replacement group had used to cross the river in March. They then pushed two Bailey bridges across the river further downstream. In June these bridges were carrying a steady stream of military and civilian traffic between the north and south sections of the city. The 187th stationed a guard at each end of the bridges with the primary task of controlling the flow of traffic. Too many heavy army vehicles on a bridge at the same time could cause one of the Baileys to collapse.

A large number of officers—most of them able and important to the war effort, some of them unimportant, and not a few of them self-important—crossed the bridges, expecting an occasional salute. Having recently departed from a combat area, our troopers were out of the habit of saluting. In any case, paratroopers are loath to salute officers, other than their own. In the continuous bumper-to-bumper stream of traffic moving across the bridges, it was not possible for officers to stop their vehicles and complain that they were not receiving their due. Then one day a short, paunchy, slovenly-dressed rear echelon colonel came through, making a round of the city. Apparently, his main contribution to the war effort was to check all of the 187th guard posts in the city and deliver lectures about this saluting business. He was probably right. Now that we weren't fighting, we should try to be exemplary soldiers.

I was on bridge guard on the Pasig early one morning when a jeep came across with a five star flag on the fender. Sitting ramrod straight next to the driver was General of the Army Douglas MacArthur. Even without the insignia or the ornate gold-encrusted cap, it would have been impossible not to recognize him. The handsome, hawk-like features were unmistakable. The sixty-five-year-old MacArthur was a general who looked the part. I saluted--smartly.

On June 9, Gen. Swing staged a division review at Lipa Airfield for his old friend, Gen. Joseph "Vinegar Joe" Stilwell who had recently been relieved as American commander in the China-Burma-India Theater--at the insistence of the Chinese ruler, Generalissimo Chiang Kai-Shek. Stillwell thought Chiang should be using all that American aid to fight the Japanese. Chiang was hoarding it for the coming struggle with Mao Tse-Tung and the Chinese Communists. It has been suggested that, had he been forced to deal with Chiang for any period of time, St.Francis of Assisi would have acquired the nickname, "Vinegar Frank."

Those members of the 187th who could be spared from duty in Manila were trucked down to Lipa to join the rest of the division in the parade. As we passed in review, the sky filled with parachutes as 324 paratroopers jumped from nine C-46 transports, jumping in double sticks from both doors. Landing just behind the marching troopers, they quickly doffed their chutes, assembled and fell in behind. As this was going on, three gliders cut loose from their tow planes over the airstrip and glided in for a landing next to the runway. A battery of artillerymen rushed from the gliders and passed in review just behind the parachutists at the end of the column. All of this accomplished with clocklike precision. I don't know if Vinegar Joe was impressed but I certainly was.

Beginning on June 23, elements of the division carried out another mission. A combat team of 1030 men, code named Gypsy Task Force, was dropped at the far northern end of Luzon near Aparri. They were to seal off the fertile Cagayan Valley and prevent Japanese forces, being pushed east by the 37th Division, from fleeing into the Sierra Madre mountain fastness.

The day before the jump Gen. Walter Krueger, 6th Army Commander, joined Gen.Swing in inspecting the preparations that were underway. Krueger had joined the Army as a private when he was seventeen. He was now sixty-four. Lt.Col.Burgess, commander of the task force, reported to the generals. Krueger looked him over and then asked how old he was. "Twenty-six, sir," Burgess replied. Krueger turned to Swing and asked, "Don't you have an older officer to command this force?" Swing replied, "Yes, sir. There's Col. Lahti who is thirty-one, but if this force runs into trouble, Lahti would take the rest of the 511th and reinforce these troops." Krueger did not pursue the subject. Older officers were almost non-existent in the 11th Airborne.

Gypsy Task Force dropped into a 20-25 mile per hour ground wind and onto a rough drop zone. This resulted in jump casualties of two killed and seventy injured. Jap resistance was light, however, and by June 26 the force had linked up with the 37th Division, completing the mission. The task force was ready to return to its base at Lipa.

Transport planes were landing on a nearby airstrip bringing in supplies for the 37th Division. Burgess contacted 6th Army Headquarters and requested that his paratroopers be flown out on these planes. A 6th Army staff officer flew in and instructed Burgess to countermarch his thousand paratroopers the fifty-five miles to the port at Aparri. There they would be picked up by naval shipping and returned to Manila. From that port they would be trucked the eighty miles back to their base near Lipa. The staff officer's plan would take weeks to return the men of Gypsy Task Force to their base.

These paratroopers had just out-marched an armored column in temperatures ranging to 120 degrees in the heat of the day. They didn't mind marching when it was necessary, but they preferred to travel by air when possible. As soon as the 6th Army staff officer had departed, Burgess went down to the airstrip where the transport planes were landing with supplies. As the C-46s were being unloaded, he talked to the pilots who were about to fly back to Clark Field with empty aircraft. In two days the young Lt.Col. had the paratroopers of Gypsy Task Force back at their base near Lipa. After all, it was only a slight 160-mile detour on the pilots' return trip to Clark Field. For their part in this unscheduled airlift, the pilots and their crews received Japanese guns, flags, helmets, and so forth to show the folks back home. And to hell with 6th Army staff officers.

The northern Luzon jump near Aparri proved to be the last major combat operation for the 11th Airborne. Overall, the Luzon campaign was the largest and bloodiest of all Pacific land operations. From the Lingayen Gulf landing on Jan. 9 to the end of the war on Aug. 15, ground forces killed in action on Luzon totaled 8300 Americans, 1100 Filipino guerrillas, and 205,000 Japanese. Best estimates indicate that, up to the time of the surrender, 1,740,000 members of the Japanese armed forces had died in all theaters of war, including the Asian continent. Of these, 425,000 died in the desperate effort to hold the Philippines. In a communiqué dated July 5, 1945, MacArthur proclaimed:

> The entire Philippine Islands are now liberated and the Philippine campaign can be regarded as virtually closed . . . Some isolated action of a guerrilla nature in the practically uninhabited mountain ranges may persist but this great land mass of 115,600 square miles with a population of 17,000,000 is now free of the invader.
> The enemy during the operations employed twenty-three divisions all of which were practically annihilated. Our forces comprised seventeen divisions. This was one of the rare instances when in a long campaign a ground force superior in numbers was destroyed by a numerically inferior opponent. . . .
> Naval and air forces shared equally with the ground troops in accomplishing the success of the campaign. Naval battles reduced the Japanese Navy to practical impotence and air losses running into many thousands have seriously crippled his air potential. Working in complete unison the three services inflicted the greatest disaster ever sustained by Japanese arms. . . .

As a summary of the Philippine campaign, this communiqué was seriously flawed. MacArthur fails to acknowledge the part played by the brave Filipino guerrillas and volunteers who fought with such extraordinary valor and zeal to liberate their homeland. Also, the unflagging support of the civilian population had been invaluable to the liberating troops. Feling and his family and all of the brave Filipinos who fought by our side should never be forgotten.

The "isolated action of a guerrilla nature" referred to in the communiqué was an obvious understatement of the facts. In the mountain wilderness of northern Luzon the men of the 6th, 32nd, and 37th Divisions and various Filipino guerrilla units were still engaged in a major struggle with Yamashita's surviving 50,000 Japanese soldiers when the war ended on Aug. 15. They would not have agreed with MacArthur's pronouncement that the campaign was "virtually closed" by July 5.

The struggle for Okinawa has been widely cited as the "last battle" of World War II. It was not.

As daylight slowly illuminated the city of Manila on the morning of July 4, a tropical downpour began. The rain never ceased falling at any time that day. At times it came in torrents, and at times it slacked off, but it never quit. After a soggy breakfast, those of us of Company E who were off duty pulled on our ponchos and helmets and headed across Manila to Rizal Stadium. Named for a Philippine national hero, the stadium had been a large, impressive structure before the war. Four months ago it had been the scene of a ferocious battle. Japanese troops took up positions under the stands using the concrete rooms as bunkers. First Cavalry Division tanks smashed their way on to the field and blasted them out. Since that battle the rubble had been cleared away, but little had been done to repair the stadium. Recently, a bulldozer had leveled the shell holes in the playing field.

On this 169th anniversary of the American Declaration of Independence, another battle was about to take place on the field at Rizal Stadium. The 11th Airborne Division football team was to face Navy in what should have been called the "Mud Bowl." Earlier in its history the division had fielded an excellent football team. Somewhere, somehow, the equipment had been found and a game scheduled with Navy for this Independence Day. For a division of nine thousand men to challenge "Navy" anywhere in the Pacific Ocean area in 1945 was evidence of audacity of a monumental magnitude. Rumor had it that Admiral Spruance had flown a Chicago Bears running back into Manila from somewhere on that vast ocean.

The 11th Airborne could counter with several former professionals and Major Tom Meserau, an All-American at West Point in 1943, now commanding a parachute infantry battalion of the 188th. By game time the torrential rain had turned the field at Rizal Stadium into a sea of mud. As the game progressed, the playing area deteriorated rapidly and soon resembled a huge buffalo wallow. As we peered through the downpour, it appeared that twenty-two big mud balls were shoving one another about. When the game ended, the 11th Airborne was satisfied to have held the high-powered Navy team to a scoreless tie.

    The ability of the officers and men at division headquarters to find the time and wherewithal to sponsor a football game is impressive when one considers all of the enterprises that the division was involved with at the time. The Gypsy Task Force had just returned from the mission on the northern tip of Luzon. The 187th was still assigned to the Provost Marshal in Manila. The units at Lipa were continuing to flush out a few Japanese in the mountains, turning volunteers into paratroopers at the jump school, and receiving and training newly arrived replacements.

Chapter XIII Regroup

When E Company returned from Manila to the Lipa base in early July, the 11th Airborne Division was rapidly reorganizing for battles to come. The 187th and 188th Regiments were being expanded from two to three battalions each. The 188th was officially designated a parachute regiment. The authorized strength of the division was increased from 8,600 to 12,000 men. In the 187th men were being transferred from the 1st and 2nd Battalions to form the nucleus of the new 3rd Battalion. Walt Lepley was one of the troopers being reassigned. It was a big loss for our machine gun squad. Few men could fill Walt's boots.

A complete parachute infantry regiment, the 541st, had just arrived from the States. The officers and men of the 541st had hoped that their regiment would continue as a unit within the 11th Airborne Division. They were to be disappointed. The 541st was deactivated and it's men assigned to the 11th as replacements. At the company, platoon, and squad levels, this caused considerable friction among the troopers. From the time the men of the former 541st arrived, the combat veterans of the 11th were not overly sympathetic toward these new replacements. The men of the 541st had been, among other activities, doing war bond rally parachuting demonstrations. They had been basking in the reflection of the renown won by the airborne troops in combat overseas while living the good life back in the States. This contrasted rather sharply with our recent activities.

There were many enlisted men in the division who were expecting to be promoted to non-commissioned officer slots left vacant by the casualties of the last five months. But the 541st was loaded with NCOs with the result that many deserving men of the original 11th Airborne would not receive the stripes they had earned. It was a bitter pill for a trooper who had been leading men in combat to be replaced by a man who had just arrived overseas and, worse still, had no combat experience. This naturally caused friction and hard feelings. The likelihood that green, unblooded non-coms would lead some of the platoons and squads of E Company into future battles was a matter of grave concern for the veterans. A number of the "old men" in the rifle platoons of Company E moved over to the weapons platoon.

Sgt. Faye was transferred to division headquarters at the time we returned to the Lipa base. When it became questionable who our next squad leader would be, one of the 60 mm mortar squad leaders urged me to move over to his squad. Whether he liked me or the fact that I could carry a lot of weight was immaterial. In any event, it was not my decision to make. Sgt. Pearson worked it out with the platoon leader and I found myself in a mortar squad, whether I wanted to be or not.

There was a lot of transferring taking place at this time, both within the company and out of the company. Men who felt that they had used up most of their luck during the past year were looking for less hazardous duty. There were exceptions, however. Two Native Americans (Indians at the time) had transferred from E Company to the Division Reconnaissance Platoon when the fighting simmered down. These two were superb combat infantrymen with physical capabilities few men possess. They transferred because it was relatively quiet in our area while the Recon Platoon was still going deep into the mountains on dangerous forays.

Two E Company sergeants, Rosen and Carabetta, transferred to the Division Military Police. Sgt. Rosen was much liked and respected by the troopers of E Company. His time of duty with the Division MPs was to be short. On the morning of July 22, he was awakened about 4:30 in the morning. A glider exercise was scheduled and Rosen was needed to take the place of a man who had suddenly fallen ill. During the flight the three C-46 transport planes towing the gliders encountered a sudden tropical storm over Manila Bay. The turbulence threw two of the gliders together and they crashed killing everyone aboard. Sgt. Rosen was among those killed-- a tragic twist of fate for a brave man who had survived two bloody campaigns during the past year.

On a more encouraging note, one of our rifle platoon sergeants was awarded an appointment to the U.S. Military Academy and departed for West Point. His fine combat record and exceptional IQ had earned him the opportunity.

The oldest man by far in the company, a trooper in his thirties, had accumulated enough points under the Army's new partial demobilization plan to go home and be discharged. He was one of the people who carried pliers and collected gold Jap teeth. Practically every combat unit in the Pacific seems to have had one of those. Pappy also possessed a Jap Nambu machine gun he had somehow stashed away. When the authorities informed him that he could not take it along home, he went down to a Bailey bridge and heaved it into the Pasig River. There was a good demand for souvenirs from sailors on liberty in Manila but Pappy wasn't interested in selling his prize.

With all of the recently arrived replacements to assimilate into the division's infantry regiments, training was intensified on all levels. Most of the men realized that what they learned today might save their lives tomorrow, so there was little complaining. In spite of the rigorous schedule, recreation and entertainment for the troops was not neglected. A natural hollow in the division area was converted into an open-air bowl by adding a stage. While fighting was still raging on Mt.Malepunyo, movies were being shown and USO shows were being staged.

Many of the films were well used, and this frequently caused problems. When a film broke or a projector malfunctioned, the operator always caught hell from the not-too-patient audience. There was consistently a call to "Put that sonuvabitch in a line company."

We were living in pyramidal tents at this time. Set up on bamboo frames with the sides open and stretched out, these six man tents were a nice improvement over the pup tents we had in Manila. Fitted out with army cots and mosquito nets, they were absolutely luxurious when compared to foxholes and slit trenches. One tent in the battalion area was set up as a day room and sparsely furnished with several folding chairs, an old table, and a few magazines and paperback books.

A USO troupe came to the division bowl and presented the popular musical, *Oklahoma*, on two consecutive nights. Early in the morning the day after the show closed, Harry Martin drove up to the weapons platoon area in a jeep. Harry was our acting squad leader, a position he held for a very short interval. "Petersen and Urish! Come over here! I need two good men for a detail."

Harry drove us to the stage area of the division bowl where a large crew was loading out the equipment needed for *Oklahoma*. Harry pulled in as though he had charge of the entire operation. The three of us hopped out, looked the situation over, loaded the show's upright piano on the back of the jeep--which was no mean feat--and drove away. When we reached the highway, Harry pulled a tarpaulin over the piano. Returning to the 2nd Bn. area, we unloaded the piano in the day room.

Harry was proud as Lucifer. He had just substantiated his ranking as top scrounger of the 187th, a rating he had first achieved back in New Guinea. There, for an extraordinarily brief time, the troopers of the 11th Airborne had been used as longshoremen. In the Oro Bay area the division soon became known as "Ali Baba Joe Swing and his 8,000 thieves."

Pete and I were not quite as thrilled as Harry with the piano operation. Harry was half Native American and his independent spirit did not blend happily with army ways. His performance on this particular morning was a manifestation of the resentment that smoldered in his spirit against the army in general and the officer-enlisted man caste system in particular. The officers, as usual, had completely monopolized the female USO personnel in the *Oklahoma* cast. Any enlisted man who might have liked to just talk briefly with a girl from back home was out of luck. *C'est la guerre. C'est la vie.*

In a secluded palm grove located a half-mile from camp, a group of enlisted men maintained their own highly unauthorized motor pool; Harry Martin had a hand in this, naturally. Half a dozen jeeps and several other vehicles, all of which had been "borrowed," were kept at this out-of-the-way location. The jeeps were used primarily for quick trips to Manila, eighty miles away. When the military authorities discovered this clandestine motor pool, there was a lot of hell raised. I never heard of anyone being court-martialed, however. With an invasion of the Japanese home islands looming in the not-too-distant future, locking up veteran paratroopers would have been significantly counterproductive.

Harry Martin was ordered to report to the Lipa Airstrip one morning not long after the piano acquisition caper. He was informed that he was to take part in a glider exercise where a new technique was being checked out.

Harry returned late in the afternoon. "What do you think those crazy bastards are doing down at the airstrip?" He proceeded to answer his own question: "They're putting the looped end of a glider tow rope up on a frame. Then a C-46 comes flying in about ten feet above the ground and hooks the loop of the towrope. The nylon rope pays out and then stretches about fifty feet. The glider snaps forward and into the air. The poor bastards in the glider go from sitting still to 115 miles an hour almost instantly."

Harry sat down on his cot and began to rub his neck. None of the paratroopers in the tent seemed to be interested in going down to the strip to get in on this glider fun. I don't believe this pick-up technique ever achieved wide popularity with the troops even though it was used frequently in Burma to recover gliders. Most glider riders or gliderists volunteered for parachute training when they got the chance. In the 11th Airborne there were few glider riders who were not also qualified parachutists. There was usually a choice: Qualify as a parachutist or transfer out.

On Aug. 1 the 2nd Bn., 187th, made a unit jump. We were in the air for an hour and a half. It was an extremely rough flight with the plane dropping precipitously as we encountered tropical air pockets. Loaded down as we were with equipment, it was not a pleasant ride. I noted that some of the troopers were looking a little green around the gills. It was the only time that I was ever glad to hear a jumpmaster order: "Stand up and hook up." When my chute opened I was surprised to be facing toward the plane I had just left. The plane seemed to be moving away almost in slow motion.

A brisk wind scattered E Company about the drop zone. I made a good landing and started looking for the weapons platoon. It took me ten minutes to locate my squad. My new platoon sergeant was not too proud of me. But then I wasn't too proud of him either. I had been on a special guard detail the previous day while the company was being briefed for the drop. No one had bothered to brief me.

I keeled over on the march the following day. Twenty-four hours later I regained consciousness in a big tent, which, I was informed, was the division medical company. The wooziness I had been feeling for the past week was apparently caused by one of the various tropical fevers that abound in the region. After two days and no particular treatment worthy of note, other than a few aspirin tablets, I was released and told to report back to my company.

I went over to the highway and stuck out my thumb, looking for a ride. The only open command car that I can remember seeing in the southwest Pacific area pulled up. A pleasant appearing major looked down from his perch in the back of the car and asked,

"Where're you headed, soldier?" "11th Airborne. 2nd Battalion, 187th", I replied. "Well, we can take you most of the way. Climb up here with me." So, the major and I, sitting up there like Very Important People, motored across southern Luzon. The major proved to be quite congenial, and we had a pleasant discussion on the war as we motored along. When I thought about it later, it occurred to me that hitching a ride on a big command car might not have been my best move. Any bypassed Jap, looking for a worthy target of opportunity, might have concluded that such an important looking vehicle must be carrying important people. He might have shot at the major and hit me.

While we were liberating southern Luzon and preparing for future battles, events were occurring worldwide that would control our destiny. On Luzon, as the tropic heat and humidity of July gave way to the tropic heat and humidity of August, it was obvious to anyone who followed the news that the final defeat of Japan was only a matter of time. That nation was doomed just as surely as those Japanese soldiers we had killed and those we had buried alive on Mt. Macolod had been doomed. They too had been given an opportunity to surrender and had spurned that offer. As the destruction of the Japanese homeland by American air and naval forces escalated from March to August of 1945, the question remained: Would the rulers of Japan allow the nation to die, rather than surrender? In its awful fury, the struggle for Okinawa foreshadowed the bloodletting that would occur during an invasion of the Japanese home islands.

During the spring and summer of 1945 the Japanese government had made an effort to persuade the Soviet Union to broker a peace in the Pacific war. The terms the Japanese were prepared to offer would have been totally unacceptable to the Allies. These peace feelers by Japanese diplomats were largely ignored by the Soviets. The United States government was first aware of these attempts only because of intelligence intercepts.

The collapse of Germany in May did not alter the mind-set of Japan's military rulers. On June 8, the Japanese cabinet, with the emperor looking on in silence, resolved to "prosecute the war to the bitter end."

On July 26 the Allied leaders, meeting in Potsdam, Germany, broadcast a message to Japan that included an ultimatum. This pronouncement, which came to be known as the Potsdam Declaration, again called for unconditional surrender. It also stated, however, that the Allies did not desire to reduce Japan to poverty or servility in the post-war world. In somewhat ambiguous language, the document called for the eventual establishment "in accordance with the freely expressed will of the Japanese people, of a peacefully inclined and responsible government." It appears that the Truman administration hoped that this wording would not be seen by Americans as abandoning "unconditional surrender" and yet would allow the Japanese leaders to discern that it might be possible to preserve the imperial system.

Point 13 of the Potsdam Declaration warned the Japanese government that the alternative to immediate and unconditional surrender would be "prompt and utter destruction." President Truman had received important top-secret information on July 17. At Los Alamos in the New Mexican desert a crucial test of the most destructive weapon ever conceived by man had been successful.

"Prompt and utter destruction" may have seemed a redundancy to a people who had been watching helplessly as their cities burned during the massive firebombing of that spring and summer. With all of the big industrial cities largely reduced to ashes, the B-29s were even now burning out the smaller cities of Japan. The American Navy, having utterly destroyed the once proud imperial fleet, was steaming up and down Japan's long coastline, bombarding at will.

The Japanese government took no action on the Potsdam Declaration, probably because the proposal did not directly address the future status of the emperor--the overriding consideration for the Japanese people. When questioned by reporters, Premier Suzuki replied that his government would "withhold comment." The word, "mokusatsu," which he used to indicate his government's attitude, translates into English as "take no notice of, treat with silent contempt, ignore." It was an unfortunate choice of words. Tokyo radio broadcast Suzuki's comments verbatim for all the world to ponder.

As August began, some American servicemen in the western Pacific were hearing a will-o'-the-wisp rumor that certain air force people in the Marianas were offering even money that the war would be over in two months. From where we stood, that possibility seemed inconceivable.

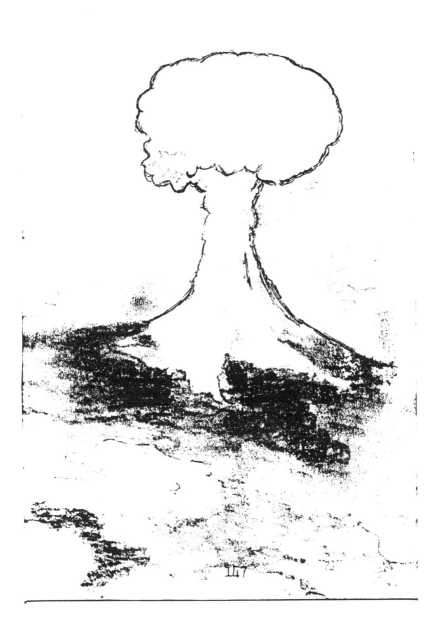

Chapter XIV Okinawa and Japan

"Urish, if this story is true, we may live through this thing after all." This from my foxhole buddy and fellow machine gunner, Norm Petersen, as he handed me a copy of *The Ripcord*, the mimeographed newsletter of the 187th, which had just been dropped off by a runner from regiment. I read it quickly, then again more slowly, attempting to comprehend the magnitude of the event that had taken place the previous day at Hiroshima. The Air Force had destroyed that large Japanese city with a single bomb. As I read of the power of this nuclear weapon, it seemed obvious that Japan must now surrender or be obliterated.

And if all this proved to be true, Pete was right. Now we would live. Now we would get to finish our lives, to go home again, to rejoin our loved ones. No combat jump into Japan. No more killing. No more dying. No more maiming and being maimed. Such were the thoughts that ran through my mind as I recalled that almost half of the men from our replacement group, assigned to E Company in March, were no longer with us. Most had been casualties of the bitter fighting in southern Luzon. Those of us who had watched the casualties mount knew, though we never talked about it, that in an invasion of Japan, there was a high probability that we would be killed or wounded. Now we dared to hope that the bloodshed might be over.

News of promising developments now began to arrive almost daily. The Soviet Union entered the war against Japan the next day, Aug. 8. The Air Force dropped an atomic bomb on Nagasaki on Aug.9. On Aug. 10, we heard that the Japanese had sued for peace. That same day, word came down that MacArthur, soon to be named Supreme Commander for the Allied Powers, had selected the 11th Airborne to spearhead the occupation when or if the Japanese surrendered.

The following day, Aug.11, aircraft began arriving at Lipa Airstrip to start flying the men of the division to Okinawa. Within twelve hours of the time division headquarters received notice of the move, the first units were airborne, on their way to Yontan Field on

Okinawa. There the division would stage for the move into the Japanese home islands.

As E Company was preparing for the move, it was announced that a volunteer honor guard company was to be formed. The mission of this guard would be to protect MacArthur when he arrived in Japan. The guard was to be composed of volunteers from the division's infantry regiments. There was a persistent rumor floating about that this Honor Guard would parachute in to seize and hold an airfield near Tokyo. Then the entire division would be flown in to this field. This rumor had a tendency to keep the number of volunteers within reason.

Perhaps I was still a little muddle-headed from my recent bout with fever. For whatever reason, I announced to my weapons platoon buddies that I was going down to headquarters to volunteer. They told me that I was crazy as hell. Volunteering was something you did only to become a paratrooper or to save a buddy. Notwithstanding this heartfelt advice, I went down and volunteered. I was told at headquarters that they would contact me when and if they needed me.

At E Company we readied our packs and equipment and stood by. The afternoon of Aug. 13 we were trucked to Nichols Field on the south edge of Manila. I noticed on the trip to the airfield that one of the rifle squad leaders had his Filipina girl friend along, dressed in full army uniform, collar turned up, helmet pulled down low. This sergeant was a nice guy who was quite ugly in the physically unattractive sense of the word. Somewhere he had found this Filipina who was just as ugly. This could not have been easy as most of the young Filipinas are slender, nice-looking women. I never heard how this world-class smuggling attempt worked out but I would guess that it came to a sudden halt at the airfield. I do know that some of the young Filipino men who had fought alongside us in southern Luzon did make the trip to Okinawa. When unit commanders found they had these extra men, they were unhappily but necessarily obliged to send them back to the Philippines. One thing that I deeply regretted about our sudden departure from the Philippines was that I had no opportunity to say farewell to Feling before we left. He had gone to visit his family in Paranaque that week, and I was never to see him again.

We spent the night at Nichols Field sleeping on the ground under the C-46 transport planes. We boarded a plane before dawn and took off at first light. After an uneventful five-hour flight, the plane landed at Kadena Airfield on Okinawa sometime before noon on Aug. 14. The airborne move to Okinawa had not gone as smoothly for all of the 11,000 men now in the division. During the hectic, full speed ahead, four-day airlift from Clark, Nichols, Nielsen, and Lipa Airfields on Luzon to Kadena and Yontan on Okinawa, forty-one men of the division died in three crashes. In addition to the 341 C-46 and 151 C-47 transport planes available, 99 B-24 bombers were pressed into service as troop carriers. On the relatively short Lipa airfield, an overloaded bomber failed to become airborne and crashed at the end of the runway, killing eleven of the men aboard. At Naha, on Okinawa, a C-46 arrived at dusk as Japanese kamikaze planes were attacking ships in the harbor. All airfields were blacked out. In the fading light, and with the ships putting up smokescreens, the pilot misjudged the end of the runway and crashed, killing all thirty-one on the plane. The division historian lamented: "Not all of us made the trip successfully. It seemed doubly tragic that men should have fought through the bloody war, only to be killed on this last leg, deprived of the glory of victory." What price glory?

Approaching Okinawa from the air, it appeared that a large part of the island was being converted into airfields, supply dumps, and campsites. A Negro truck company was waiting to haul us to a campsite. I hopped into the cab of a truck with Sgt. Pearson and the driver. The road was a series of potholes connected by short stretches of washboard. Pearson, a take-charge North Carolinian, found it necessary to provide a driving critique as we bounced along.

As we were setting up pup tents, word came down for Honor Guard volunteers to report to division headquarters. A platoon-sized group from each of the three infantry regiments checked in. Any decent campsites on southern Okinawa had already been taken by earlier arrivals, so the Honor Guard was assigned a hillside just above the beach on which to pitch our two man pup tents. The area was loose sand, which made a better sleeping surface than hard ground. On the downside, strong winds sometimes took a tent up like a kite. I drew a nineteen-year-old Californian for a tent-mate.

While the men of the 11th Airborne were engaging in the hectic, hurry-up airlift from Luzon, then waiting restlessly in pup-tent camps on Okinawa, Japanese government officials and military leaders in Tokyo were wrangling over the bitter choice of surrendering or continuing the war. The shock of the nuclear destruction of Hiroshima on Aug. 6 and of Nagasaki on Aug. 9, combined with the Soviet entry into the war on Aug. 8, had given the peace advocates in the Japanese leadership their opportunity. They urged Emperor Hirohito to exercise his imperial authority and overrule the bitter-end military leaders. There was a fear that an atomic bomb detonated over Tokyo might destroy the government and the imperial household leaving no central authority to deal with the Allies. This fear was heightened by a rumor, rampant in Tokyo at the time, that the city was targeted for an atomic bomb to be delivered on Aug. 12. This raised the specter that, with no national government in Japan, the war would end only when the home islands had been ground into dust and the far-flung Japanese armies totally destroyed.

Emperor Hirohito, meeting with the Supreme Council late in the evening of Aug. 9, indicated that he wished his government to immediately accept the terms of the Potsdam Declaration if the imperial system would be preserved. The following day the Japanese government announced that it would accept the terms of the Potsdam Declaration "if it does not compromise . . . the prerogatives of his majesty as a sovereign ruler."

President Truman met with his advisers to discuss this unexpected offer as soon as the radio announcement was picked up. By the time the formal note was received through the Swiss Embassy, they had discussed the Japanese proposal and Secretary of State Byrnes had been instructed to prepare a reply. This reply read in part:

> "From the moment of surrender, the authority of the Emperor and the Japanese government to rule the state shall be subject to the Supreme Commander of the Allied Powers who will take such steps as he deems proper to effectuate the surrender terms."

The note also repeated the clause in the Potsdam Declaration that stated: "The ultimate form of the Government of Japan shall be established in accordance with the freely expressed will of the Japanese people."

Quickly approved by Britain, China, and the Soviet Union, the note was forwarded to Japan on Aug. 11. That same day President Truman directed that naval and air attacks against Japan be continued until a satisfactory reply was received from that government. He further directed that no more atomic bombs be used.

Almost forgotten down in the Philippines, Americans in the rugged, disease and insect infested mountains and jungles of northern Luzon continued to slug it out with Yamashita and his remaining 50,000 dogged Japanese. In some of the bitterest fighting of the Pacific war, American and Japanese infantrymen continued to kill one another, day after day.

When word of the Japanese note reached the air bases in the Marianas on Aug. 10, the B-29s stood down. In part due to weather conditions, they remained inactive until Aug. 13. When it appeared that the Japanese might be stalling, a "maximum effort" was ordered. Every available B-29 would go. From Washington, top Air Force brass pushed to put 1,000 of the big bombers over Japan. There were 800 available in the Marianas. On Okinawa, 200 more, only recently deployed there, did not participate in this last raid.

On Aug. 14, Emperor Hirohito met with the Japanese cabinet in a bomb shelter under the Imperial Palace. The cabinet divided equally on the question of accepting the terms of the Allied note. The military chiefs wanted to fight on. Generals Anami and Umezu and Admiral Toyoda held on to the forlorn hope that they could make the coming invasion of Kyushu so bloody that America would grant Japan better terms. At this point the emperor invoked his imperial prerogative and instructed his ministers to end the war. He would take the unprecedented action of recording a message to be broadcast to his subjects the following day.

Unwilling or unable to believe that the nation should capitulate, a group of young officers in Tokyo attempted to incite the army to take over the government. These rebels attempted to assassinate the Prime Minister and other high government officials. In an attempt to seize the recording of the Emperor's surrender address, they invaded the palace grounds and killed the commander of the Imperial Guard when he refused to cooperate. They failed to find the recording, and it was broadcast to the Japanese people a few hours later. Unable to enlist Gen. Anami or any other senior officers in their cause, the leaders of the revolt committed hara-kiri and the Tokyo revolt fizzled out. Even so, many army and navy officers throughout the empire were calling for continued resistance.

At 7:00 AM on Aug. 15 an Air Force communiqué from the Marianas proclaimed: "More than 1,000 aircraft of the U.S. Army

Strategic Air Force operated against Japan in the last twenty-four hours." They had included the escort fighter planes from Iwo Jima in the count. Among the eight primary targets burned out and destroyed on this final raid were Isezaki (pop. 40,000) and Kumagaya (pop. 49,000). Large, intact targets had become scarce in Japan. When definitive news that the war had ended reached the Marianas at 8:00 AM on the 15th, half the planes from the night portion of the raid were still on the return leg of the 14-16 hour flight, spread out as far back as Iwo Jima. Ten thousand fliers had participated in the raid. They had dropped 6,000 tons of bombs on Japan. There had been one American casualty, a fighter pilot downed by anti-aircraft fire.

As the 7:00 AM cease-fire neared in the mountains of northern Luzon, Pfc. Ed Mullins of A Company, 128th Inf. Regiment, 32nd Inf. Division, was on patrol with his squad near Bagabag in the Cagayan Valley. The patrol was disengaging from a firefight with the Japanese. Minutes before the cease-fire was to take effect, Pfc. Edward O'Dell Mullins gave that last full measure of devotion, killed by a Japanese sniper's bullet. His squad had been ordered to patrol to the end.

That afternoon in Japan, one hundred miles north of Nagasaki, sixteen B-29 crewmen who had been shot down weeks earlier, were taken to a deserted field where they were tortured and then beheaded by Japanese army officers. The fliers never knew the war was over. Many captured American airmen had met a similar fate during the war.

During the weeks following the surrender, over a thousand Japanese army officers, from War Minister Anami down to field grade level, committed suicide, as did hundreds of navy officers and civilians. Most were making atonement for their guilt in having failed the emperor and the nation. For others it was the ultimate act of protest against the decision to surrender.

The entry of the Soviet Union into the war on Aug. 8 has been characterized as an opportunistic move to gain territorial spoils after the United States had defeated Japan. It was that. But the Soviet onslaught also contributed mightily to the Japanese desire to end the war quickly. The peace advocates in the Japanese government wanted to surrender while the US remained the chief enemy and before there was an invasion of their home islands. They knew that Japan would have a better future under Uncle Sam if Uncle Joe could be kept out. The Soviets had an old score to settle dating from the 1904-05 humbling of Russia in the Russo-Japanese war.

Comrade Stalin had pledged, while meeting with Roosevelt and Churchill at Yalta in early February 1945, that he would enter the war against Japan within three months after Germany surrendered. He met that deadline precisely, spurred on perhaps by the dropping of the atom bomb on Hiroshima. Soviet armies, with one and a half million men, 5500 tanks, 28,000 guns, and 4,370 aircraft, outclassed and swiftly defeated the one million man Japanese Kwantung Army in Manchuria, an army that had been weakened by the transfer of men and materiel to other fronts. On Sakhalin and in the Kurile Islands off Hokkaido, the Japanese resisted fiercely, demonstrating to the Soviets how difficult it could be to dislodge a well-entrenched island force ready to die to the last man.

The Soviet armies captured an estimated 594,000 Japanese soldiers. Many of these prisoners disappeared into the Gulag, the Soviet slave labor camps in Siberia. Some would never be accounted for.

Even after the Japanese surrendered in Manchuria on Aug. 17, the fighting continued. When the Soviet troops ceased their advance on Sept. 1, they had seized Manchuria, a large part of northern China, northern Korea, south Sakhalin Island, all of the Kurile Islands, and were poised on the doorstep of Hokkaido.

Stalin had, in fact, planned an invasion of Hokkaido, as the island was thought to be lightly garrisoned. On Aug. 15 President Truman had sent a message to Stalin covering plans for receiving the Japanese surrender. The following day Stalin proposed that the Soviet Union take the surrender of Japanese forces in the northern half of Hokkaido. Truman tersely reminded Stalin that their Potsdam agreement had set a demarcation line north of Hokkaido. Further, the United States strongly rejected any changes in that agreement. Stalin, already at odds with the western Allies over Poland and Eastern Europe, and with his troops in the Hokkaido area bogged down by the stubborn Japanese resistance in the Kuriles, did not press the issue. Thus the territorial and political divisions that were to cause such long-enduring problems in post-war Germany and Korea were averted in Japan.

Soviet troops invading Manchuria, Korea, and northern China showed little mercy to civilian Japanese administrators and colonists caught up in the maelstrom of war. Small wonder. These veterans of the war in Europe had seen their homeland horrendously ravaged. Over 25 million of their fellow citizens had died from a population of 180 million. Of all Soviet males born in 1923, it was estimated that only three per cent were alive in 1946. At terrible cost the Red Army had ripped the guts from the invading German Wehrmacht. Of 13.6 million German casualties and prisoners in WW II, the Red Army claimed to have accounted for 10 million.

In the vast territories of the Soviet Union that the Germans overran, fifty per cent of all urban living space was destroyed, the equivalent of 1.2 million houses. In rural areas, 3.5 million houses were destroyed and the towns and villages were left in ruins. In many battle ravaged areas the people were reduced to living in holes in the ground. The transportation infrastructure was equally hard hit. In the agricultural sector, horses were a prime source of power. Of 11.6 million head in the occupied areas at the beginning of the invasion, 7 million were killed or confiscated. Of 23 million hogs, 20 million disappeared. A large percentage of the farm buildings and most of the machinery was destroyed, including 137,000 tractors and 49,000 combines.

The troopers of the 11th Airborne were under the impression that they would be on Okinawa for only a few days. It didn't work out that way. First, the Japanese were slow to get their negotiators on the way to Manila. Then there were complications with the weather as a series of typhoons moved across the western Pacific. Our camp-out on Okinawa was to last over two weeks.

In retrospect, it was fortunate for all concerned, Americans and Japanese alike, that this delay occurred. It was on Aug. 14, the day we flew to Okinawa, that the Emperor instructed his ministers to end the war. It took some time to convince the military hard-liners in the home islands to accept the bitter fact that they must surrender. In a number of instances this was achieved only through the use of force. Had we moved into Japan earlier, there might well have been clashes with Japanese army and navy diehards.

When, on the morning of Aug. 15, we received word that the surrender had been finalized, the news was greeted at the Honor Guard with little show of emotion. We had felt from the day the first atomic bomb was dropped that the final capitulation of Japan would be only a matter of time. There was a feeling of great relief that the bloodshed was now over. I said a silent prayer of thanks as the surrender message was read to the Honor Guard. Our remembrance of those who had not lived to see this day muted the joy of the occasion.

The Japanese people listened in shock that afternoon as the high-pitched voice of their emperor emanated from every radio and public address system in the empire. When the emperor told his subjects, "The war situation has developed, not necessarily to Japan's advantage . . . ," he could have been credited with the understatement of the millennium. When he continued, the emperor gave his people a reason to justify the surrender:

> The enemy has begun to employ a new and most cruel bomb, the power of which to do damage is indeed incalculable, taking the toll of many innocent lives. Should we continue to fight, it would only result in an ultimate collapse and obliteration of the Japanese nation.

He concluded with an admonition:

> Beware most strictly of any outbursts of emotion which may engender needless complications. . . . Unite your total strength to be devoted to the construction of the future. Cultivate the ways of rectitude; foster nobility of spirit; and work with resolution so ye may enhance the innate glory of the Imperial State and keep pace with the progress of the world.

Despite the emperor's message of surrender, many bitter-enders in the Japanese army and navy called for continued resistance. They discounted the emperor's address as the work of "traitors around the throne." Among the navy holdouts was Captain Minoru Genda, the man who had planned the Pearl Harbor attack. Only after flying to Tokyo and determining that it was the emperor's will that Japan surrender, did he fly to the navy airfields and use his personal prestige to convince the fliers that the war was over.

On Aug. 16 the emperor issued a special Imperial Rescript, in effect a cease-fire order, to the Japanese armed forces:

> The Soviet Union has now entered the war, and in view of the state of affairs both here and abroad, we feel that the prolongation of the struggle will merely serve to further the evil and may eventually result in the loss of the very foundation on which our Empire exists. Therefore, in spite of the fact that the fighting spirit of the Imperial Army and Navy are still high, we hereupon intend to negotiate a peace . . . for the sake of maintaining our glorious national polity.

Emperor Hirohito did not mention the atomic bombs that had destroyed Hiroshima and Nagasaki in this message to the Japanese armed forces. In addition to the Imperial Rescript, three imperial princes were dispatched to the commanders overseas. The prestige of the throne would be used to bring the military into line.

For many of the officers and men of the Japanese armed forces there was a dark, compelling reason for their desire to fight to the finish. Would they be punished in kind for the wholesale atrocities they had committed against defenseless civilians and prisoners of war wherever their arms had been victorious? The blood of millions of Chinese, Filipinos, and other victimized peoples cried out for vengeance. Would the treatment the Japanese had meted out be the treatment they would receive?

While the battered *Pittsburgh* was being repaired and refitted at the Puget Sound Navy Yard, Wayne had been given leave and had arrived home. Mother saved the Aug.17 issue of *The Pekin Daily Times-Tazewell County's Only Daily*, which briefly noted this event along with the now outdated information that Wayne's brother Earl was with the 11th Airborne Division in the Philippines.

This copy of the *Times* was replete with information of interest. The headline story:

> Manila, Saturday, Aug. 18-The Japanese Government, reacting to a stern "hurry-up" order from Gen. Douglas MacArthur, broadcast today that its surrender envoy would fly to Manila for armistice terms tomorrow. . . It was heard in Manila only a few hours after MacArthur had warned the Japanese bluntly to stop stalling and send their surrender delegation to Manila "without further delay."

> At the same time, Japanese general headquarters notified MacArthur by radio that members of the Emperor's family had left by plane for Manchuria, China, and French Indo-China to inform Japanese forces there of Hirohito's cease-fire order.
> Japan formally asked MacArthur to halt the Russian offensive in Manchuria on the ground that it was making compliance with a cease-fire order difficult.

The *Times* contained several items from Washington DC which would have been of great interest to us:

> Congressional sources predicted today that President Truman and congress will have their first major clash over continued drafting of men for the army. Mr. Truman has ordered continued induction of 50,000 men a month, compared with the recent rate of 80,000.
> Senate and house military affairs committee leaders have expressed a desire to stop inductions immediately. But the President told reporters yesterday that he saw no reason why some of the young men who aren't doing anything right now shouldn't relieve men at the front so they can return. He said the draft would be continued until replacements are sufficient to send veterans home from the occupation fronts.

[HEY, WE'RE WITH YOU ALL THE WAY ON THAT ONE, HARRY!]

And another story from Washington DC:

> The War Department promised today that every one of the 5,000,000 soldiers scheduled for demobilization within the next year will receive a "helpful shove" in his reorientation back to civilian life. By the end of this year, American troops will be pouring into twenty-seven separation centers at the rate of 500,000 per month . . . .

And then a story for the home front:

> The office of price administration said today that consumers shouldn't throw away their gas ration books and the green stamps in their food ration books. While no longer

needed for buying gasoline, those A, B, and C books will be of help to motorists wanting tires. . . .

As for the green stamps in ration book four, you had better hang on because these are the future meat rationing stamps. The green stamps originally were intended to replace the blue stamps which became obsolete when canned goods rationing ended.

No more ration books will be printed. OPA advised that airplane stamps for buying shoes will be wisely used until it is determined how long shoe rationing will continue.

And on the Tazewell County scene:

The Red Cross published a list of prisoners of war from the Central Illinois area, believed to be held by the Japanese. Instructions followed informing next of kin how to send a message to former POWs through the local Red Cross chapter.

Mothers were warned that a young boy attending a children's party a week earlier in Pekin had been stricken with polio.

The price of corn settled at $1.13, down three cents in the first day of peacetime operations on the Chicago Board of Trade.

The county 4-H show was only a week away.

Meanwhile, on Okinawa, the troopers of the 11th Airborne were discovering that the climate was only marginally better than that of tropical Luzon. It was hot and humid for most of our stay with frequent storms moving through the area. Early one morning the sound of low flying aircraft brought us scurrying out of our pup tents just in time to be sprayed with a solution of DDT in oil-- mosquito control units in action.

While most men of the division were taking it fairly easy, the Honor Guard had immediately gone into a program to sharpen up the members on close order drill and the manual of arms. Part of the mission of the Guard would be ceremonial. If we were to represent the 11th Airborne, we had to look sharp. The Honor Guard had been honed into a proficient drill team by the time we left Okinawa. Along with the rest of the men in the division, we were lectured on the

Japanese people, their customs, and the problems likely to be encountered during the early stages of the occupation.

Because the entire division was combat loaded, we were not only back to sleeping on the ground in pup tents but were also living exclusively on field rations again. The division's field kitchens were somewhere on a slow boat in the western Pacific between Luzon and Okinawa. C, 10-in-1, and K field rations would challenge our digestive tracts once more. And here there were no friendly Filipinos with fruit to sell or trade. We were eventually issued squad burners on which some portion of our 10-in-1 field rations could be cooked.

Many of the Okinawan hillsides were dotted with family tombs. These had small, low entrances leading to underground rooms that were actually man-made caves. During one exceptionally severe storm, we used the tombs for shelter. There was room for a dozen men in the underground room where I sought refuge from the typhoon raging outside. Urns containing the bones of deceased Okinawans stood all about the dank interior of the room. We stayed in the tomb no longer than was absolutely necessary.

Word filtered down that our departure for Japan was scheduled for Aug. 28. Typhoons in this area of the western Pacific resulted in a two-day delay. We took advantage of the time to have a look around southern Okinawa. The hills, ridges, and caves that we saw had made this part of the island a hard nut for the American forces to crack. The scars from the recent bitter battle were already partially covered with the vegetation that flourishes in that warm, humid climate. The island was rapidly being transformed into an enormous military complex. Airfields were dispersed about the area. Sea-Bees and service troops were setting up bases and supply depots. Okinawa would be a key American bastion in the western Pacific for decades to come.

Viewed from the high ground above Kadena Airfield, big silver four-motored airplanes seemed to be parked from horizon to horizon. During the past weeks the Air Transport Command had assembled these C-54 transport planes from every corner of the globe. They would carry the 11th Airborne and then the 27th Infantry Division on the last leg of the largest, longest air-landed troop movement ever executed up to that time.

The Honor Guard Company was trucked to Kadena Airfield during the afternoon of Aug. 29. That night we slept under the C-54 that would fly us to Japan. About midnight we were awakened and told to start loading the plane. Our C-54 was to take off at 1:15 and land at Atsugi airdrome on Honshu at 6:15. Gen. Swing, with Div. Hqs. and Signal Corps equipment was on the first plane, scheduled to set down at 6:00. The C-54 Skymasters, pride of the Air Transport Command, were taking off at three minute intervals and flying in single file to Atsugi Airfield, a Japanese kamikaze base and training center located twenty miles west of Yokohama and twenty-three miles southwest of Tokyo. MacArthur had selected Atsugi because it was the airport nearest Tokyo that could handle the C-54s. The Japanese had warned that Atsugi was a training base for kamikaze pilots who had refused to lay down their arms and were reported to still be holding out in the vicinity of the airfield.

After four and one-half hours in the air, we sighted the coast of Honshu in the early morning light. Soon, the majestic cone of Fujiyama, sacred mountain of Japan, came into view. Flying over Sugami and Tokyo Bays, we looked down on a fantastic display of naval might. A large part of the Pacific Fleet spread out below us in what must have been one of the greatest concentrations of naval power ever assembled. A part of the fleet was covering the landing of a Marine regiment at the huge Yokosuka Naval Base. This amphibious force was scheduled to hit the beach simultaneously with our aerial landing at Atsugi. Gen. Eichelberger, commander of all occupying forces, wrote later that an amused Marine officer reported, "The first landing wave was made up entirely of admirals trying to get ashore before MacArthur."

As our plane approached Atsugi, we pulled on our packs and checked our rifles a final time. Few of us were contemplating the fact that we would be the first foreign conquerors in her 2600-year history to tread on the soil of imperial Japan. More mundane questions came to mind. Could the Japanese really be trusted? After fighting so ferociously these past years, would they now accept defeat so calmly?

Our pilot made a smooth landing and taxied to a line of planes unloading in front of a row of large, weather-beaten hangars. The C-54s were landing with clock-like precision, one every three minutes, just as planned. The last eighteen minutes of each hour was reserved for departures. One of the big planes would take off each minute.
The troopers in our plane quickly scrambled out and took up defensive positions around the hangar. As more troops arrived, Gen. Swing enlarged the defense perimeter to include the entire airfield.

Adjacent to the airfield stood row after row of stubby kamikaze planes, gleaming in the morning sun. Their propellers had recently been removed.

Gen. Swing was the first man out of the lead airplane. He was soon greeted by a group of Japanese army officers who offered their hands. Swing refused to shake hands and ordered them to remove the swords and daggers they were wearing. They protested that these were symbols of their authority. Swing replied that he was now the authority and the weapons would come off. After removing their weapons, the Japanese officers reported that there were kamikaze pilots in the area from the 302d Air Group of the Japanese navy. These diehards had refused to acknowledge defeat and had not given up their arms. The Japanese officers urged Swing to keep his troops within the previously agreed area in order to avoid any clashes. With MacArthur scheduled to arrive at 2:00 PM, this report was the cause of some consternation. Swing radioed this news to Eichelberger who in turn radioed MacArthur urging him to delay his entry into Japan for several days. MacArthur refused, of course.

Shortly before noon, word came that the kamikaze pilots had laid down their arms and departed for their homes. By noon, when 8th Army Commander Eichelberger arrived at Atsugi, the 11th Airborne had 2400 combat ready paratroopers on the ground. Eichelberger, as he wrote later, was deeply concerned with the small size of the force he would have at Atsugi when MacArthur arrived. In England, Winston Churchill was moved to remark, "Of all the amazing deeds in the war, I regard General MacArthur's personal landing at Atsugi as the bravest of the lot."

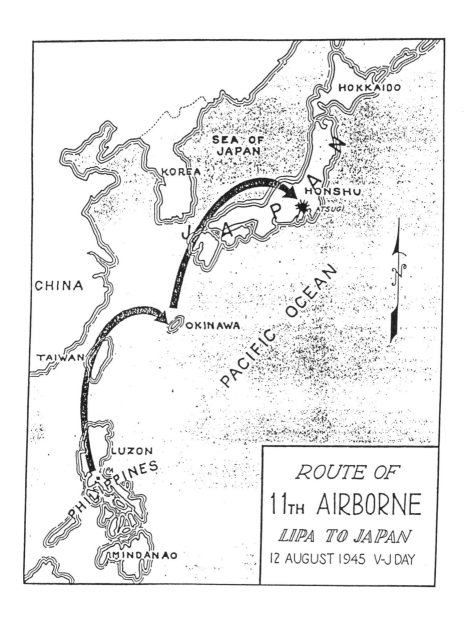

Chapter XV Atsugi and Yokohama

As more paratroopers arrived to shore up the perimeter defense around Atsugi Airfield, the Honor Guard was pulled back and mustered in front of the main hangar. At 2:05 PM a special C-54 came in for a landing. Inscribed on its fuselage was the word *Bataan* and an outline map of the Philippines. The plane taxied to the hangar area where Gen. Eichelberger, Gen. Swing, the Honor Guard, the 11th Airborne Division band, and a host of photographers and reporters awaited. To my surprise, about two-thirds of the reporters and photographers were Japanese. On Okinawa we had heard that all Japanese were to be removed from an area extending three miles from the airfield. The new ruler of Japan obviously wanted the news of his arrival to be headlined throughout the Japanese homeland.

The door of the plane opened and a ramp was lowered to the runway. General of the Army Douglas MacArthur stepped out into the brilliant summer sunlight. He paused dramatically to give the photographers and newsreel cameramen adequate opportunity to record this historic moment. With the gold braid encrusted cap, the sunglasses, the oversized corncob pipe, the faded khaki uniform with the shirt open at the neck, and with no decoration save the five star insignia of rank, MacArthur made a striking picture—a picture that would appear in newspapers and newsreels around the world in short order. Atsugi must have been the most coveted destination in the world that afternoon. Reporters, photographers, generals, and VIPs of various stripe all vied to get aboard a plane to Atsugi. Among the famous war correspondents on the scene were Theodore White, Carl Mydans, and George Silk, all covering the event for *Life* and *Time*.

MacArthur descended from the plane while taking a few puffs on his oversized corncob pipe. He returned Gen. Eichelberger's salute, stepped forward and shook his hand briskly. MacArthur inquired "How are you, Bob?" then added, "This looks like the payoff." The 11th Airborne Division band had been playing appropriate music in the background. MacArthur strode over and spoke to the bandleader: "I want you to tell the band that that is about the sweetest music I've ever heard." MacArthur then gave a brief statement to the eager American and Japanese reporters crowding around him, "From Melbourne to Tokyo is a long road . . . but this looks like the payoff . . . the Japs seem to be acting in complete good faith." MacArthur briefly inspected the Honor Guard, and then moved toward his waiting car. The photographers wanted more pictures. An overeager Japanese newsreel cameraman pushed in ahead of an angry American photographer. MacArthur, a stern look on his face, remarked, "You'll have to make him capitulate."

As MacArthur passed within a few feet of me, I reflected that, despite the verdict of my weapons platoon friends, I hadn't been crazy as hell to volunteer for the Honor Guard. After all, it isn't every day that a nineteen-year-old farm boy gets a ringside seat to see history being made.

MacArthur, flanked by the Honor Guard, moved on to a line of vehicles waiting to escort him to Yokohama. The Japanese had been ordered to supply 400 trucks and 100 sedans for the use of the 11th Airborne. At first glance the field where they were parked could easily have been mistaken for a junkyard. Almost all of the dilapidated vehicles were powered by charcoal burners. There was at least one exotic model with a steam engine. The best of those that burned gasoline or diesel fuel were selected for use in escorting MacArthur. It did not help the situation when the Japanese army drivers disappeared. Their superiors had told them that, as soon as the Americans arrived, they could leave the army and go home. The Japanese drivers wasted no time in getting away from Atsugi.

MacArthur and Eichelberger climbed into the big shiny black Lincoln that was to take them to Yokohama. The Honor Guard clambered aboard their waiting trucks. With a roar of well-worn motors and a grinding of gears, we sputtered off. The twenty-mile trip to the New Grand Hotel in Yokohama was to take almost two hours. Japanese soldiers lined both sides of the road at intervals of about fifty yards. They were facing away from the road, standing at parade rest, bayonets fixed on their rifles. The soldiers and their equipment appeared to be in good condition. The rifles and bayonets gleamed in the bright summer sunlight. The army undoubtedly had priority on all supplies, especially food. As I surveyed our truck convoy of 200 paratroopers, I was hoping that these 30,000 Japanese soldiers lining the road would all remember that they were there to protect MacArthur.

These 30,000 soldiers guarding our route were only a small fraction of the Japanese military manpower in the area. Twenty-two Japanese infantry divisions—300,000 soldiers—still under arms, were stationed within a few hours marching time as our column wheezed and sputtered up the road. The 11th Airborne had just over 3,000 paratroopers in the Yokohama area at this time.

The paratroopers were in great spirits, not particularly concerned that their necks were out a considerable distance. The entire division had been in a state of euphoria since the sudden end of the war. While not entirely comparable, the cessation of hostilities had a certain similarity to being granted a stay of execution for all of those infantrymen, parachute or otherwise, who had been destined for the invasion of Japan. On this day, for the men of the Honor Guard, the presence of General of the Army Douglas MacArthur at the center of our column added immeasurably to our feeling of security. Never mind the fact that MacArthur had been the greatest of personal risk-takers throughout his long military career.

Our route to Yokohama, which had been selected by the Japanese, took us through quiet green countryside where there was little sign of the ravages of war. There was no human activity around the homes and buildings that we passed. Occasionally I would see someone furtively peeking through a window as we neared a house. There was considerable fear and trepidation prevalent in the land of the rising sun on that bright, sun-drenched day in late August.

Would this occupying army rape and kill and torture and loot as Japanese soldiers had in Asia and the western Pacific lands? I wondered if Japanese civilians knew that their sons and brothers and fathers had participated in such inhuman outrages as the Rape of Nanking. On Dec. 13, 1937, that unfortunate Chinese city fell to the Imperial Army. The Japanese soldiers immediately embarked on an orgy of murder, torture, rape, and pillage, the like of which had not been seen since the Mongols under Genghis Khan invaded China in 1213. The Japanese butchered two to three hundred thousand Chinese men, women, and children in savagery that continued for weeks. Such barbaric conduct was to be common practice for the Japanese armed forces in the years that followed.

So the Japanese had good reason to be worried about the coming occupation, fearing that the American troops might behave as savagely as their own soldiers had in the areas Japan conquered. Many civilians sought refuge in the countryside until it became apparent that MacArthur would preside over a benevolent occupation. Strict rules of conduct were enforced for the occupying forces. Slapping a civilian could incur a five-year prison sentence. Rapists would be eligible for the death penalty.

As our truck column moved from the countryside into the city of Yokohama, we drove through block after block and mile after mile of the burned out city. Three months earlier, on May 29, a B-29 firebomb raid had destroyed 80% of this industrial seaport. Only masonry structures and the dock area had survived. One of the buildings still intact was the New Grand Hotel. It was to be MacArthur's headquarters for the next three weeks.

Immediately upon our arrival at the hotel, the Honor Guard was deployed to protect the area. My platoon was assigned the main entrance. During the remainder of the afternoon, the top army brass from the Pacific war continued to arrive. Stilwell, Sutherland, Kenney, Spaatz, Willoughby, and Whitney were among those I could recognize. Vinegar Joe Stilwell, apparently no man to risk going hungry unnecessarily, arrived with two cases of 10-in-1 field rations. Our platoon was relieved in the evening and spent the night in defensive positions on the perimeter around the hotel.

The following morning the Honor Guard again loaded aboard our decrepit Japanese trucks. We were driven to an area known as the Bluff, a cliff top site overlooking Tokyo. Our truck column wound through the gates of a large estate and halted at a house and some outbuildings. A large, expertly landscaped mansion stood nearby. Previously occupied by an executive of Sun Oil Company, it would serve as MacArthur's residence until he moved to the American Embassy in Tokyo three weeks later.

The Honor Guard was quartered in the guesthouse and several outbuildings. It was extremely crowded, and we slept on the floor, but it was the first time we had been billeted under a genuine roof in eight months. The members of the Honor Guard continued to subsist on field rations until we returned to our regiments in late September.

There was no furniture in the guesthouse, but a fine watercolor painting of Mt. Fuji adorned one wall of the main room. I managed to save this prize from the souvenir collectors by liberating it and wrapping it around a broom handle. I mailed this personal war reparation home a month later. Fortunately, the army postal workers must have thought someone was mailing a souvenir Japanese broomstick home, and therefore did not bother to confiscate it for their own use.

The first night on guard at the mansion, I was walking a post along the edge of the bluff as a streak of light on the eastern horizon indicated the coming of a misty dawn. As I scanned the area below and ahead, I was startled to see a Japanese machine gun position materializing through the mist and fog about four hundred yards to my front. The hair on the back of my neck stood up as I quickly took cover and leveled my rifle toward the machine gunners. Just as I prepared to summon the other guards from nearby, the steadily improving light revealed that the gunners were in position to fire away from the mansion. Their uniforms were black rather than the mustard drab of the Japanese army. It dawned on me that the Japanese police had a defense cordon set up to protect MacArthur.

This protective line was about 300 yards outside our Honor Guard perimeter. So far as I knew, no one had briefed the members of the Honor Guard on the existence of this Japanese police cordon. Not long ago we had been destroying similar machine gun positions, no questions asked.

Several nights later I had a guard post twenty-five feet from the big front window of the mansion. A tall box hedge hid this post from the view of anyone in the large drawing room. I could peer through the hedge without being seen from the mansion. On this evening MacArthur was relaxing with several guests. I decided that they were Generals Willoughby and Whitney, his favorite staff members, and his personal physician, Col. Egeberg. MacArthur's Filipino houseboy was serving the group.

Later in the night when I came on duty again, the mansion was dark. The adjacent guard whose post included the kitchen area soon greeted me. He was carrying a bottle of two-liter capacity, which he handed to me. "I'm sure Mac would want to share a little of this good Jap beer with a couple of thirsty paratroopers," he remarked. The beer was cold and an excellent brew, but I wasn't as sure as my friend that Mac was into this kind of sharing, even with thirsty paratroopers. I was sure that our Honor Guard officers would not consider this activity to be "walking my post in a military manner." I convinced my friend that he should hustle the empty bottle back to the kitchen before the Officer of the Day came by on his rounds.

On another day I drew the guard post that included the kitchen area. On the kitchen staff was a Japanese chef who spoke excellent

English. He struck up a conversation so I questioned him about conditions in the country. He gave me a vivid description of the firebomb raids that had destroyed Tokyo. The most terrifying and most destructive raid had occured on the night of March 10-11. He described this raid, which killed 100,000 and burned out sixteen square miles of the heart of the city, "The first of the B-29s came in about midnight and started fires in numerous locations. The bombers came in a steady stream until 3:00 AM. As each plane dropped its bombs the fires grew in intensity until the firestorm consumed the oxygen in the atmosphere. People in shelters died of asphyxiation. Cut off from escape by the raging inferno, many jumped into the canals that run through the city and died there. Asphalt streets burned and the water in the canals steamed. It took over three weeks to gather and bury the dead." The B-29s returned on five more raids during the spring and summer to complete the destruction of Tokyo. The chef told me that the devastation that I had seen in Yokohama and Tokyo had been repeated throughout Japan.

I asked the chef about the food situation. He replied that the outlook was bleak. Unless food was brought in, much of the country would be facing starvation during the coming winter. This was my first conversation with a Japanese civilian, and I was surprised at the man's resignation to the situation and his candor in discussing it. I had to remind myself that he was probably one of the top chefs in the country and not the average man on the street.

Early in the morning on September 2, the members of the Honor Guard who had not been on night duty climbed aboard the now familiar Japanese trucks. We fell in behind the big black Lincoln and escorted MacArthur to the Yokohama docks. A new destroyer, the *Nicholas*, awaited, ready to transport the General eighteen miles up Tokyo Bay to the battleship *Missouri*.

And thereon hangs a tale. The announcement that MacArthur, as the Supreme Commander for the Allied Powers, would receive the surrender of Imperial Japan came as a distressing blow to the Navy brass. Feeling, as they did, that theirs had been the primary force in the defeat of Japan, this decision was a bitter pill for the admirals to swallow. Had Roosevelt still been Commander-in-Chief, things might well have been different. FDR had served as Assistant Secretary of the Navy during World War I, and his favorite garment ever after had been a navy cape. But now the office of president was occupied by a staunch former army captain who had served as a field artillery battery commander in the trenches of France.

There were reports that Admiral Nimitz was so incensed that he would decline to participate in the surrender ceremony. When the Navy was partially consoled by the decision to hold the ceremony on the battleship *Missouri*, he relented. Or so the story goes.

While arrangements for the ceremony were being made, Nimitz had given orders to prepare an infantry landing craft by painting five stars on the bow. These clumsy appearing, hard riding, but extremely useful vessels had been used in large numbers for amphibious assaults in every theater of war. This particular landing craft, spruced up by Navy Seabees with the five star insignia and bright red and white seats, was to be used to transport MacArthur from the Yokohama docks eighteen miles down Tokyo Bay to the *Missouri*. At no small expenditure of time and effort, the Navy prepared and transported this landing barge from Guam to Tokyo Bay.

This was the same type of landing craft that had carried MacArthur almost to the beach during the landing on Leyte that day he fulfilled his pledge to the people of the Philippines, "I shall return." That landing craft hit a sandbar just offshore and MacArthur and his party had been forced to wade ashore through the knee-deep surf. MacArthur was so well pleased with the resulting pictures and newsreels that he repeated the performance on several occasions. He was not pleased, however, with the prospect of a cold, rough, eighteen-mile ride down Tokyo Bay to the *Missouri* in an open vessel

MacArthur, when he heard of the Navy's plan, let it be known in no uncertain terms that he was not about to go to the *Missouri* on "that thing." "I want a destroyer and I want a new destroyer," thundered the Supreme Commander, the American Caesar who was even now tightening his control over Japan, reducing Hirohito to de facto deputy emperor. With most of the participants in the surrender ceremony--including the Japanese delegation--being transported to the *Missouri* on four American destroyers, it would be difficult to criticize the General for looking askance at the Navy's plan to use a barge to transport him to the scene of his finest hour.

MacArthur presided over the surrender ceremony in what must have been the zenith of his career. Back on the Yokohama docks, the sky was overcast, and it was breezy and quite cool. The members of the Honor Guard spent most of the morning in a warehouse, out of the chill morning wind. About 2:00 PM the sun came out and the remainder of the day was very pleasant. Far out over the bay, fifty B-29s and 450 naval aircraft flew over the *Missouri* marking the end of the surrender proceedings. We saw the planes as they headed up the bay and swung over the Tokyo area. This was the only part of the ceremony that we witnessed or heard. It was many years later that I read MacArthur's stirring speech, delivered after the signing of the surrender document. MacArthur returned to the docks late in the afternoon, and we escorted him back to the mansion.

One bright morning when we were to be off for the day, two Honor Guard troopers from California and I decided to go up to Tokyo. The city had not been officially occupied so it was technically off limits. Despite this ban, a good many reporters and members of the military had been visiting the city. The trains seemed to be running on schedule so we went down to the Yokohama station. We caught the first train headed north and soon arrived at the big central Tokyo station. As we stepped off the train, I was startled by what I saw when I looked across the vast station. Covering every available space were what must have been ten acres of Japanese soldiers. They were lounging about, some eating, some sleeping.

These Japanese soldiers were as surprised to see us as we were to see them. And no more delighted. We were probably the first American troops they had encountered. It would be more correct to refer to these Japanese as ex-soldiers. They were part of the army of 330,000 men that had been stationed in the Tokyo area to oppose the anticipated American invasion. They had been demobilized during the last few days by their own commanders under the supervision of American officers. This army, deployed to defend the Japanese home islands, had never been defeated in the field. Many of the soldiers were veterans of fighting in Asia, brought home to strengthen the defenses on Honshu and Kyushu. Now they were waiting in this station for trains to take them back to their homes, many of which no longer existed, and to an uncertain future.

Cox and O'Hara and I were carrying our rifles. We might have walked through this multitude without any trouble. Then again, maybe not. Sgt. Faye's frequent admonition, "Don't do anything dumb," flashed through my mind. Perhaps because I had seen Errol Flynn and the 7th Cavalry cut down by a host of Sioux and Cheyenne warriors, I looked at all those blinking Japs and thought of Custer at the Little Big Horn. A whistle shrieked behind us. I looked around.

It was a train rolling toward Yokohama. We jumped aboard as the train picked up speed. Discretion is still the better part of valor.

I still felt a deep hostility toward these Japanese whose fellow soldiers had killed, wounded, and maimed my friends. Despite this, I could not help thinking about their fate as the train carried us back to Yokohama. In addition to the troops in the home islands, almost 7,000,000 servicemen and civilians would be returning to Japan from China, Manchuria, Korea, the Philippines, Indonesia, Malaya, Indo-China, and the Pacific islands. For these sullen, dispirited troops, the prospect was bleak. There would be no celebrations when they returned home; no mustering out pay to ease the transition to civilian life; no G.I. Bill to help them get an education; no V.A. loans to assist them in starting a business or buying a home.

They and their countrymen would be on the ragged edge of starvation during the rapidly approaching winter. Shelter would be a problem for many. Twenty per cent of the housing in the country had been destroyed. The cities of Japan lay in ashes. In and around the ruins of these cities were shacks and lean-tos of corrugated metal and scraps scrounged from the rubble. Fuel and clothing supplies were practically non-existent. Coal production was at 12% of pre-war levels. These ex-soldiers would wear their uniforms, stripped of insignia, until they were in tatters because they would have no other clothes.

MacArthur moved swiftly to prevent the food shortage from becoming a major crisis. First, he ordered the occupation forces to refrain from requisitioning any of the civilian food supply. Then he alerted Washington that food imports would be essential if domestic tranquility were to be maintained in Japan. There was bureaucratic hemming and hawing. MacArthur grimly wired Washington once more, "Give me bread or give me bullets." The food eventually arrived.

The sight of all those Japanese troops lying about the Tokyo railway station brought to mind another image; the scene in the movie, *Gone With the Wind*, which depicts the Atlanta railway station where row on row of wounded Confederate soldiers lie suffering in the noon-day sun.

When we returned to Yokohama, we spent the rest of the day looking around what was left of the city. At the waterfront, the docks were crowded with vehicles and equipment being swiftly offloaded from a variety of ships. The army was arriving in force.

United States Navy photo by Wayne Miller

Demobilized Japanese soldiers crowd trains that will return them to their homes after the end of the war in September 1945.

Late in the day on Sept. 2, an advance unit of the 1st Cavalry Division came ashore from transports, landing on the Yokohama docks. The 11th Airborne Band was on hand to welcome the cavalrymen with a rousing rendition of "The Old Gray Mare, She Aint What She Used To Be." On Sept. 8, when the cavalrymen marched into Tokyo to begin the formal occupation, photographers asked paratroopers, standing along the way, to please step aside. They needed pictures of the first American troops to enter Tokyo. Undaunted by friendly heckling from the paratroopers, the cavalrymen immediately erected a huge billboard proclaiming in over-sized letters, "1st Cavalry Division-1st in Manila-1st in Tokyo." An around-the-clock armed guard of four cavalrymen protected the sign until the 11th Airborne Division was shipped north.

A few days after the surrender ceremony on the *Missouri*, I was assigned the guard post at the entrance to the estate where we were guarding MacArthur. At mid-morning, MacArthur's big black car came rolling down the drive. The other guard and I saluted as the car passed, then looked at one another in disbelief. MacArthur, accompanied only by his driver, was on his way to headquarters. He apparently felt that he had no need for a guard. I remarked about this when I returned to quarters that evening. The platoon sergeant informed me that MacArthur had not used a guard while commuting since his return from the surrender ceremony. I shouldn't have been too surprised as this squared with stories I had heard back in the islands. MacArthur frequently walked about the battlefront as though he were bulletproof.

The 11th Airborne Division was relieved from occupation duties in the Tokyo-Yokohama area on Sept.14 and ordered to occupy northeastern Honshu. The move, principally by rail, began on Sept. 15 and was completed on Sept.17. This left the Honor Guard as the only element of the 11th Airborne remaining in the Tokyo area.

Jean Faircloth MacArthur and son, Arthur, flew to Atsugi from Manila on Sept. 19. The MacArthur family moved into the American Embassy in Tokyo that afternoon. SCAP Headquarters moved from the New Grand Hotel to downtown Tokyo. MacArthur would now rule Japan from the Dai Ichi (number one) Building. It seemed appropriate that this six story office building overlooked the Imperial Plaza and the Imperial Palace, Emperor Hirohito's residence. Ironically, Tokyo Rose, notorious for her wartime propaganda broadcasts beamed at American servicemen in the Pacific, had predicted that MacArthur would be publicly hanged in the Imperial Plaza at the end of the war.

MacArthur would make his greatest contribution to history as the ruler of Japan. Ambassador Sebald, who was with him during those years, has written, "Never before in the history of the United States had such enormous and absolute power been placed in the hands of a single individual." MacArthur had his mandate from the President, "You will exercise your authority as you deem proper to carry out your mission. Our relations with Japan do not rest on a contractual basis, but on unconditional surrender...Our authority is supreme." The conversion of Japan from a militaristic totalitarian society to a flourishing democracy is evidence of the wisdom and skill MacArthur exercised. For the Japanese people he secured civil liberties and universal suffrage, insisted on equal rights for women, permitted labor unions to flourish, forced land reform that allowed the long-suffering farmers to buy the land they tilled, and instituted a public health program of sanitation and immunization that saved an estimated 2.1 million lives during the first two years of the Occupation. The constitution that MacArthur introduced remained unchanged after half a century.

When, after five years, MacArthur was relieved of his duties in Japan, he had won the admiration and respect, even the affection, of the Japanese people. A leading newspaper editorialized: "Japan's recovery must be attributed solely to his guidance. We feel as if we had lost a kind and loving father...." Prime Minister Yoshida, in a radio address to his countrymen said, " It is he who has firmly implanted democracy in all segments of our society....No wonder he is looked upon by our people with the profoundest veneration and affection." Earlier, the people of the Yokohama area had erected a statue of MacArthur bearing the inscription: "General Douglas MacArthur-Liberator of Japan."

MacArthur was, and always will be, controversial. He seems to be and to have been either admired and praised or hated and excoriated. There is little middle ground. His detractors dismiss and diminish the accomplishments of a long, brilliant military career while emphasizing his mistakes and shortcomings. We are fortunate that two outstanding scholars, D. Clayton James and William Manchester, have given us even-handed biographies of MacArthur.

The meticulous and exhaustive research evident in these two biographies makes them the definitive work on the General.

In considering MacArthur's contribution in World War II, it might be instructive to consider the comments of a few experts in the field of wartime generalship. Field Marshal Lord Alanbrooke, Chief of the British Imperial Staff during the war, called MacArthur "the greatest general and best strategist the war produced." General George C. Marshall, American Chief of Staff, referred to him as "our most brilliant general." Internationally respected British historian B.H.Lidell Hart wrote, "MacArthur was supreme among the generals. His combination of strong personality, strategic grasp, tactical skill, operative mobility, and vision put him in a class above other allied commanders in any theater." A ranking Japanese intelligence officer, questioned soon after the war ended, stated, "MacArthur's envelopment of our strong points was the strategy we hated most. MacArthur, with minimum losses, attacked and seized a relatively weak area, constructed airfields, and then proceeded to cut the supply lines to our troops in that area. Our strongpoints were gradually starved out. . . the Americans flowed into our weaker points and submerged us. . . This strategy gained the most while losing the least."

MacArthur's use of the bypass strategy was a crucial factor in keeping American losses to a minimum. The saving of American blood was phenomenal. For each Allied serviceman lost in MacArthur's theater, ten Japanese were killed. Total casualties in his theater from Australia to the end of the war were less than those suffered by Eisenhower's troops in the Battle of the Bulge.

The advance on Leyte was slowed at one point by the monsoon season and the ability of the Japanese to bring in reinforcements from nearby islands. MacArthur's old friend, the Filipino reporter, Carlos Romulo, asked him, "What shall I tell the press by way of explanation?" MacArthur shook his finger in Romulo's face and replied, "Tell them that if I like I can finish Leyte in two weeks, but I wont! I have too great a responsibility to the mothers and wives in America to do that to their men. I will not take by sacrifice what I can achieve by strategy."

Among MacArthur's manifold personality flaws was his penchant for self-glorification. Communiqués from his SWPA Headquarters were replete with references to MacArthur who wrote many of the communiqués himself. His generals were seldom mentioned and were discouraged from giving interviews. Reporters were kept on a short leash. If they wrote anything considered negative, it would likely be censored. Fighting units in the theater received little recognition and were usually identified only as "MacArthur's troops." This did not improve MacArthur's popularity with the combat soldiers.

In mid-December of 1944, two paratroopers of the 11th Airborne Division were temporarily stranded in Tacloban, Leyte's capital and MacArthur's headquarters at the time. They had been wounded while fighting in the mountains of central Leyte, had been released from the hospital when they recovered, and were now awaiting an opportunity to return to their units. They were put to work loading transport planes with supplies that were being airdropped to their fellow paratroopers, fighting deep in the mountains. When Pfc. Feuerisen and Pfc. Merisieki got a few hours off, they went into Tacloban and soon found themselves in front of GHQ. Addressing an officer who was leaving, they asked if it would be possible to see Gen. MacArthur. They were told that MacArthur was extremely busy and there was no chance at all for them to see the General. Something about a chain of command was mentioned. By chance, MacArthur had heard the conversation through his open office window. He ordered that the two be shown in.

MacArthur inquired as to their reason for wishing to see him. The two paratroopers explained that their division, the 11th Airborne, had been fighting the Japs for months in the mountains, yet had never been mentioned in any communiqué or news report. They had received letters from home where friends and relatives were wondering if the paratroopers were sitting out the war. The General proceeded to show them the entire battle situation on his operations map including the part the 11th was playing. He explained that, for the time being, he wanted to conceal from the enemy the presence and disposition of the 11th Airborne. He then gave them a message to take back to Gen. Swing and the men of the Division. He wanted them to know that he was aware of the great fight they were making against the enemy, the terrain, and the weather. As soon as possible he would publicly give them full credit for their contribution. The two went on their way, satisfied that they and their division were appreciated. The story of their visit with the Commander in Chief, SWPA, was soon known throughout the division. MacArthur's popularity rating with the men of the 11th Airborne improved considerably.

We can only speculate on the reception these two audacious privates might have received from other famous World War II generals. They would likely have been hustled away from Eisenhower's wary headquarters, never having gotten within half a mile. Patton would have had them disciplined or fined. Perhaps Omar Bradley would have been interested in their story.

At the time the Japanese agreed to surrender, the 11th Airborne Division was the logical unit to spearhead the occupation. With their expertise and experience in airborne operations, the officers and men of the Division were able to begin the move almost instantly. And time was of the essence. The last thing MacArthur wanted was to have sailors and marines landing in Japan ahead of his army.

After all, MacArthur and the men of the 11th Airborne shared many qualities, some admirable and some not so admirable: self-confident to the point of arrogance; proud of the uniform they wore; brave, even reckless on occasion; borderline insubordinate at times; jealous of their reputation; sometimes given to hyperbole; striving for their place in history.

And now, as of Sept. 20, the mission of the Honor Guard was completed. MacArthur was permanently established in the American Embassy and the Dai Ichi Building. The time of danger was past. The military police could now handle the situation. The Honor Guard was ordered to proceed by rail to 11th Airborne Headquarters at Sendai, there to be disbanded and the members returned to their regiments and companies.

Accompanied by one of my California friends, I went into Yokohama a final time the day before we moved north to Sendai. Traffic was heavy in the dock area. The busier intersections were each manned by an American MP and a Japanese policeman, working together to keep things moving. Civilians had learned that the Americans were not the monsters that Japanese government propaganda had pictured. They had emerged from the debris of the city to resume their lives.

The children and the G.I.s had already reached a degree of rapport. The little Japanese had the innocent, ingenuous quality of children all over the world. It had been no surprise in the Philippines to see little Filipinos, along the streets of Manila, give the V for victory sign and shout, "Veectoree, Joe!" It was something else to see little Japanese urchins on the streets in Yokohama, raising their stubby, grubby little fingers in a V and yelling, "Victly, Joe! Tojo eat shit." Somehow, it seemed a bit incongruous. Never underestimate the power of a chocolate bar to influence the political views of a little tyke. But I was told that not even that sweet of a reward could persuade the little Nips to include Emperor Hirohito with Tojo.

Japanese men and women were working in the burned out areas of the city, clearing away debris, and salvaging everything that might be useful. The women were wearing baggy clothes and slacks. The men were wearing old, badly worn uniforms and threadbare western style clothing. They all appeared thin, weary, drained. It was not only their cities that had been burned out.

Back in the States, President Truman's proposal to continue the draft at a level that would provide replacements for the troops on occupation duty went largely unheeded by Congress. On Sept. 6, Truman announced that he would soon propose a comprehensive program of national military security. Before Truman could send his proposal to Congress, MacArthur, on Sept. 17, without consulting his superiors in Washington, announced that, in another six months the strength of the occupation force could be reduced to 200,000 from the half million he now commanded. The President, the State Department, and the Joint Chiefs of Staff first learned of this announcement through the press. President Truman wrote in his *Memoirs*: "This was not only embarrassing but actually affected the position the administration could take, both at home and abroad." Truman's argument that the draft should be continued at a reasonable level because of occupation requirements in Japan and Germany had been badly undercut.

Artillery Captain Harry S. Truman had been on the line in France at the end of World War I. He was then stationed near Verdun until April of 1919. He hated the waiting. In letters home to friends in Missouri he wished "Woodie [President Woodrow Wilson] would stop galevanting in France and go home" so the rest of the American soldiers could too. Truman's personal experience could account for his calling for prompt replacement of combat veterans on occupation duty after World War II. MacArthur's surprise announcement on Sept. 17 had torpedoed Truman's plans, a program that was already facing rough sailing in congress. The man who had driven mules on a Missouri farm in his youth was not likely to forget.

Chapter XVI Sendai and Northern Honshu

Japan's cities were burned out and destroyed but somehow the Japanese had managed to maintain some semblance of a rail network. The train that was to transport the Honor Guard back to the 11th Airborne Division arrived at the Yokohama station on time. The coaches we boarded bore a resemblance to the "40 and 8" cars used in France during World War I.

As the train moved toward Sendai, we passed through forty miles of burned out area that had been the cities of Yokohama. Kawasaki, and Tokyo. Together with Nagoya, Osaka, and Kobe, these cities had been the early targets of the low-level firebomb raids. The first of these was the raid on Tokyo on the night of March 9-10, 1945. This most devastating bombing attack in history marked a turning point in the air war against Japan. Up to that point the B-29 Superfortresses had not performed up to expectations. High altitude precision bombing, first from China, then from the Mariana Islands, had achieved limited results. The stormy weather and cloudy skies, coupled with the strong winds of the jet stream over Japan, rendered high altitude precision bombing chancy at best, impossible on most days. The 3,000 mile round trip, requiring 14-16 hours, flown at altitudes up to 30,000 feet, taxed the aircraft engines to the utmost, resulting in many mechanical problems with heavy losses of men and aircraft.

Gen. Curtis LeMay, who had won his spurs in the bombing of Germany and had recently been commanding the B-29 force based in China, was ordered to take command in the Marianas. He arrived in January 1945. He studied the situation, experimented, and by early March was ready with a bold, radical plan. He would send the B-29s at night, at low altitude, with most of the guns and ammunition removed. Flying at reduced altitudes would save fuel and reduce stress on the aircraft. Additional bombs would replace the weight of guns and ammunition. To hold losses of his crews and aircraft within acceptable limits, LeMay was counting on the element of surprise, the lack of night fighters in the Japanese Air Force, and the fact that enemy anti-aircraft guns were not radar controlled.

Through the twilight hours of March 9, 1945, three hundred and twenty-five B-29s took off from the airfields in the Marianas. The first of the 279 planes that reached the target arrived over central Tokyo just after 12:00 midnight. When the crew of the last plane released their bombs about 3:00 AM, the B-29s had delivered ten times the weight of bombs that the Germans had dropped on London in the biggest raid of the "Blitz."

The man who led the raid, Gen. Tom Power, later wrote that it was "the greatest single disaster incurred by an enemy in military history. It was greater than the combined damage of Hiroshima and Nagasaki. There were more casualties than in any other military action in the history of the world." The US Strategic Bombing Survey estimated that "probably more persons lost their lives by fire at Tokyo in a six hour period than at any time in the history of man." The great Tokyo Earthquake, the Chicago fire, the San Francisco Earthquake all pale in comparison.

Estimates of casualties vary. Tokyo police records eventually listed 83,793 dead (most authorities estimate 100,000), 40,918 wounded, 267,171 buildings destroyed. One fourth of Tokyo—sixteen square miles--was gone. Over one million people were left homeless. It took workers twenty-five days to remove the dead.

In his mission report LeMay wrote that the object of the attack "was not to bomb indiscriminately civilian populations." Military and industrial targets were dispersed throughout the urban areas. Looking at the results of the raid, LeMay concluded that he had the formula that would break the Japanese will to resist.

LeMay was a warrior as hard as Grant or Sherman. Long after the war he was quoted as saying, "I'll tell you what war is about. You've got to kill people, and when you've killed enough, they stop fighting." A conclusion reached a century earlier by another hard realist. William Tecumseh Sherman, following the Civil War, defended Grant's huge losses in battling his way to Richmond. Sherman concluded that the South would not give up so long as it had an army of any reasonable size. The Confederacy had a certain number of men–300,000 was the figure he used several times--who would not stop fighting. If the North were to reunite the Nation, these would have to be killed. To do this, many Union soldiers would also die in battle. This, Sherman said, was the "awful fact" of the war. Those who believed otherwise deceived themselves.

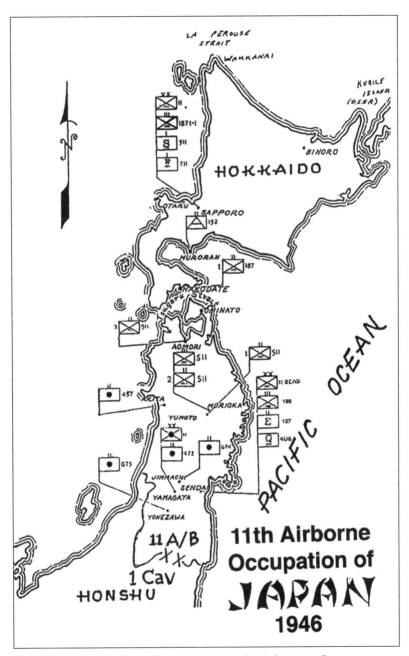

The 11th Airborne Division occupied the northern section of Honshu and the island of Hokkaido at the end of World War II.

Following the massive firebomb raid on Tokyo, LeMay sent his planes to burn out the other big industrial cities, firebombing until the supply of firebombs was temporarily exhausted. There was an interlude in April while the B-29s bombed airfields on Kyushu and mined the Japanese waterways in support of the Okinawa invasion. On May 14, they returned to firebombing the big industrial cities.

LeMay sent in nine 500-plane raids during the following weeks. By June 15 the six large industrial cities had been largely destroyed. Next came the secondary targets. Cities of 100,000 and more were bombed and incinerated. By late July and early August, smaller cities such as Tokoyuma (pop. 38,000), Isezaki (pop. 40,000), and Tsuruga (pop. 31,000) were being targeted and burned out.

Fantastic as it may seem, in the six months beginning March 9, 1945, Japan suffered damage from air attack equal to that sustained by Germany in the last three years of the war in Europe. Several factors contributed to this outcome. The cities of Japan were densely populated and had streets that were extremely narrow. Nearly all of the buildings were constructed of wood, bamboo, and paper making them highly flammable. Recently developed firebombs made with napalm, magnesium, and phosphorus were practically impossible to extinguish. Japan had been the first nation in World War II to use firebombs against a civilian population. In Shanghai and other defenseless Chinese cities, the Japanese had sown the wind. In 1945 they would reap the whirlwind.

But the Japanese economy had not been destroyed by aerial bombardment alone. Other forces had been at work since early in the war. Japan, at the time of the Pearl Harbor attack, had 6 million tons of merchant shipping. This tonnage was augmented by ships seized in the conquered areas and by production in Japanese shipyards during the early years of the war. By January of 1945 American submarines, surface vessels, and aerial forces had reduced the Japanese merchant fleet to 2.75 million tons. When the war ended in August, that figure had dropped to 1.5 million tons and was being rapidly reduced. In addition, three-fourths of the Japanese fishing fleet had been destroyed. The Japanese home islands, always dependent on imported oil, raw materials, and food, had been isolated and their essential supplies cut off.

Japanese coastal shipping was vital to inter-island commerce. Toward the end of the war this coastal shipping was at a virtual standstill. B-29s and naval forces had laid 12,000 mines in the harbors and crucial waterways of the home islands. Only the railways remained useable and they had been reduced to 25% of pre-war capacity by the bombing. Japan no longer had the resources necessary to sustain her people through the winter that lay ahead.

Much has been written of the horror of the atomic bombing of Hiroshima and Nagasaki. It was horrible. All war is horrible. The totality of World War II multiplied that horror. It was horrible that 200,000 men, women, and children were killed and injured by the atomic bombs. But it should be remembered that these two bombs hastened the end of a horrendous war that cost the lives of 57,000,000 people worldwide. China alone counted 15,000,000 dead as a direct result of Japanese lust for conquest.

The U.S. Strategic Bombing Survey, headed by Paul Nitze, operated in Japan immediately following the war. The Survey attempted to determine the effectiveness of the strategic bombing campaign and, as an important part of that study, the effectiveness of the atomic bombs. The survey concluded that to equal the destruction caused by a single atomic bomb would have required 210 B-29s at Hiroshima and 120 at Nagasaki, each carrying their usual load of ten tons of incendiary and high explosive bombs. Bomber command could and regularly did send 400 to 500 B-29s into the night skies over Japan that spring and summer.

These numbers serve only to place in perspective the two nuclear weapons and the damage they wrought in August of 1945. Powerful as they were, their destructive force was almost insignificant when compared to the nuclear arsenals developed during the Cold War. The desolation that a nuclear war between the superpowers could have created is terrible to contemplate.

The nuclear genie unbottled at Hiroshima and Nagasaki would cast a long, dark shadow over the world during the years that lay ahead. After the Soviet Union's development of an A-bomb, the nuclear race escalated until man's continued habitation of planet Earth seemed in some doubt. During the Eisenhower-Dulles years America seemed to be relying on a deterrent policy of mutually assured destruction. When John F. Kennedy campaigned for the presidency in 1960, he pledged to redress a "missile gap" created by laxity in the face of ominous Soviet advances. President Eisenhower remarked that it was militarily "fantastic, crazy, and unconscionable" for the United States to have built some 5,000 nuclear weapons averaging 100 times the power of the Hiroshima bomb, to be cranking out two more thermonuclear bombs every calendar day, and to still push for more. Yet he characterized himself as helpless against the tide of arms. One of his final speeches as President was a warning to Americans of the dangers inherent in the "military-industrial complex."

Following Kennedy's election, an investigation by his Secretary of Defense, Robert McNamara, revealed that a "missile gap" did indeed exist, but it was in America's favor by a wide margin. When the world teetered on the brink of the abyss during the 1962 Cuban missile crisis, Kennedy controlled over 6,000 nuclear weapons while Soviet General Secretary Nikita Khruschev had about 800 nuclear bombs and warheads. The doomsday clock was ticking.

Estimates of the consequences of all out nuclear war have varied from a generally accepted figure of about 200,000,000 dead to a World Health Organization assumption that if ten thousand megatons were exploded 1,100,000,000 people would die at once and 1,100,000,000 more would be seriously injured and a majority of these would die for lack of medical care. Over 30% of the people on earth would perish.

Some members of the scientific community were to predict the possibility of even more cataclysmic consequences. In 1983 Carl Sagan and a group of fellow scientists came to the conclusion that the explosion of 100 megatons over 100 cities might produce a climatic catastrophe, obscuring the sun for a period of time up to six months, lowering the earth's temperature, destroying plants and animals, and leading to the possible extinction of *Homo sapiens*.

By 1990, there were 23,000 nuclear warheads held by eight nations. The end of the Cold War resulted in some reduction of this number. The possibility of nuclear disarmament at any time in the foreseeable future appears to be extremely remote.

The wisdom of the decision to employ the atomic bombs against Japan is a subject that continues to occupy writers and historians. It is true that Japan was already a defeated nation. Any rational government would have long since sued for peace, but it took two atomic bombs and the entry of the Soviet Union into the war to shock the military-dominated Japanese government into reality. Only this series of events made it possible for the peace advocates to prevail and thus present the opportunity for the emperor to end the war. Even then, a large part of the Japanese military establishment wanted to continue the war.

There were, of course, other possible ways to end the war without using the atomic bombs. With the massive and ever increasing destructive power that the Air Force and Navy were bringing to bear on Japan, the air force generals and the admirals were convinced that they could end the war without an invasion. They would accomplish this by continuing the blockade and bombardment of Japan, if it proved necessary, until all of the cities and villages were reduced to ashes and rubble, and the people who had survived the shells, the bombs, and the fires were succumbing to starvation, exposure, and disease. It is difficult to comprehend how this option would have been more humane than the course that was taken. This bombardment of Japan was well along when hostilities ceased. The larger cities had been burned out with one-fifth of all housing destroyed, fuel supplies were almost non-existent, and the food supply was reduced to the point where it would be inadequate for the coming winter.

MacArthur and the Army maintained that there was no certainty that the bombardment would succeed within any reasonable period of time. MacArthur's staff continued to prepare plans for an invasion. The Joint Chiefs of Staff, meeting with the President on June 18, recommended an invasion of Kyushu in November. President Truman was worried about casualties: "I hope there is a possibility of preventing an Okinawa from one end of Japan to the other." Secretary of War Stimson pointed out that the casualty rate on Okinawa had been 35%. If Kyushu were no worse, 268,000 of the 767,000 men involved in the operation would be killed or wounded. And Kyushu might actually be worse.

Kyushu is a mountainous island with terrain similar to that which the Japanese had exploited so doggedly on Luzon and Okinawa. Fourteen Japanese divisions and five brigades stood ready to defend the area around the landing beaches. This army was equal in size to MacArthur's invasion force and could possibly be reinforced from Honshu. Over five thousand kamikaze planes had been hoarded to savage the invasion fleet.

On Okinawa, three Japanese divisions, isolated and cut off from resupply, never out of range of the big guns of American battleships, had inflicted appalling losses on an American force over twice their size. Admiral Nimitz stated:

> We must be prepared to accept heavy casualties whenever we invade Japan. Our previous successes against ill-fed and poorly supplied units, cut down by our overpowering naval and air action, should not be used as a sole basis of estimating the type of resistance we will meet in the Japanese homeland where the enemy lines of communication will be short and enemy supplies more adequate.

It is an easy thing to look back over half a century and, from the vantage point of an ivory tower, second-guess the hard decisions that had to be made that high summer of 1945. The soldiers, sailors, and marines whose lives and limbs and eyes would have been forfeited invading the islands of Kyushu and Honshu had few doubts concerning the wisdom of Truman's decision to use the atomic bombs.

The Tokyo-Yokohama-Kawasaki area, which, on this late September day in 1945, was a vast, burned out wasteland, would, in fifty years, become the most populous metropolitan area in the world with a population of over 28,000,000. Only a few brick and mortar islands now stood in what would be transformed into a vast industrial complex and one of the most important centers of economic power and influence on earth.

The train carrying the Honor Guard moved north out of Tokyo. Leaving the war-wracked cities behind and moving into the green, unspoiled countryside was as refreshing as leaving a stuffy room and stepping out into the fresh, cool air of a brisk September morning.

Our train was now entering the Kanto Plain, a highly productive agricultural region. Men, women, and children were at work in the gardens, fields, and rice paddies. There was a critical need for all the food they could produce. The villages we passed were neat and peaceful, showing no sign of the catastrophe that had engulfed the nation. The sun was bright, but the weather had turned cooler, and there was a hint of fall in the air. For men whose eyes were weary of ruin and rubble, the trip through the green, quiet countryside was a rare pleasure.

As the train entered the city of Sendai, we again beheld the devastation of war. The turn of Sendai had come on the night of July 10, when B-29s burned out the center of this city of 234,000 people. The 11th Airborne Division Headquarters and the 187th Regiment were stationed in and around the city. The 187th was quartered in an immense Japanese army arsenal just outside the city. The other units of the division were on occupation duty throughout northeastern Honshu.

It was with mixed feelings that I reported in at the E Company orderly room that late September evening. The days with the Honor Guard had been an exciting time. I did not relish the garrison duty that we now had coming up.

At E Company quarters, Petersen, Walker, Ward, and the old members of the weapons platoon greeted me. It was good to see them again. They informed me that the battalion had quite a wild time after arriving in Japan. Some of the troopers, using Jap vehicles from Atsugi, had raided the breweries and distilleries in the Yokohama area. They had hauled truckloads of booze back to the area where they were quartered, and a good many of the troopers had gone on a twenty-four hour celebration. I understood that this celebrating took place throughout the division. Early the next morning, the officers took their hung-over troops on a ten-mile forced march with full field equipment. The troopers took the hint and kept their celebrating under control from that time on.

Sgt. Denny Faye appeared on the scene the day after I returned to the company. He was splendidly attired in a complete paratrooper combat uniform. I had seen pictures of this uniform but never the real thing. It was apparently what a paratrooper would wear into battle in a world of perfect supply services. It was the one and only such uniform I saw during my time as a paratrooper.

Sgt. Faye related his most recent exploits. He had flown up from Manila to Atsugi on a plane with Mrs. MacArthur, her son Arthur, and Arthur's Chinese nanny. He was part of a detail protecting them on the trip from the Philippines. Denny was hoping to continue with this duty in Japan. I was glad to see the big redhead again and to learn that he had such a promising assignment.

Mail call was usually a morale booster, but the backlog of letters I received after returning from the Honor Guard had the opposite effect. A letter from home contained the news that my cousin and former high school classmate, Adam Urish, had been killed in action on July 24 when his ship was sunk in Philippine waters. Adam had served in the Atlantic for a year. Then, in January of 1945 his ship, the destroyer escort USS *Underhill*, had been transferred to the Pacific.

While on convoy duty between Leyte and Okinawa, the *Underhill* had detected a Japanese submarine. As they depth-charged the sub, another periscope was sighted nearby. They increased speed and rammed the second submarine, which exploded, ripping the *Underhill* in two. The explosion demolished the forward fire room where Boilermaker 3/C Adam Urish was on duty. Ten officers and one hundred and two enlisted men were killed. It saddened me to realize that while most Americans were celebrating the victorious conclusion of the war, Adam's family was grieving their recent loss. They were not alone.

The Japanese army barracks in which we were quartered were run down and vermin infested. Fleas were the most offensive pests. They seemed to prefer their victims clean, so we gave up showering for a few days. Supply eventually came through with canisters of DDT enabling us to eliminate the fleas.

If there ever had been a decent heating system in the barracks, it had long since ceased to function. As cold weather came on, potbellied oil stoves were installed in the squad rooms with metal stove pipes sticking out through holes in the windows--a surefire setup. During the winter, reports telling of burning barracks arrived regularly from units all over northeastern Honshu. It was fortunate that there was a surplus of old Japanese barracks in the area.

The plumbing was typically Japanese with rectangular slots in the toilet floor, to be used in the same manner as a slit trench. The waste falls into a holding tank and is regularly dipped into "honey carts" and hauled to the fields where it is used as fertilizer--night soil.

These "honey carts," moving through the streets and along the roads, did more to promote careful jeep driving than any number of whistle-tooting MPs.

The army, out to prove that any crappy situation can be made worse, eliminated the Japanese toilets and set up outdoor privies. These consisted of shacks containing oil drums cut in half with seats over them. Every morning the drums were moved out, oil was poured into them, and they were burned off. As company punishment, nothing could compare with the task of burning off the toilet drums.

The squad rooms were adequate for six men. They were equipped with built in shelves that had apparently been used as bunks by the Japanese. These shelves were too small for American soldiers to use for sleeping, but they did make convenient storage areas. During the next month, when we were not on guard or patrol, we spent much of our time cleaning up the area and making our quarters as livable as possible.

When the war in Europe ended, a point system had been instituted to provide for the orderly release of men from the armed forces. It was probably about as fair a system as could be devised, giving points for time served, time overseas, certain decorations, and marital status. For those of us who had been shipped overseas after a short period of training in the States, then immediately thrust into combat with a rifle company, it appeared that we might be in Japan far longer than we really cared to stay. We had something in common with American servicemen all over the world. We wanted to go home. There were reports of troops rioting in Europe and in the Philippines. Parents and wives were harassing their representatives in congress. Troopships from Europe were double loaded for the trip home. Half the troops slept in the daytime, half at night.

The kind of instant demobilization that would have satisfied most servicemen was neither practical nor possible. America's armed forces had important responsibilities all over the world. One part of the global mission that America shouldered was the disarming and occupation of Japan. So far, this was going much better than anyone had thought possible. Many of the occupying troops came to Japan from battlefields where, a few weeks earlier, they had been engaged in mortal combat with the unyielding and barbaric Japanese army. That they were able to exhibit civility and restraint in dealing with the Japanese during the critical early days of the occupation reflected great credit upon these American servicemen and their leaders.

MacArthur was working through the government structure that was in place to bend the Japanese to his will. The highly disciplined Japanese, ever subservient to their God-ruler, Emperor Hirohito, were cooperating with the Americans to produce an occupation far more peaceful and successful than either side had anticipated. Even though many of the Allies wanted to try the Emperor as a war criminal, MacArthur's decision to keep him in place undoubtedly made for a more tranquil occupation. The evidence would seem to indicate that throughout the years of Japanese aggression Hirohito was much more than the ineffectual figurehead his post-war apologists depicted.

The officers and many of the ranking enlisted men left E Company soon after we arrived in Japan. The officers and enlisted men who were citizen soldiers and had enough points returned home to civilian life. The West Pointers and Regular Army officers were off on well-deserved furloughs. They would then receive new assignments. With the departure of these veteran officers and key ranking non-coms, the mood of the troopers in E Company changed significantly. The departing officers were replaced by new arrivals who had not seen combat. Some were recent officer candidate school graduates. The close relationship, based on mutual respect and loyalty, which the troopers had enjoyed with the wartime officers, no longer existed. There was also an undercurrent of friction between the "old men" and the non-coms who had arrived with the 541st after the fighting was over.

The troopers had a number of gripes. The combat veterans were of the opinion that, since they had won the war, someone else should handle the occupation. The weather was consistently raw and rainy. Temperatures were dropping as winter approached. Mail, so important for troop morale, was slow and erratic in arriving. The Air Transport Command was hampered in carrying the mail due to the inclement fall weather over Japan and personnel problems caused by demobilization. A battalion mess had been set up. The variety and quality of the food left much to be desired. The Japanese beer, which had been of excellent quality when we arrived, was now coming through green and poorly brewed. High-octane sake and other alcoholic beverages of doubtful origin were readily available. Some of the troopers were becoming borderline alcoholics. A few had crossed the border. It was fortunate that the troopers were kept busy with guard duty, patrolling, and searching caves, villages, and former military installations for war materiel.

Division commanders were involved in a genuine effort to make life more agreeable for the troops. One of the largest buildings on the arsenal grounds was converted into a recreation center. It housed basketball courts, a theater seating 2500, and a large arena for boxing matches. USO shows occasionally came to camp. An indication of the prevailing mental attitude of the men in the ranks is apparent in a letter I wrote home at the time. Danny Kaye and Leo

Durocher had appeared in person for a performance at the camp. My only comment: "What a pair of big-mouths."

Late one rainy, windy afternoon, long after duty hours, a member of the weapons platoon was seated on his cot, drinking a can of beer. Our new company commander, a postwar arrival from the States, entered the squad room. Harris, deep in his cups, looked up at him through bleary eyes. The captain, from what we had observed, had the idea that his bars elevated him to something approaching divinity. He began berating Harris for failing to stand and snap to attention. Harris, unable or perhaps unwilling to stand, politely told the captain to go to hell.

Harris was given company punishment and stripped of his Pfc. stripe. There can be no doubt that he deserved this. The extent and manner of the company punishment was questionable, however. A quiet man, Harris had never been in trouble before. He had been a good soldier and a skillful mortar man in combat. Had the incident occurred with one of our wartime officers, he would have had the squad sober Harris up, reprimanded him severely, and given him several nasty work details. Then, if Harris straightened up, the incident would have been forgotten.

Our company commander evidently decided to make an example of Harris. Here was an opportunity to show the all too cocky combat veterans in his company that they had better stay in line. The troopers did not like this martinet of a captain, and he sensed their heartfelt disdain. The incident with Harris was the culmination of a series of events that had made the captain the most hated man ever to hit E Company.

The company grade officers on the base were quartered in small cottages that had been Japanese officer billets during the war. The army hired a number of Japanese men and women to do janitorial work and various other tasks around the base. Among these employees were maids hired to do the cleaning, washing, and other chores for the officers' cottages. The Japanese workers told that our captain was forcing the maid who took care of his cottage to have sex with him. This in spite of her attempts to fend off his attentions. Desperately needing the job to help feed her family, the maid felt she had little choice but to submit.

Harris' company punishment had developed into an ongoing thing. The captain still had him restricted to the company area. He was being required to handle every dirty detail the captain could devise. And our captain had a fertile imagination. Harris' friends in the weapons platoon were becoming concerned about his mental state. Always reserved, he had grown silent and morose under the incessant badgering.

In the small hours of a foggy night, two members of the weapons platoon were making their way back to the barracks. They were returning to the company area after a Saturday night of serious drinking. The shortcut they took led them through dimly lighted officer's country. As they walked along, something at the entrance to one of the cottages caught their attention. There, sprawled across the gate in a drunken stupor, was our captain.

These two men were Harris' closest friends. The three had been together since the time the division was activated. Together, they had lived and trained, fought and bled, suffered and survived, grieved and celebrated, for three long years. The bonds that bound them had been forged in the sweat and drudgery of training, in the mud and mountains of Leyte, in the bloody assaults on Nichols Field and Ft. McKinley, in the treacherous mountain jungles of Macolod and Malepunyo. They were closer than brothers.

One of the men walked over to see if the captain had passed out. Satisfied, he backed up as if to punt and kicked the captain in the face with all his might. The captain was sent away for extensive repairs. On Monday morning it was announced that our company commander had sustained serious injuries in a fall and was being replaced. He never ever returned to E Company.

Checking former Japanese military installations to make sure that all arms and munitions had been destroyed was one of the primary missions for the 11th Airborne in the division's area of responsibility. Even though the Japanese were cooperating, there were still a large number of caves, factories, arsenals, and bases that had to be checked.

A patrol, consisting of four members of the weapons platoon and their leader, was sent inland one gray October day to check some caves that were possible repositories for arms and ammunition. If there ever had been any contraband in the caves, it had been removed before we arrived there. We were out in the hinterland longer than the patrol leader had anticipated, and the early onset of darkness caught us shortly after we started the return trip to Sendai.

As we drove into a village on our route back to camp, we noticed a large building with lights blazing over the entrance and people going inside. The Army was wary of any large gathering of Japanese citizens at this early stage of the Occupation, so we stopped to investigate.

A rush of steamy air struck us as we stepped inside the building. When our eyes became adjusted to the dim light and the steam, we could see what looked like a large, shallow swimming pool that had been divided into sections. Several hundred naked people of all ages and genders were soaking in the pool. There was a sudden hush in the hubbub we had heard when we entered the building. Two hundred heads turned to look at the intruders. There was a certain embarrassment on both sides. A chance encounter of discrete cultures. Since it appeared that no seditious activity, aimed at undermining the occupation, was taking place, we did an about face and resumed our journey.

Imagine, if you will, the two hundred people living nearest to you, all getting together and soaking naked in hot, steamy water in a shallow pool. The Japanese still have the largest hot tubs in the world.

During the first year of the occupation, the 2nd Battaliom, 187th, had the dubious distinction of being continually stationed adjacent to 11th Airborne Division and 187th Regimental Headquarters. There were a number of disadvantages to this situation. Headquarters had a lot of officers. So there was more chicken to contend with. More officers, more chicken. It's a direct ratio. Also, it is inevitable that there will be more guard duty to pull. Division always has lots and lots of things to guard.

On the cold, stormy night of Oct. 20, E Company was again standing guard. The post I was assigned was in a remote part of the base, located at the far end of a building complex where division supplies were stored. It was raining heavily, the downpour driven by a 25 mph gale. My four hour shift should have ended an hour earlier, but my relief was nowhere in sight. I hesitated to leave my post, but finally decided to search the area. Eventually, I found the man who should have relieved me. A recently arrived replacement, he was staying dry by holing up in a shack beyond the post area.

Cold, soaking wet, and furious by this time, I dressed him down in language that would have made a mule blush. He made no reply, obviously aware that one of us was very close to getting the hell kicked out of him. But the blame should have been placed primarily on the Officer of the Day and the Sergeant of the Guard for not properly changing the guard. They were staying inside at the guardhouse, keeping their butts dry, and failing to carry out their duties. Reflecting on recent events as we headed back to the company quarters that morning, I came to the sad conclusion that once proud E Company was really going to hell for lack of leadership.

I was soaked to the skin after the night of guard duty in the storm. The jungle rot that had plagued me in the Philippines had recently erupted again on my feet and lower legs. As I pulled off my boots and socks, my legs, from ankles to boot tops, were raw. I was preparing to shower and get a little rest when the First Sergeant walked into the squad room, "Urish, as soon as you get cleaned up, go down to Regimental Headquarters and report to the officer in charge of personnel." This sounded like an order rather than a request. Well, I thought, things can only get better.

Reporting in at Regimental Headquarters, I was referred to the officer in charge of records. He interviewed me briefly, and then told me that, pending approval by my company commander, I would be placed on temporary duty to Regimental Headquarters. The need for more help in the personnel section was obvious. With half of the men in the Division scheduled to go home during the next two months, the amount of paperwork had multiplied.

E Company was quartered near Regimental Headquarters, so I could continue to live with my friends in the weapons platoon as before and go to work at regiment each morning. I ate and slept at E Company but did not have to stand reveille or other formations, stand guard, or pull details. The assignment to Regimental Personnel was a providential break that came at a most opportune time--inside work with no heavy lifting. Now I could wear low shoes and keep my feet and legs dry. This would give the jungle rot sores on my feet and legs a chance to heal.

The people at the regimental personnel office were a mix of new assignees, as I was, and men who had been doing this work since the activation of the Division in 1943. They were a congenial group, and a minimum of formality was observed. The emphasis was on getting the work done as accurately and expeditiously as possible. The first weeks consisted of training in the morning and working with records in the afternoon. I enjoyed the change of duty and was soon doing the work of a corporal or buck sergeant. I did not get promoted, however, for several months. No problem. I would probably have taken a cut in pay, if necessary, just to stay in a position where my jungle rot could be cleared up.

There was another reason working at regiment proved to be a good assignment. In November the 2nd Battalion was assigned the duty of guarding the geisha house district in Sendai--foxes guarding the hen houses. Most of these so-called geisha houses were little more than brothels. The incidence of VD in the regiment was increasing.

The regimental medical officer convoked a seminar for all members of the 187th. As we filed into the field house, we could see that the "Doc" had assembled a group of geishas, all dressed in their finest kimonos. With them was their "headmaster." The Doc called the troopers to order and began his presentation: "Good morning, men. Our guests, who, by the way, do not understand English, are under the impression that they are here for a demonstration of geisha attire, and that I am going to give a lecture on the role of the geisha in Japanese culture. I'm going to provide a little more information than they realize. Now, let's start with the headmaster. You can translate that 'pimp' if you wish. Notice the scars around his mouth. They are the result of syphilis chancres from past infections." The Doc then proceeded to introduce the girls and to reveal, not the nuances of the geisha culture, but, instead, the various venereal diseases with which they were infected. Some of the troopers who had made the acquaintance of these geisha girls while on guard duty in Sendai were beginning to break out in a cold sweat.

The doctor next introduced a trooper from the 187th. This soldier had been scheduled to go home a month earlier but had been held back. He was still in Japan because he had contracted a strain of gonorrhea that was resistant to penicillin. He was now receiving a lengthy treatment. Prognosis: uncertain.

The Doc had given the troopers a good bit to think about. Admired and respected by officers and enlisted men alike, the doctor came to the 187th after the deactivation of the 503rd Parachute Inf, the regiment that liberated Corregidor.

There was little merchandise in the shops of Sendai and the surrounding villages when the occupation troops arrived. When the shopkeepers found that the Americans would buy rather than confiscate their goods, the situation changed. Silk, lacquerware, and other items of interest soon surfaced. Occasionally a trooper would insist that a merchant accept the worthless peso currency that the Japanese had foisted upon the Filipinos. He would explain that these pesos had the full faith and fidelity of the Japanese government behind them.

One of my fellow workers at regimental personnel had made friends with a Japanese family in Sendai. He urged me to come along one Saturday when he was going to visit them. We took some food and a few other items along so that we would not be depleting their meager supply of food. Judging by the house and the furnishings, this was an upper class family. The patriarch of the family appeared to be about sixty years old. We were served sake and a fish dish prepared on a small charcoal hibachi. I was extremely uncomfortable for the entire time. The young Japanese I could tolerate, even get to like. With the older Japs, I still had a problem. I was not yet ready to break bread with our recent enemies. My attitude would mellow as the months went by.

On Thanksgiving Day our cooks, making good use of their primary culinary tool, the can-opener, managed to provide the traditional holiday meal of turkey, dressing, cranberry sauce, candied yams, and pumpkin pie. When the troopers had finished eating this lavish meal and were leaving the mess hall, they would again behold a scene that had become a part of camp life. It was a scene that was duplicated at many American installations throughout Japan. As they had at every mealtime since early in the Occupation, the Japanese waifs were waiting near the garbage cans. At most army mess halls, there was a series of garbage cans near the exit. The first can was for the disposal of food left in a soldier's mess kit or tray; the second held soapy water in which to wash the kit or tray; and the third held scalding water for a final rinse. It was the first can that drew the young Japanese. These thin, pitiful children would stand in a row behind the garbage cans, shivering on cold days, their threadbare clothes hardly sufficient for this harsh climate. In their hands they held tin cans, retrieved from an army junk pile. They stood there mute, silently hoping against hope that a soldier would place his leftover food in one of their cans, rather than throwing it in the garbage. When these children first showed up, I still had a lot of battlefield bitterness in my heart, and I ignored them. Blaming the children for the sins of the fathers, no doubt. But how could I hold hungry, innocent children responsible for the stupidity of Japan's military dictators? I was soon taking all the food I could get in the chow line. That way I always had quite a bit left for one of the children.

The food situation was critical everywhere in Japan. In Tokyo, the local Japanese authorities asked for, and were given, the garbage from the ships in the harbor to help feed the people. Every bit of food and every grain of rice was precious that winter. Japan's former sources of food in Asia had been cut off, first by the blockade and bombardment, then by the Soviet and communist Chinese subjugation of those food-producing areas. The situation worsened when the Japanese rice harvest of 1945 fell 40% below the normal yield. Food shipments from America prevented disaster, but hunger and malnutrition continued to haunt almost the entire population. Inflation was rampant, black markets flourished, and city dwellers were forced to go to the countryside and barter their possessions for food in order to survive. The food situation remained critical for several years and American aid programs continued until the end of the occupation.

One evening in November, a group of troopers from the weapons platoon went down to the auditorium to see a movie. As we waited in the dim light for the show to begin, the trooper on my right turned and said, "Urish, there's another guy from Green Valley sitting on the other side of me." Sensing a practical joke, I replied, "Sure there is. There're a lot of us around Sendai." Just to be sure, I looked around the trooper and came face to face with Steve Hopkins. Steve was another farm boy I had known from a neighboring community near home. He entered the service shortly before I did, had served as a rifleman with the Americal Division in the Philippines and had been wounded during the battle for the island of Cebu. In the original occupation force, the Americal Division had replaced the 11th Airborne in the Yokohama area. The Americal had later been disbanded, and Steve was assigned to an engineer outfit stationed at Sendai. Steve and I had a good session, catching up on the events of the past year and exchanging news from home.

During the first week of December most of the "old men" departed for home. They had served with the 11th Airborne Division since its activation in early 1943. During their nineteen months overseas they had survived two grueling campaigns and had spearheaded the occupation of Japan. Their departure was a time of mixed emotions. Those of us who had come into the division as replacements at Mt. Macolod were beholden to them. During those traumatic days when we were first thrust into combat, these men had helped us survive. Strong friendships had been forged during the following months. We were glad that they could now return to their homes, yet it was with some regret that we bade them farewell, knowing that we would probably never see some of them again. Those of us who had joined the 11th Airborne at the base of Mt.Macolod were now the combat veterans of E Company, all of nineteen or twenty years of age.

As the climactic year of 1945 wound down, MacArthur's prediction that the occupation force could be reduced to 200,000 men had proven to be correct. There were now just 152,000 American and 38,000 British soldiers in Japan. Much of the work of the occupation forces had been completed; many of the 6,500,000 Japanese servicemen and civilians who had been abroad were in the process of being repatriated from Japan's lost empire; the military bases and the arms industry had been dismantled; the weapons of war destroyed, dumped into the sea, or shipped to America as souvenirs. The United States had taken nothing from Japan for war reparations. Some of our allies had not been as generous. In Manchuria, the Soviets had shipped everything home that could be moved. In the bomb ravaged home islands, there was little worth taking.

Relations between the occupying troops and the Japanese people became more relaxed as time passed. The Japanese had discovered early on that the Americans were not oversized savages come to loot and destroy, but were, in most instances, friendly and generous. The occupying troops were amazed by the tractable, cooperative behavior of the Japanese people. There was no sign of the barbarous brutality that the Japanese soldiers had displayed during the war. The occupying troops could go about the land of the rising sun without arms and without fear of harm.

At the end of the war, the President had called upon congress to continue selective service inductions at a reasonable rate in order to replace combat veterans who were overseas on occupation duty.

Congress' shortsighted failure to do so meant that my buddies and I would be obliged to spend a good part of the next year in Japan. It also deprived many other worthy young men of the opportunity to replace us and visit scenic Japan. From time to time we would get word that the demobilization and the rotation of troops stationed in Japan was being slowed down. The troopers could then be heard singing in their beer:

> "When the plans we've made
> Need a helping hand,
> I'll be in Japan,
> Always, always."

    By mid-December the snows had begun in earnest at Sendai. The company, with a high percentage of new replacements, started twelve weeks of basic training on Dec. 23. Merry Christmas, fellas. The sergeant I had been working with at regiment had gone home in early December, so my workload had increased. No complaints, though. It still beat hell out of that basic training the company was undergoing.

    For New Years, practically all of the troops at Sendai went down to Tokyo by special train to attend the Rice Bowl football game. The 11th Airborne Angels were scheduled to play our old friends, the 1st Cavalry Division. While most of E Company made the trip, Gene Walker and I had been assigned essential duties at the base, now officially Camp Schimmelpfennig, named for the division chief of staff who had been killed during the drive on Manila.

    Not very happy at missing the trip, Walker and I lingered a bit too long at the beer hall the evening before the troops were to return. After finding our way back to the barracks, we suffered a sudden, severe attack of stupidity. Inside the entrance to E Company's quarters was an interior wall of plaster and lath that we decided to go through rather than around.

    The company returned from Tokyo during the night. As I went down the hall the next morning on my way to Regimental Headquarters, I came up behind the First Sergeant and a platoon sergeant. They were surveying a badly damaged wall and a large pile of broken plaster and lath. I looked down at my boots, the toes of which were badly scuffed, did a quiet about face, and cleared the area at flank speed.

Our football team had won: 11th Airborne 35-First Cavalry 6. There was a general supposition that the new opening in the wall in E Company's barracks was the result of the victory celebration that occurred when the troops returned from Tokyo. The Angels would go on to win the Japanese Occupation title, then the All Pacific Championship by defeating the Hawaiian All Stars.

In addition to my other duties at Regimental Personnel, I was responsible for monitoring the morning reports, orders, and other paperwork coming in from E Company. During the past several months--since shortly after our arrival in Japan--a succession of semi-literate first sergeants had been running the company. They were men who had been assigned to the company as replacements from the disbanded 541st, arriving overseas just before the war ended. They came into the company wearing four or five stripes, much to the chagrin of some of our combat veterans who could see their chances for promotion evaporate. That most sacred of army documents, the Morning Report, would arrive from E Company each day, scribbled in an unintelligible manner. The officer in charge at regiment would curse and fire the reports back to the company for clarification.

The latest of the E Company First Sergeants had been sought out late one night by the Officer of the Day on some urgent company business. The OD located the Sergeant at his quarters in his sleeping bag, where he should have been. In his sleeping bag with him, where she shouldn't have been, was a Japanese woman. The First Sergeant was scheduled to leave for home the following week. And now it looked as though he might also have a court-martial coming up. I had already prepared his papers for the trip home, and he departed from Sendai on schedule. But, in the meantime, the military court had met to consider his case and had decided to reduce the sergeant to private, stripping him of his six stripes. I had heard through the Regimental Personnel grapevine that the order had been cut reducing him to private, but the papers had not yet reached my desk when the Sergeant left for Tokyo. I was watching with some interest and no little amusement as I waited to see how this would all play out.

One week later the former first sergeant, now clean-sleeved, walked into Regimental Personnel. He had made it as far as the 5th Repl. Depot near Tokyo. Orders were waiting there to ship him back to Sendai immediately. From remarks I heard around the area, it was obvious that the outcome of this episode did not result in widespread despondency among the troopers of E Company.

Chapter XVII Hokkaido and Home

A new company commander had been assigned to E Company in December. First Lieutenant Edmund Donnelly hailed from Lexington, Mass., was a graduate of Boston College and had been a CPA in civilian life. My friends in the weapons platoon reported that he was shaping up the company in a quiet, businesslike manner. No yelling or storming about, just making sure that the members of E Company, officers and men alike, were doing their jobs--and doing them well.

I had been keeping an extremely low profile around E Company while working at Regimental Headquarters, believing that such conduct was in my best interest. Out of sight, out of mind, and that sort of thing. And so it came as something of a surprise when I arrived at the company barracks one evening in late January to find that I had orders to report to the company commander first thing in the morning.

"Sgt. Urish, I'm bringing you back from regiment to the company as acting First Sgt., beginning immediately." I was greatly surprised and not too overjoyed with this proclamation from Company Commander Donnelly when I reported to the orderly room the next morning. I was quite well satisfied with the job I had at Regimental Personnel. I had recently been promoted from corporal to sergeant and thought I had it made for the rest of my army career. Since I had no choice in the matter, I thanked the Lieutenant for his confidence in my ability to handle the job and went to work. The fact that Lt. Donnelly had just relieved an acting first sergeant the day before assigning me to the job would not make it any easier. Fortunately, many of the non-coms had joined E Company as replacements back in the Philippines and were my friends. I was sure I could count on their support.

Because I was a buck sergeant (three stripes) who now had authority over staff and tech sergeants (four and five stripes), I decided that it would be better not to wear any stripes. There was a Staff Sgt. Shoger in the company who had transferred in during the time I was at Regiment. When we were off duty, he would refer to me as a "Model T Sergeant." My promotion at Regiment had been as a technician and stripes for that position had a T below them. I ignored his comments but decided that, in the interest of good order and discipline, it might be wise to make a point with this sergeant. I immediately began to give close attention to my duty assignments for the non-coms.

The company was still sending out patrols to check buildings and caves for weapons and other contraband. From time to time we maintained outposts in the countryside. There was guard duty every third night. It seemed obvious to me that Sgt. Shoger was the ideal choice to lead the patrols on stormy days; to man the coldest, most remote outposts; to take charge of the least desirable work details; and to serve as Sergeant of the Guard as often as possible.

Not terminally stupid, Sgt. Shoger soon got the message. There was a price to be paid for any overt lack of respect for the new acting First Sgt., whether on or off duty. This series of events did not go unnoticed by the other non-coms and the troopers of E Company. Never again did I hear the expression, "Model T Sergeant." For reasons too numerous to itemize, Sgt. Shoger was never promoted.

Shortly after I took over as First Sergeant, orders came down that all personnel would be given dental inspections, and any problems would be corrected. Troopers having the longest interval of time since their last dental exam were to go first. This put my buddies and me at the top of the list. We had last seen a dentist immediately before being shipped overseas, more than a year ago. On that occasion the perfunctory dental exam we were given could only have been described as a sham. During the months that followed, dental care did not have a high priority.

I was among the first to report for my dental examination. I soon discovered that the dentist was operating with a type of equipment rarely seen since the days of the Spanish Inquisition. The dentist's drill was powered by a soldier turning a wheel that rotated the instrument by means of a series of belts. When I figured out what this Rube Goldberg contraption was to be used for, my first impulse was to jump out of the dentist's chair and run as fast and as far as my legs would carry me. Realizing that this would set a bad example for the men in the company, I stayed, much against my natural inclination toward self-preservation. The dental officer decided that I had two molars that were in urgent need of help. After he drilled the first, an operation that sent clouds of steam issuing from my mouth, I decided that the best alternative was to have him pull that second molar.

The word soon spread regarding Captain Torquemada and his equipment, making it increasingly difficult to get men to go for their dental examinations. One of the company cooks was particularly challenging in this respect. He had been scheduled to go on several occasions, but he would disappear, as if by magic, only to show up later in the day with some more or less plausible reason for having missed the appointment. Finally, with my patience wearing thin, I decided that he would not be allowed to miss another appointment. The day of his appointment, I saw him return to his squad room after lunch and followed, determined to send him on his way to the dentist even if it required an armed escort.

When I entered the room, there was nobody in sight. The windows were tightly closed and locked on the inside. Pfc. Mulcahy seemed to have disappeared into thin air. No believer in the occult, I started to search the room. In addition to an army cot, each trooper had a plywood closet, 3 by 3 by 6 feet, open at the front. The trooper's footlocker stood just in front of his closet. Overcoats had been issued earlier in the season and these hung down below the top of the footlocker. Looking about the room, I noticed that the overcoat in one of the closets was bulging suspiciously. I unbuttoned the overcoat and there was Pfc. Mulcahy crouched inside, invisible to anyone casually glancing into the room.

Had there been a choice between going to our dentist or being flogged, I'm not sure which the troopers would have chosen. After only a small percentage of the men had been to the dentist, we moved north and I heard no more of the dental rehabilitation program.

There had been no official announcement, but it was common knowledge that elements of the 11th Airborne would soon be moving north. The 77th Infantry Division, stationed on the island of Hokkaido since the beginning of the occupation, was scheduled for deactivation. Units from the 11th Airborne would replace the 77th on this northernmost Japanese island. It was soon made official when orders came down for the 187th Regiment and Division Headquarters to prepare for the move. The 2nd Battalion was scheduled to go on Feb. 8. It was a busy time, especially for a newly assigned First Sergeant.

The train ferry between Honshu and Hokkaido was temporarily out of service because of engine trouble, and our departure was delayed until Feb. 10. We moved by train from Sendai to Aomori near the northern tip of Honshu. The train was rolled aboard a ferry for the trip across the Tsugaru Strait to the city of Hakodate on the southwestern coast of Hokkaido. The train ferry encountered extremely rough water during the six-hour crossing. All of the transport in Japan was badly worn and in need of overhaul or replacement at the time, and our train ferry was no exception. As the ferry groaned along through the heavy seas, it occurred to me that survival time for a man in those frigid northern waters would be limited to a few minutes. Several years later one of the train ferries sank with considerable loss of life. It was not carrying a battalion of American paratroopers. With the completion of the Seikan Tunnel in 1988, the Japanese greatly simplified inter-island transportation between Honshu and Hokkaido.

Our train was rolled off the ferry at the port of Hakodate. We were on Hokkaido, the second largest of the Japanese home islands. In 1946 the island had a population of about 3.5 million, which was less than 5% of Japan's population, scattered over 21% of the nation's land area. Forests covered 75% of the island and about 15% was considered suitable for agriculture although less than half of that was being utilized for farming in 1946. The climate was considered unsuitable for rice production. This, plus the severity of the winters, had resulted in the slow colonization of the island. Hokkaido, the name given the island in 1869, translates into English as "region of the northern sea." Siberia lies across the Sea of Japan to the west and the Sea of Okhotsk to the north. The climate resembles that of eastern Siberia more than that of lower Japan.

With the Meiji restoration in 1868, the Japanese government made a determined effort to increase the population of the island but had very limited success. Sapporo, the capital and principal city, was laid out in a rectangular pattern with broad streets. In 1872 an American, Horace Capron, was brought in by the government to introduce scientific methods of farming and to establish an agricultural college in Sapporo.

With our train back on land, we resumed our ride on the rails. The train passed through a winter landscape of spectacular beauty as it chugged through southern Hokkaido on the way to Sapporo. The pine-covered mountains were blanketed with seven feet of snow.

Great drifts lined the railroad right-of-way. Small wonder that Sapporo was sometimes isolated for days at a time when avalanches of snow covered the tracks. We arrived at the Sapporo station at mid-morning of Feb. 12. Trucks were waiting and we were at our new camp before noon. The men of the company spent the remainder of the day unloading equipment and settling into their new quarters.

That evening the troopers all headed for a nearby field house where a movie was being shown. I completed my company reports and went to a nearby bathhouse. I had just finished showering when a bright glow in the window caught my attention. The barracks that we had just moved into were going up in flames. The old frame buildings burned to the ground in a matter of minutes. Fortunately, no one was injured in the fire, but E and F Companies lost most of their equipment, clothes, personal effects, and company records. Many of the troopers lost personal items that were irreplaceable. Photographs, letters, and souvenirs, which I had carried since Luzon, had gone up in smoke.

E and F Companies were quartered in the field house until they could be resupplied and moved into permanent quarters. To keep the men busy and fit, we had calisthenics and started a wrestling tournament. My Company E troopers wanted to get me involved in the tournament. Here was a little problem. Regardless of the troopers' motives, which in some instances were suspect, I would appear to be chicken if I refused to compete. If I entered the fray and got clobbered, I would probably lose face—not an insignificant factor when running an airborne company.

A consistent winner in the tournament was a tall, muscular, eighteen year old trooper from E Company who had been winning all of his matches on sheer strength. He had joined the company at Sendai--a clean-cut, intelligent, well-adjusted young man we all appreciated having in the company. I studied his wrestling style and concluded that he should be susceptible to a figure four scissors and a grapevine if I were just fast enough to get him before he got a hold on me. It worked. I earned considerably increased respect from my Company E troopers that afternoon.

While we were living in the field house, the company had to march a quarter of a mile to the nearest mess hall for meals. As we marched up the street the morning after the fire, a prisoner was picking up refuse under the watchful eye of his guard.

The G. I. prisoner stopped work to observe our passing column, then remarked, "So that's those paratroopers I been hearing about. They don't look so tough to me." Immediately from behind me came a voice I recognized as Pvt. Haseltine, "First Sergeant, I request permission to show this stupid bastard how tough we really are." "Denied." I informed the guard that he had better make his prisoner shut up if he wanted to get him back to the stockade unbruised. Those paratroopers had just lost most of their personal possessions and were not in a very forgiving mood.

The company soon moved into barracks previously occupied by members of the 77th Division. Covered walkways, ten feet high at the peak, connected the buildings in the company area. Before the winter ended, snow had drifted over the top of these walkways covering them completely. The troop quarters were heated with coal stoves, a marginal improvement over the hazardous pot-bellied oil burners at Sendai. The barracks were constructed with a central hallway, which allowed anyone walking down the hall to observe the squad rooms on either side. Each company would have its own kitchen and mess hall, and the food, prepared in smaller quantities, would, with any luck, be more palatable than that provided by the battalion mess at Sendai. Overall, it appeared that Camp Siedenburg would be a somewhat better setup for the troops than Camp Schimmelpfennig had been--which really isn't much of an endorsement. Division officers took over the best hotel in Sapporo, recently vacated by 77th Division officers.

As usual, the 2nd Bn., 187th, was stationed near regimental and division headquarters. I was never able to discern whether the division leaders considered the 2nd Bn. 187th to be the best of the infantry battalions and kept us nearby for show purposes or thought we were the worst and wanted us where they could keep an eye on our activities. Whatever the reason for our being near these headquarters, it meant that we would again be saddled with an excessive amount of guard duty. As the harsh winter wore on, with blizzards piling the snowdrifts higher and higher, the men were becoming weary, both physically and mentally.

The E Company barracks were so large that we had three times the number of squad rooms that we needed for company personnel. Because we had this extra room, division would regularly quarter replacements with us until transportation could be arranged to take them to the outlying units, scattered throughout Hokkaido, an island about the size of Ireland though far more irregular in shape. Because of the snowstorms and avalanches that frequently caused disruptions in travel, the replacements would sometimes be with us for a week or so.

The replacements had been traveling by ship, train, and truck from the States for various periods of time ranging up to one and one-half months. The military discipline instilled during training had usually eroded to some extent during this time. When a detachment arrived, I would send reliable Sgt. Smith to meet them. He would take their names, acquaint them with the facilities, and show them to their quarters. I would then welcome them and go on to explain that their government-sponsored ocean cruise and tour of scenic Japan was over. They would now start earning their pay by sharing in the activities of E Company. I would put them on the duty roster and they would go on guard within a few days. On one occasion, several of the replacements wised off during the orientation. Five minutes later they were busy in the kitchen, rendering valuable assistance to the mess sergeant. Placing the transient replacements on the duty roster had several beneficial effects. It not only lessened slightly the burden on E Company troopers but also kept the replacements occupied and out of trouble.

Shortly after we started receiving the transient replacements, Sgt. Smith came to me with a question, "Technically, Sgt., according to Army Regulations, when these new replacements arrive, shouldn't they be put at the bottom of the duty roster rather than at the top?"

"Sgt. Smith, you know that and I know that and the company commander undoubtedly knows it. But these replacements don't know it. They have been taking it easy for several months. Our men are getting tired and run down with all of this guard duty and need a little relief. So long as we have the responsibility for overseeing, housing, and feeding these transient replacements, we will continue to operate in the present manner until I receive a direct order to do otherwise. Understood?"

"Understood."

The division stockade had become something of a problem. The prisoners were, for the most part, real hardcases. At the same time, many of the guards were new men who had joined the division during the last few months. A situation developed where the prisoners were causing trouble and intimidating some of the guards. The problem was resolved one March night while E Company was on guard at the stockade. A prisoner on a work detail attempted to seize the weapon of his guard, E Company's Pfc. Olson. Olson wrestled the carbine free, stepped back, and shot the prisoner through the thigh.

Early the following morning, I had just received word of the incident when Lt. Donnelly entered the orderly room. He had already heard about the shooting.

"Sgt., let's promote Olson to Corporal."

"Good idea, sir."

Ten minutes later the telephone rang. It was Regimental Headquarters.

"Col. Wilson for Sgt. Urish."

"Sgt. Urish speaking, sir."

"Sgt. Urish, I want your Pfc. Olson promoted to sergeant."

"Yes, sir."

"Sgt., I want that order cut this morning."

"Yes, sir."

And the word went out. Shoot a recalcitrant, trouble-making prisoner and get an instant promotion to sergeant. The atmosphere at the stockade changed immediately. It had just become extremely dangerous for a prisoner to disobey a guard.

Among the prisoners in the Division Stockade was a former E Company soldier. He and an accomplice had entered a small Japanese workshop and relieved the workers of their watches and other valuables at gunpoint. The two soldiers had been apprehended, incarcerated, and court-martialed. They were now standing trial in Sapporo.

One of the things that MacArthur considered most essential to the success of the Occupation was the proper treatment of the civilian population. Down through history, most occupations had failed because the people came to hate the occupiers. MacArthur was determined that this would not happen in Japan. A soldier who slapped a civilian could receive five years imprisonment, and more serious crimes drew proportionate punishment.

Captain Donnelly--he had been promoted--and I went into Sapporo to observe the court-martial proceedings. Judging from the information I had, I knew the defendants were in deep trouble.

How deep became more obvious as the day wore on. Only officers sat on military courts at that time. Presiding over this trial was the division artillery commander, a large, heavyset colonel with short-cropped, steel-gray hair and a brusque manner.

The first witness was one of the workers who allegedly had been robbed. A Nisei Sergeant, in interpreting the testimony of the Japanese witness, referred to the accused men as G.I.s. The Colonel interrupted, sharply informing the Nisei interpreter that the accused men were soldiers and would henceforth be referred to as such.

When it came time for the defense, counsel for the accused presented a unique rationalization of the events that had taken place on the night of the alleged robbery. The captain in charge of the defense set out to show that the defendants had entered the workshop only to observe the operation. When they said "watch", they actually wanted only to watch the workers. And then, when the Japanese gave them watches and other valuables, the soldiers thought the workers were being friendly and were offering gifts. Not wishing to seem impolite, they had accepted. The fact that the soldiers were waving pistols around during this one-way exchange of gifts did not enter into the defense scenario. The officers of the court retired to determine their verdict.

During the recess I took the opportunity to inquire of the captain in charge of the defense as to his opinion on what the verdict might be. He was enthusiastically optimistic, explaining that he had successfully countered the charges. Yeah, sure, I thought. You're the next Clarence Darrow and I'm Alice in Wonderland.

The officers of the court required little time for their deliberations. The two amateur hold-up men were to be returned to the States. Ft. Leavenworth, Kansas, location of a notorious federal prison, would be their address for a considerable period of time.

The swift, sure justice that was meted out to members of the American Occupation forces stands in sharp contrast to the barbarous conduct permitted Japanese soldiers by their commanders throughout the areas Japan conquered. Many of these Japanese commanders were tried as war criminals.

Article 10 of the Potsdam Declaration stated: "We do not intend that the Japanese shall be enslaved as a race or destroyed as a nation, but stern justice shall be meted out to all war criminals, including those who have visited cruelties upon our prisoners."

Among these war criminals were Generals Homma and Yamashita. Homma was in command of the Japanese forces that overran the Philippines in 1942. Troops under his command committed the atrocities of the Bataan Death March. When General Wainwright attempted to surrender the beleaguered defenders of Corregidor, Homma insisted that he surrender all American and Filipino forces throughout the Philippine archipelago. Otherwise, he would continue the attack until his troops had overrun Corregidor. Nurses, soldiers, sailors, marines, and civilians, all would be victims of the onslaught. A humiliated Wainwright was forced to comply.

Yamashita, arguably Japan's most talented field commander, was the Japanese commander in the Philippines during the period when the islands were being liberated by American forces. Early in the war, this "Tiger of Malaya"—later dubbed the "Gopher of Luzon" by US infantrymen--had presided over the surrender of the British at Singapore. Shortly thereafter, 5,000 inhabitants of that area were slain for no other reason than the fact that they were Chinese.

The captured British troops, over 95,000 men, were marched into the jungles to toil in forced labor gangs. Many of these prisoners of war perished while working on the Siam-Burma railway project. The fictional bridge over the River Kwai was supposedly part of that project. The motion picture *The Bridge Over the River Kwai* does not begin to accurately depict the appalling suffering of these hapless prisoners at the hands of their brutish guards. Over 12,000 Allied prisoners of war died while constructing the railway, six deaths for each mile of track laid. And this was only a fraction of the cost in human suffering. The Japanese forced hundreds of thousands of Malayan and Indonesian coolies to labor on the construction of the railway. Of those slave laborers, it is estimated that over 100,000 died while toiling under the Japanese lash in those insect and disease-ridden jungles.

During his trial, Yamashita's defense rested in part on the claim that he had no control over the Japanese who ran amok in Manila, destroying the city and causing the death of 100,000 Filipino citizens. It seems unlikely that the Japanese commanders had no control or knowledge of the actions of their troops. There was a pattern of conduct in every area that the Japanese conquered. It is obvious that the barbaric behavior of Japanese soldiers was overlooked, was condoned, and was even encouraged by Japanese commanders. The Japanese army had used terror as an instrument of war continually since they started World War II by invading China in 1937.

It is a well-chronicled fact that Homma and Yamashita were tried and convicted by a military court in Manila that ignored many of the niceties of western jurisprudence. But the Generals' "I had no knowledge . . ." and "I had no control . . ." line of defense provides no reasonable excuse for the atrocities committed by troops under their command. If there is to be any responsibility at all in war, there must be "command responsibility." A commander who cannot control the actions of his troops is no commander at all. And these two were among the highest-ranking Japanese generals, commanding men of a highly disciplined race.

I had walked through the smoldering ruins and smelled the stench of a hundred thousand dead civilians in Manila. I had talked with the grieving families of Filipinos murdered in the barrios and cities of southern Luzon. I had seen emaciated survivors of the Bataan Death March shortly after their liberation and listened to their gruesome stories of inhuman Japanese savagery. I feel in my heart and in my bones that justice was served by the conviction and execution of Homma and Yamashita. For the military tribunal in Manila to have found them other than guilty would have been an abominable affront to the hundreds of thousands of brave men, women, and children, living and dead, American and Filipino alike, who suffered and died so grievously at the hands of the Japanese troops these two men commanded.

Up in the Dai Ichi building in Tokyo, MacArthur granted an audience to Mrs. Homma, allowing her to plead for her convicted husband. Although he denied her plea for clemency, MacArthur did order that Homma face a firing squad, considered by the Japanese to be a more honorable death than the hangman's noose that ended Yamashita's career. It appears that MacArthur was for "doing justice and leaving mercy to Heaven."

The final week of February, I developed a severe case of laryngitis. I went down to see the Regimental Doc, he of the Geisha VD production back at Sendai. He examined my raw, inflamed throat and chuckled, "You know, Sgt. Urish, you're every enlisted man's ideal First Sergeant; one who can't even talk, let alone shout." I could only shake my head in agreement, having been shouted at by a few First Sergeants, myself, in the not too distant past.

March came in like a lion and kept right on roaring on Hokkaido. Snowstorms were an almost daily occurrence. Japanese laborers were used to shovel out the most essential streets and walks at Camp Siedenberg. In Sapporo, no attempt was made to remove the snow from most of the streets. By spring, vehicles and pedestrians had packed it down into a layer of ice up to six feet thick. Shopkeepers would cut steps in the ice down to their doorways.

On March 17 Captain Donnelly informed me that E Company had orders to send two men to Wakkanai. I had studied the maps enough to know that Wakkanai was a remote fishing village located at the extreme northern tip of Hokkaido, an estimated two hundred road miles from Sapporo.

As he was with most projects, the Captain was enthusiastic about this mission. "We need to send men who can be goodwill ambassadors as they carry out their mission. During the final weeks of the war, the Soviet Army captured half a million Japanese soldiers, mainly in Manchuria. Most of these prisoners disappeared into Siberian slave labor camps. A number of the prisoners were sent to Communist indoctrination schools. Those that the commisars deemed sufficiently fanatical in their allegiance to communist doctrine are now being infiltrated back into Japan. It is suspected that one of the infiltration routes is from Sakhalin Island across the La Perouse Strait to the northern tip of Hokkaido around the town of Wakkanai. This is why division has ordered us to send two men there."

I had heard the old story about the Texas Rangers sending only one man because there was only one riot to bring under control. Still, to send two paratroopers out to defend two hundred miles of rugged coastline against infiltration seemed like a considerable stretch. I voiced my misgivings to the Captain. He smiled and continued, "The mission is not to repel any infiltrators. It is to observe the situation and to determine the number and nationality of people coming across the strait. Reports indicate that many of them are Koreans who were used as slave laborers by the Japanese in the mines and forests of Sakhalin. Not wishing to play the same role for the Soviets, a number of them are making their escape across the La Perouse Strait. The two men we send are going into an area where the only previous contact with American troops occurred last fall when a few patrols passed through. Most Japanese have come to regard MacArthur and the occupation troops as liberators rather than as conquerors.

We are hoping that our two men can build on this and make friends with the people in the area. That is about the only way we can get the information we want. The natives will know who belongs in the area and who is a stranger passing through."

We sent two of our finest, Alabamian Sgt. Hartzog and Virginian Pfc. Gibson. They were extremely dependable, drank only socially if at all, and had arrived overseas after the war ended. Some of our combat veterans still had bitter memories haunting them.

During the weeks that followed, Hartzog and Gibson monitored a steady trickle of people coming down from the north. Most were Koreans and Japanese crossing the dangerous strait to escape the "worker's paradise" the Soviets were inflicting on the southern half of Sakhalin, an area the Japanese had wrested from Russia in 1904-05, then lost to the Soviets in 1945. Our two men performed the goodwill ambassador part of their mission even beyond Captain Donnelly's expectations. When they returned to E Company later in the spring, I got the distinct impression that they would gladly have spent the remainder of their army time at Wakkanai.

Spring came late to Hokkaido. After the severity of the winter, it was appreciated all the more. Conditions had steadily improved at E Company since our arrival at Camp Siedenburg. As the season changed, the guard duty became less onerous. A program was initiated which emphasized training but also allocated more time for organized athletic activity, including basketball and volleyball at the field house or skiing in the nearby hills. With no ski lifts in the immediate area, this meant cross country or very limited downhill skiing.

Replacements for Company E arrived periodically and those who had not completed parachute training were sent down to the jump school that had been reactivated at an airfield near Sendai. One of the troopers returned from jump school with an interesting story. It was a story that was believable only because someone on the drop zone recorded the event on film.

A trooper named Welch jumped from a plane, only to have his parachute streamer, failing to open properly. He pulled the handle on his reserve chute which also streamered, wrapping tightly around the main chute. Cpl. Newcomb, one of the troopers who had jumped just ahead of Welch, saw what was happening. He was able to maneuver enough to grab the lines of the streamer as Welch plummeted by. The suspension lines burned Newcomb's hands, and his shoulder was dislocated by the strain, but he managed to wrap the canopy and lines around his legs and hang on. The two rode Newcomb's parachute down to a safe landing. Newcomb was given the Soldier's Medal. He had given Welch life itself.

On another occasion, a student jumper's parachute streamered and his reserve parachute failed to open. One hundred would-be paratroopers were waiting by the airfield for a later lift, already wearing their parachutes and equipment. When they saw the unfortunate jumper hurtle to his death, they quietly removed their parachutes. With a few exceptions, however, they went up and jumped the next day, qualifying as paratroopers. While in operation, from March through June of 1946, the jump school at Sendai graduated 3,376 men, 75% of those who had volunteered, with serious injuries of less than one per cent.

Camp Siedenburg became a sea of mud when the sun finally melted the huge drifts of snow that had covered the area. One fine spring morning, when the sun was bright, the air clear and brisk, and the mud and water at their worst, E Company troopers were being taught ju-jitsu as part of their training. Their instructor was a Japanese expert in that ancient martial art. The paved company street in front of our barracks was serving as the classroom because it was high and dry, even though the ditches on either side were filled with mud and water.

Captain Donnelly returned from a meeting at Regimental Headquarters just as the troops were preparing to break for lunch. For whatever reason, he was attired in full dress uniform. The Captain stopped to observe the training. Nearby, Haseltine and Sucharzewski were practicing some of the moves they had been shown. Here were two of our most rugged men--in more ways than one. They each stood about 5' 8" tall and measured about half that across the shoulders. Captain Donnelly approached the pair, "Pvt. Haseltine, show me what you've learned this morning." Unfortunate request. Or was it an order? In something like a nanosecond, the Captain was flying through the air to land broadside in twelve inches of mud and water alongside the road. The Captain might have been less likely to ask Haseltine for a demonstration, had he known that the main lesson that morning had to do with subduing an opponent by applying a body slam. As Haseltine and Sucharzewski helped brush the mud and crud off his once impeccable uniform, Captain Donnelly muttered, "Well, I asked."

With the arrival of more temperate spring weather, the mud around camp dried up and the men spent most of their off duty hours engaged in outdoor sports. We cleared the area behind our barracks for a volleyball court. Being in a convenient, protected location, the court saw a lot of use.

Baseball and softball were also popular off-duty pastimes. As soon as the roads were clear of ice and snow, the company resumed the airborne tradition of running several miles each morning immediately after reveille.

The company sent patrols out into the countryside when the roads became passable for vehicles. There were rumors that the Japanese had hidden arms and ammunition in the area north of Sapporo as the war ended. With the snow reported to be twenty feet deep in places during the winter, it was necessary to wait for the spring thaw before checking the outlying areas.

During the clear, invigorating days of spring, I occasionally led a patrol into the hinterlands. This provided an opportunity to get out of the orderly room and to see how the rural Japanese lived. To withstand the heavy snowfall, the houses and other buildings were more sturdily built than those in lower Japan. The farmers and workmen we encountered were courteous and respectful but very reserved. In many instances, we were the first Americans they had encountered. The good news that the Americans were more like liberators than enemies had spread into every corner of Japan, so the people showed little sign of fear. They appeared to be hardier and healthier than the inhabitants of the lower islands. Living in a largely agricultural area, they had not suffered to the same extent from the food shortage. Also, Hokkaido had been out of the range of the B-29s and had escaped the immediate consequences of the bombing campaign.

The farmers we saw on our patrols, indeed all of the tenant farmers of Japan were soon to have the financial opportunity of their lives. Down in Tokyo, MacArthur was pushing land reform. He would break up the ancient feudal landholdings and sell the land to the long-suffering tenant farmers at extremely low prices and with generous terms. They would be allowed to buy seven and one-half acres on the lower islands, thirty acres on Hokkaido. In a few years the people who tilled it would own 90% of Japanese farmland. This was a brilliant stroke. By mandating land reform, MacArthur converted millions of downtrodden peasants into land-owning capitalists, who, from that time forward, would have a tremendous stake in making democracy succeed.

On one of the patrols, we came across a group of neat, well constructed buildings set in a pine forest. All around the area were trees growing in straight, orderly rows, indicating that they had been planted and cared for.

While the other troopers looked around, I went to the door of the main building. A dignified elderly gentleman opened the door and invited me into his office. He motioned for me to sit down and offered me a cup of tea, which I politely declined. Looking around, I decided that this was the office of the administrator of a forestry experiment station. The operation seemed to be connected in some way with the agricultural college in Sapporo. The language barrier made communication difficult, but my host knew a little English, and I had acquired a number of words of Japanese, so our conversation wasn't a total fiasco. He attempted to point out some of the research being carried on at the station. In turn, I indicated that back home in the US, I had attended a university agricultural college that included a forestry department and numerous experiment stations. He seemed pleased when I told him I hoped to get back to that university before another year passed. We spent an interesting half hour, then I had to move on, impressed by the enthusiasm the old man had for his work. I would guess that he had several degrees in forestry management.

The old Japanese base at Camp Siedenburg had been built for a much larger force than the 11th Airborne had stationed there. Many of the buildings stood vacant because we had no use for them. When the snow had melted and the mud had dried, these surplus buildings were turned over to the Japanese living in the area. The local people, men, women, and children, worked diligently, dismantling the buildings, preserving the lumber for use in repairing their homes and other buildings, and saving any scraps for fuel. It was not unusual to see a man or woman carrying a load on their back that would have filled a medium-size American pickup truck.

One afternoon during the time this demolition was taking place, Sergeant Walker stopped at the orderly room to report that some young Japanese were making a lot of noise and behaving strangely at a nearby building that they were dismantling. We walked over to see what was going on. The boys, who appeared to be in their early and middle teens, were laughing happily as they staggered about while attempting to take down a wall of the building. It didn't take a Sherlock Holmes to deduce that the boys had discovered a cache of sake and other alcoholic beverages. Empty bottles were strewn about, and it was evident from their unusual behavior that the boys had spent the day wetting their whistles while they worked.

The scene reminded me of a time before the war, when my brothers and I were about the age of these boys. For some reason our parents were suddenly called away for a few days, and we were left at home to watch the farm and care for the livestock. While exploring in the cellar we discovered a barrel of our Dad's potent rhubarb wine, carried over from Prohibition days. We ended up in about the same condition as these Japanese boys.

Walker and I watched their antics as they attempted to continue their work. We decided that it would be in the best interest of the boys if they turned in any future discoveries of this nature at the E Company orderly room. We attempted to explain this to the young Japanese. However, with no interpreter available, it was impossible to get our message across to this well-loaded group.

Beginning on the first day of the occupation, it was not unusual to see the Japanese smile, almost in a ceremonial manner, as they bowed and addressed members of the occupation force. I always doubted the sincerity of these smiles as the Japanese had little to smile about at this point in their history. I had never heard a hearty, gleeful laugh from any of them until we encountered the boys with the booze. Though the laughter may have been inspired by alcohol, it was reassuring to find that the people of this staid and industrious race were capable of such mirth.

Captain Donnelly arrived at the company one morning with news that a fire had broken out at the 187th Regimental Officers' Club during the night. The local Japanese fire department, with a station only a block from the club, had supposedly extinguished the fire. As we discussed E Company's agenda for the day, the telephone rang. The caller informed Captain Donnelly that the fire had rekindled and was threatening the entire structure. We jumped into the company jeep and sped to the scene.

The Japanese firemen were running about like a company of Keystone Cops, having little effect on the progress of the fire, which was soon burning out of control. It appeared that morning that they would have had trouble organizing the proverbial two-car parade. I had a feeling that their hearts weren't really in this endeavor. After all, these were the people who had, in the recent past, conquered most of the far eastern world and who would, during the next forty years, rise Phoenix-like out of the bitter ashes of defeat to build the second most powerful economy in the world. They managed this phenomenal economic revival in their little island nation, geographically the size of Montana, lacking in almost every natural resource save the industry and intelligence of the people.

The old Japanese barracks we occupied at Camp Siedenburg had a long central hall with squad rooms on each side. These squad rooms had large windows facing the hallway so that anyone passing through could check the rooms on either side. In the center, next to the main entrance, was the orderly room--company headquarters. Adjacent to the orderly room was a smaller room with no window on the hallway. This room served as quarters for the First Sergeant, the Communications Sergeant, and the Company Clerk. One brisk spring morning, as I was dressing for reveille and our two-mile run, one of the platoon sergeants came into the room. He had a question,
"Sergeant, you sleep pretty sound, don't you?"
"Yeah, I try."
"Didn't hear anything around here about midnight, I guess."
"Nope."
"Didn't hear the patter of little feet?"
"What the hell are you talking about? If you've got something to say, spit it out."
The sergeant proceeded to tell me that there had been an invasion of the barracks about midnight by a group of geisha girls offering curb service, as it were.
"Sergeant, fall the company out. I don't give a damn if they're dressed or not. I want them on the company street in thirty seconds."
The company formed up in various degrees of dress in the cold morning breeze. I proceeded to give them a short, pointed lecture along these lines:
"This is the home of a parachute infantry rifle company, not a cathouse. What you do off the base on your own time is your business.

What you do here in the company area is my responsibility. I'm your First Sergeant, not your warden. I'm deeply disappointed in the non-commissioned officers of this company. If there is another report of unauthorized people being in the company area, I will have the stripes of any squad leader who does not take immediate action to remove them. I will also break any platoon sergeant back to private if he does not take action should this situation arise again."

The problem never occurred again. The sergeants had worked hard for those stripes. They could be depended on to do whatever was necessary to keep them, especially at this point when many of them would be going home within six months. They knew me well enough to know that I would not hesitate to do what I had promised. They also knew that the company commander would support me in whatever action I took.

As happens with almost any group of servicemen far from home in a foreign land, there were men who frequented the brothels, which, if not already in existence, soon materialize near military installations. I had observed in the Philippines that there was, in general, a non-judgmental attitude among the men of the company in regard to these matters. They were considered strictly personal issues with an individual's beliefs and attitudes being respected or at least tolerated.

I was appalled that security was so lax at Camp Siedenburg that unauthorized groups of civilians could wander about the base at night without being challenged. During the winter, the deep snow had been an effective barrier around the camp. Now the drifts were gone and the perimeter security was badly in need of improvement.

Memorial Day, 1945. With brass and boots gleaming, uniforms and weapons spotless, the troopers of E Company joined the other units of the 11th Airborne stationed nearby in a review and parade down the main thoroughfare of the city of Sapporo. During the ceremony, General Swing inspected the troops. Accompanied by a retinue of officers, he passed down the line looking the men over carefully, stopping occasionally to ask a question or make a comment. When he came abreast of the position where I stood as company guide, he stopped. The sharp blue-gray eyes quickly scanned me, hesitating slightly at the Paratrooper wings, the Combat Infantryman's Badge, and the ribbons with two battle stars, and then shifting to my unadorned sleeves. The old warrior looked me in the eye and asked,

After serving on General MacArthur's Honor Guard, Earl Urish, right, ended up as E. Company First Sergeant in the 187th. He is with Sgt. Cornin in Sapporo, Japan during the spring of 1946.

"Aren't you a sergeant?"

"Yes, sir."

"Where are your stripes?"

"They haven't been available through supply, sir," I replied, truthfully.

"That's no excuse. Get some."

I didn't feel the General's suggestion indicated that a verbal response was necessary so I gave none. I figured, correctly as it turned out, that our paths were unlikely to cross again for some time. I delayed sewing on stripes until several months later when they became available through supply. On occasion, as First Sergeant of E Company, I would have contact with Colonel Wilson, the regimental commander, and Major Ewing, the bn. commander. Neither seemed concerned that I was not wearing stripes. Perhaps they recalled combat days when it was almost suicidal to wear any insignia of rank.

The 2nd Bn. had, for a time, as battalion executive officer, a self-important Captain Sinclair who was something of a prig and a pest when he visited E Company. When he entered the orderly room, I would greet him with "What can I do for you, Captain?" He would chew around awhile, complaining that when he entered the room all activity should cease, we should snap to attention and report to him. I never bothered to tell him that we did that only for field grade officers. We would go through this routine with Captain Sinclair periodically while he was battalion executive officer. I could get away with this borderline insubordinate behavior only because Captain Donnelly thoroughly disliked Sinclair.

Captain Donnelly had the respect and confidence of the men of E Company, earned through months of dedicated leadership. A man possessing great common sense, a virtue not obvious in every member of the officer corps, Donnelly was genuinely interested in the welfare of the men he commanded. The troopers realized this and the old army maxim, "loyalty up, loyalty down", applied. Every officer and enlisted man in the company was expected to fulfill his duties in a manner worthy of the airborne tradition—or else.

Since moving to Hokkaido, E Company had been fortunate in being assigned two more outstanding officers. The first was Lt. Haynes, a career officer and a veteran of the D-day jump into Normandy. Wounded in the European campaign, he was now fully recovered. Haynes served as company executive officer and became company commander when Donnelly departed in June.

Lt. Harold Moore came to E Company by way of the US Military Academy at West Point and the Ft. Benning Infantry and Parachute Schools. Most people who came to know Moore expected him to make his mark in the army. They were not disappointed. Moore served with distinction in the Korean Conflict. A Lt.Col. when he arrived in Viet Nam, Moore led an Air Cavalry Battalion into the first major engagement with North Vietnamese Army regulars, the Battle of the Ia Drang. Without Moore's heroic leadership, his battalion would likely have been overrun and annihilated. When the bloody battle ended, Moore and his surviving men held the field. With war correspondent Joseph Galloway, he recorded the battle in the book *We Were Soldiers Once...And Young,* adapted for filming in 2002. Lt. Gen. Moore retired in 1977.

In the spring of 1946, the Army of Occupation, or perhaps it was only the 11th Airborne Division, made the wise decision that it would be better to supply the troops with a little legitimate stateside booze rather than have them run the risks involved in drinking the potentially hazardous indigenous rotgut available in occupied northern Japan. Each trooper was given the opportunity to purchase five bottles of liquor.

The booze arrived late in July. To control the consumption of the liquor, it was kept at the bar of the beer hall which was a part of the Post Exchange. It was available only after duty hours. When a trooper wanted a drink, he gave the bartender his order. The bartender would take the trooper's bottle from a set of alphabetized pigeonholes and pour him a drink. A large majority of the troopers seldom drank anything stronger than beer. Nevertheless, on the evening that the stateside liquor became available, many of the troopers made a valiant attempt to drink several months ration.

One of my platoon sergeants was in uncommonly sorry condition the next morning. As I headed up the barracks hallway for reveille, I glanced into his squad room and noticed that he was draped across the windowsill with his head and shoulders hanging outside the building.

After reveille the company went for the usual two mile run. When we returned, Captain Donnelly turned the company over to me and I dismissed them. The Captain, who seemed to have an uncanny sense of his company's off duty activities, was waiting with a question for me,

"Where was Sgt. Nelson this morning?"

"Well, sir, he wasn't feeling too well this morning, and he's scheduled to go home next week, so I excused him."

"Sergeant, I'm leaving for home tomorrow and I was out there, running, this morning."

Captain Donnelly could see that I was having a little trouble coming up with a logical response. With half a grin on his face, he changed the subject, "By the way, Lt. Haynes and I are going out to look over the new camp site this morning. If you can get away from the orderly room, round up Sgt. Hartzog and come with us."

The new camp was being constructed four miles from Sapporo in a beautiful valley. Mountains formed a backdrop and a river ran alongside. Lt. Moore greeted us when we arrived at the construction site. He was currently on temporary duty, supervising Japanese workers who were in the early stages of the project. The plans Lt. Moore showed us indicated that the camp would be superior to most stateside facilities. The barracks were to be one story and constructed of brick. During the tour he gave us, Lt. Moore pointed out that athletic and recreational facilities would be an important part of the camp. The new facilities would contrast quite sharply with the primitive, vermin infested, dirty old Japanese barracks we had moved into during the early days of the Occupation.

It had been an enjoyable day. When we returned to the company area, it was time to bid Capt. Donnelly farewell as he was leaving for home early the next morning. Donnelly was indeed an officer and a gentleman. He left E Company far, far better than he had found it at the time he took command back at Sendai. The fierce airborne pride and esprit de corps, which had wavered under incompetent leadership shortly after the end of the war, had been restored.

Lt. Haynes assumed command of E Company without a hitch. He had served with the company long enough to be completely familiar with the operation and with the personnel. His war record was a testimonial to his previous service to his country. The fact that he had parachuted into Normandy on D-Day and had been wounded in the subsequent battle assured the respect and esteem of airborne soldiers wherever he might go. More important than this, so far as E Company was concerned, Lt. Haynes was an effective commander who took his work seriously and did it well.

My promotion to First Sergeant had come through on May 2. Several months later the Pentagon announced that henceforth all First Sergeants must be promoted from the Regular Army. As the time neared for my return home, Lt. Haynes suggested the possibility of a field commission if I would stay in the service. The Army was offering generous incentives for men to re-enlist at the time. I had little trouble resisting these recruiting ploys. It had been a year and a half since I came overseas. I was looking forward to returning home and resuming my studies at the university.

In July, all personnel on parachute pay were required to participate in a jump in order to maintain that status. This meant that everyone in the company would make the jump with the exception of men who were scheduled to go home within the next two months. For them the jump was optional. It had been the better part of a year since our last jump. A few of the men who were soon to depart for home were a little uneasy about taking the risk. At $50 a month, however, there was about $150 in pay involved. In 1946, that was an exceptionally good day's wage.

On July 29, E Company traveled sixty miles down to the air base at Chitose where C-46 transport planes were waiting to take us up. It was an ideal day for parachuting. There was no wind, the skies were not cloudy all day, and the spacious drop zone was covered with a heavy growth of soft grass. Every jump should be made on such a field on such a day.

On a warm, sunny morning in early August, I departed from E Company to begin the trip home. Petersen, Walker, Sanchez, and the other five men I had served with for eighteen months were on hand to say farewell, along with most of the other members of the company. Even Teruo Aoki, our likeable teen-aged company houseboy and factotum, was there to see me off. As I shook their hands, I had a feeling of great pride in Company E, in the 187th, and in the 11th Airborne Division-- pride in what they had been, pride in what they had accomplished, and pride in what they were that day. The average age of the troopers in the company that day was less than twenty. The oldest man, one of the few enlisted men over twenty-one, was the supply sergeant who was twenty-five.

Company E had been home and family for what seemed like an age. We had known some of the highest highs and lowest lows possible within the human experience. The lows must include that first day in combat when we were ambushed on Mt. Macolod, the hell of the artillery barrage in front of the Malepunyo hill mass, and the days we lost some of our closest friends. The times of joy and exhilaration include that fifth jump that qualified us as paratroopers, the day we heard the news of the atomic bomb and realized that we would not need to make a combat jump on Japan, flying into Japan that first day of the Occupation, and the month spent guarding MacArthur.

The company roster had changed many times while I was with E Company. First, there were the proud, highly motivated, superbly trained, but battle weary men of the original division. They had instilled their fierce pride in the 11th Airborne in my replacement group and in the other replacements who joined the company later during combat on Luzon. Then there were the men from the deactivated 541st Parachute Inf. Regt. who joined us shortly before we went into Japan. During the Occupation there was a continuing parade of replacements coming in and veterans leaving for home.

My journey home took me down to the 4th Replacement Depot, now located near Tokyo. At Yokohama we boarded the ship that would take us to Seattle via the great circle route. I watched the majestic gray cone of Fujiyama fade away in the distance and then settled down in a quiet spot on the deck with a book. Suddenly, there was a loud "Whoopee!" followed by "Ureesh! You made it!" Tony Turietta gave me a big slap on the back and a hearty handshake. Obviously, Tony had also survived. It seemed that we had each lived a lifetime since our paths last crossed eighteen months earlier at Ft. Ord. Tony had not lost the happy-go-lucky exuberance he had shown at Camp Hood. While in Manila, I had seen a Time magazine report on the large number of eighteen-year-old boys being killed and wounded in action while serving with infantry divisions. Former U.S. Senate Page Tony Turietta was among those cited as examples.

As the ship plowed through the north Pacific that first afternoon of the voyage, I went below to check my belongings. Two officers were waiting by my bunk. They handed me a thick pile of troop rosters and informed me that I was in charge of this section of the ship. They proceeded to tell me that they needed some men for a work detail right away. I immediately ripped two pages off the top roster, handed the pages back to the two lieutenants and told them to help themselves and have at it. Looking somewhat surprised, they took the sheets and departed. I never saw those two shave-tails again. Apparently they hadn't realized before that a paratroop First Sergeant with a Combat Infantryman's Badge far outranked them.

Being in charge of the men in a part of the ship was not difficult when handled properly. It was all in knowing how to delegate responsibility. There were five other first sergeants in the troop compartment so I rotated them in taking charge of the details. Aside from cleaning the compartment each morning, there were few tasks that the troops were called on to perform.

About one-third of the troops in the compartment were black as was one of the first sergeants. I called him over the first morning while I was assigning details and informed him that he and his men were going to be first in line this time. He looked me over thoughtfully, then smiled and remarked, "Well, that makes once." While visiting with him, I learned that this bright young first sergeant's home was in Chicago. On the long journey home, across one ocean and two-thirds of a continent, we became good friends.

We disembarked from the ship at the Port of Seattle. The men were all extremely happy to be back on land and well on their way home. The first night back in the U.S., we were quartered at nearby Ft. Lewis. For some unknown reason, the troops were restricted to the base. This seemed like another unnecessary serving of army chicken. Many of the men went over the camp fence in search of a place to properly celebrate their first night back in the land of the free and the home of the brave. When a group of these celebrants returned to the barracks about 2:00 AM, they awakened me so that I could share a homecoming drink or two with them. If it hadn't been for the fellowship of the thing, I would have much preferred to keep on sleeping.

The following morning all of the men destined for the Middle West and the Northeast boarded a troop train on the Great Northern Railway and traveled eastward over the Rocky Mountains and across the wide-open spaces of the Great Plains. From eastern North Dakota on, we were in farming country. It looked like home.

At Ft.Sheridan I was separated from the service on Aug. 29, 1946 "for the convenience of the government." My army days ended where they had begun after five months and twenty-two days of service in the United States and nineteen months of foreign service all around the Pacific.

A year had passed since the war ended so suddenly and so opportunely. With the passing of time, the mental trauma of battle healed, though never completely. Only a receding glimmer now, those days when we had passed through the valley of the shadow of death; those times when we had pondered at dawn whether we would be alive to see that day's sunset. The more painful images now mercifully suppressed, to be recalled with some effort on rare occasion, or to intrude as specters in the night to disturb our rest, only to be summoned forth purposely, with some qualified pride, half a century later.

Wayne had been discharged from the Navy several months earlier and was on hand with Mother and Dad when I stepped off the *Rocket* at the Rock Island Station in Peoria. It was a joyous reunion for all of us. Mom and Dad were looking well but were grayer than I remembered from that cold night, nineteen months earlier, when we had said good-bye at another railway station.

Army regulations stated that separated soldiers should wear the uniform for no longer than three days after being discharged. I wore mine for three weeks. I was inordinately proud of that uniform with the 11th Airborne shoulder patch, the Paratrooper's Wings, the Combat Infantryman's Badge, the rows of ribbons, and the three Overseas Bars. Eventually my Navy veteran brothers suggested that I either re-enlist or get some civilian clothes.

Millions of servicemen had returned home during the past year and the citizens of the good old USA were just about satiated with returning veterans. Understandably, most Americans wanted to forget the war and get on with the good life. And it was a prosperous and bountiful land to which we returned. When the war ended, the manufacturing capacity of the United States equaled that of all other countries in the world combined. Wages had been high, farm prices profitable, industry booming. For many, it had indeed been the "good war." Now, in the post-war period, American genius for production was at work supplying the pent-up demand for every kind of consumer goods. With vivid images of the carnage and devastation in the Philippines, the burned out cities and hungry people of Japan, all imprinted forever in my memory, I could only thank God and wonder at the good fortune of America.

Veterans of World War II, an estimated two-thirds of whom had never heard a shot fired in anger, were better rewarded by a grateful nation than any who served before or after that time. Legislated in part to prevent large-scale unemployment during the immediate post-war period, the Servicemen's Readjustment Act of 1944, popularly known as the "G.I. Bill of Rights," proved to be an unqualified success. The opportunities that were afforded veterans to continue their education and to make a fresh start paid off many times over for America.

I was among the millions who would benefit from our nation's generosity. Receiving my discharge at the end of August, I had only a few weeks to prepare to enroll for my sophomore year at the University of Illinois. With this time restraint, I did not feel it necessary to sign up for the "52-20 Club" which eight million veterans joined for weeks or months immediately upon being discharged from the service. Under this program, which was a part of the G I Bill, the government paid returning veterans $20 a week for up to 52 weeks while they were seeking employment. Jim Robison, a four year navy veteran and soon to be a college friend of mine, signed up, indicating on the application that he was a diamond cutter with two weeks experience desiring employment in that occupation in Tremont, a small nearby village. When he departed for the university six months later, the Veterans Administration had as yet been unable to secure such a position for him.

With the deluge of veterans enrolling at the University of Illinois, housing became the number one problem. I was fortunate in having a Green Valley friend and neighbor, John Phillips, who saved me a place in Alpha Gamma Rho, a professional agricultural fraternity. This serendipitous event was to lead to friendships that I would cherish through the years. The fraternity house was just reopening after being rented to the Army during the war years. Practically all of the members were men who had returned from the armed services during the past year. Over half were enrolling in college for the first time.

While registering for the coming semester, I encountered an acquaintance from my previous year on campus. The young lady informed me that she was now enrolled in Graduate School. I called later and invited her out to dinner. On that occasion I ordered a bottle of wine. The waiter somewhat apologetically explained that the local authorities were conducting one of their periodic crackdowns on underage drinking. He would have to see some identification.

"Sorry, sir, but I can't serve you any alcoholic beverages."

It was two months before my twenty-first birthday.

Written in memory of Ollie and Adam and Potts and Woerz and Short who were my friends, and for all of those young men who were killed in the springtime of their lives while fighting for our country and for a better world for all the human race.

"When you go home, tell them of us and say,
'For your tomorrow, these gave their today.'

John Maxwell Edmonds, 1945

Fecund America—today
Thou art all over set in births and joys!
Thou groan'st with riches, thy wealth clothes thee as a
 swathing-garment,
Thou laughest loud with ache of great possessions.
A myriad-twining life like interlacing vines binds all thy vast
 demesne,
As some huge ship freighted to water's edge thou ridest into
 port,
As rain falls from the heaven and vapors rise from the earth, so
 have the precious values fallen upon thee and risen out
 of thee;
Thou envy of the globe! thou miracle!
Thou, bathed, choked, swimming in plenty,
Thou lucky Mistress of the tranquil barns,
Thou Prairie Dame that sittest in the middle and lookest out
 upon thy world, and lookest East and lookest West.
Dispensatress, that by a word givest a thousand miles, a
 million farms, and missest nothing,
Thou all-acceptress—thou hospitable, (Thou only art
 hospitable as God is hospitable.)

--Walt Whitman, 1865, at the end of the Civil War

EPILOGUE

In the fall of 1946 when I returned to the University of Illinois, the atmosphere on campus had undergone a marked change since that day I departed for home during the wartime spring of 1943. The Champaign-Urbana campus seemed almost ready to burst at the seams. This bastion of higher learning was gearing up to meet the challenge of educating and housing the flood of returning veterans, all eager to get an education with the assistance of the G.I. Bill. The enormous number of veterans seeking entry astounded university and college administrators across the nation. Enrollment at the University of Illinois soared to 26,000 for the fall term in 1946. There were 11,000 veterans on the Champaign-Urbana campus with thousands more enrolled at temporary branches in Galesburg and at Navy Pier on Chicago's Lakefront. The University suspended housing requirements so that men could live wherever they could find a room, an attic, or a basement in the area. Many small war surplus prefabricated dwellings were moved in for married students.

In January of 1949 I graduated with a Bachelor of Science degree in Agriculture *Summa cum Laude* with University Honors and entered a purebred livestock and farming partnership with my father.

The entire 11th Airborne Division returned to the U.S. in May of 1949 after four years of occupation duty. On Sept. 1, 1950, the 187th was broken out of the division and ordered to Korea. The only paratroop unit to serve in the Korean conflict, the 187th Regimental Combat Team made two combat jumps and was awarded two Presidential Unit Citations, one honoring E Company: "Company E, 187th Airborne Infantry Regiment is cited for outstanding performance of duty and extraordinary heroism against the armed enemy in the vicinity of Wonju, Korea on 14 February 1951. Company E was assigned the mission of repulsing a Chinese Communist force [of battalion size] which had overrun elements of the United Nations regiment. First and third platoons closed on the enemy in hand-to-hand combat, the enemy suffering appalling casualties was forced to fall back in disorder..." E Company killed 442 Chinese soldiers in the attack but 61 of the paratroopers died in the battle and many more were wounded.

After the Korean War the 187th was made a component of the 101st Airborne, a division that had achieved fame in WW II for the jump into Normandy and for the heroic stand at Bastogne during the Battle of the Bulge. The weapons platoon of Company E, 187th was assigned a new West Pointer in early 1957. Lt. H. Norman Schwarzkopf, upon graduation from the Military Academy had attended the Ft.Benning Infantry and Paratroop Schools, then asked for assignment to the 101st which had recently been designated the first "Pentomic Division." He was assigned to that division's 2nd Battle Group. The group's commander had requested Schwarzkopf under the impression that big Norman was a football player who could be added to the sizeable stable of athletes the battle group already had on special duty. Disappointed that he was not getting a football star, he assigned Schwarzkopf to Company E of the 187th. The new lieutenant was put in charge of the weapons platoon where Petersen and I had served during WW II. Schwarzkopf apparently soon discovered that the army wasn't exactly as he had envisioned it while a cadet at West Point. In June 1959, after an enlightening tour of duty with the 187th, Schwarzkopf left Ft. Campbell, Kentucky and the airborne for an assignment in Berlin.

In the 1960s a battle group of the 187th was deployed to Lebanon as part of a peacekeeping force. During the Viet Nam War, the 3rd Battalion, serving with the 101st Airborne Division, was in action once again, notably during the bloody battle for Ap Bia Mountain, better known as "Hamburger Hill." In the 1990's as the 3rd Brigade of the 101st, the 187th conducted the longest helicopter assault in military history during the Persian Gulf War. The "Rakkasans" were next stationed at Ft. Campbell, Kentucky as a part of the rapid deployment Force. In 2002 the brigade is in Afghanistan, air assaulting the Taliban in their mountain strongholds.

Gen. Swing retired from the Army in 1954. Shortly thereafter his former West Point classmate, President Dwight D. Eisenhower, appointed him U.S. Commissioner of Immigration and Naturalization. Nate Ewing, wartime commander of the 2nd Bn, 187th, was appointed Deputy Commissioner. "Jumping Joe" Swing died in 1984 at the age of 90. Gen. George Pearson, commander of the 187th during the battle for southern Luzon, died in 1998 at the age of 94.

Ten years after the war I drove through the Southwest on my way to California. I stopped in Wichita for a few days to visit Gene Walker and his family. Continuing on my way, I arrived in Albuquerque about mid-morning and decided to see if I could contact Tony. There was no Tony Turietta in the phone book so I dialed the first Turietta listed. A member of Tony's family answered. She told me that Tony was dead. It was a sad story. Shortly after Tony returned from the war, a blood enemy of the family had accosted and humiliated him in a public bar. Tony had procured a gun, returned to the bar, shot the man, then gone to a remote canyon and shot himself.

In 1976 I unintentionally broke my 1944 vow to never again visit the fair city of Temple, Texas. My wife, daughter, and I were on our way to Padre Island on the south Texas Gulf Coast for a winter vacation. We had not made reservations ahead; we were just rolling along until we were tired. Spotting a Holiday Inn ahead, we wheeled in. I discovered that we were on the outskirts of Temple. As I registered, the desk clerk, noting my Illinois address, remarked, "You should go out to Fort Hood. It's quite a place. "Yeah," I replied, " I know. I've been there."

Bibliography and References

From the vast array of books on World War II, here are a few of the many that I found interesting and informative:

The Angels: A History of the 11th Airborne Division, by Major Edward M. Flanagan, Jr (Infantry Journal Press, Washington DC 1948)—for obvious reasons.

Dear General (a collection of the wartime letters of Gen. Swing to his father-in-law, Gen. March), published in 1987 by Swing's daughter, Mary Ann Swing Fullilove, gives insight into the General's problems and thoughts as he leads the 11th Airborne Division through the Philippine Campaign.

The Years of MacArthur, Clayton James (Houghton Mifflin, Boston 1975) and William Manchester's *American Caesar (*Little, Brown and Co., Boston 1978) are the definitive biographies of that fascinating enigma who may well have been the most gifted general America has produced.

Each biography contains an excellent account of the campaigns in the Philippines.

John Keegan's *The Second World War* (Viking Penguin NY 1990) presents broad coverage of the conflict.

For a comprehensive global history of World War II, *A World at Arms* (Cambridge University Press, NY 1994) by Gerhard L. Weinberg is excellent.

Memoirs by Harry S Truman, Vol. I Year of Decisions (Doubleday, Garden City, NY 1955) covers the critical first year of the Truman administration.

Theres A War To Be Won, Geoffrey Perret (Random House, NY 1991) offers a lively and readable history of the U.S.Army in World War II.

Eagle Against the Sun (Free Press, NY 1984) by Ronald Spector is a concise, thoughtful, and well-written account of the Pacific War.

War in the Pacific (Military Press, NY 1990) by Clark G. Reynolds includes a vivid portrayal of the naval war and the great carrier battles.

Battle for Batangas (Yale University Press, New Haven 1991) by Glenn Anthony Wayne is a fascinating account of the Philippine-American War of 1899-1902 in Southern Luzon and the effect it had on the Filipino population and the American invaders.

The Battle for Manila (Presidio Press, Novato, CA 1995) details the tragic struggle that cost the lives of 100,000 Filipinos and destroyed a beautiful city.

For a complete history of the Philippine Islands from the landing by Magellan in 1521 to the present era, Stanley Karnow's *In Our Image* (Random House, NY 1990) is outstanding.

The trials and tribulations of infantrymen in combat are covered from varying perspectives by:

Stephen E. Ambrose in *Citizen Soldiers* (Simon and Schuster, NY 1997), a gripping account of the ground war in Western Europe as experienced by the men on the battle-lines.

By Gerald F. Linderman, who in *The World Within War* (Free Press, NY 1997) attempts—with considerable success—to view battle experiences through the eyes of American combat soldiers and Marines.

And by that premier infantryman's advocate, Bill Mauldin, who in *Up Front* (Henry Holt and Company, NY 1945) produced a work that will never cease to bring back memories—good and bad—to any reader who once upon a time dug a foxhole in a far-off battlefield.

Haruko Taya Cook and Theodore F. Cook's *Japan at War: An Oral History* (New Press, NY 1992) records the remarkable, sometimes chilling, personal narratives of Japanese individuals, military and civilian, during and after the war.

Blankets of Fire (Smithsonian Institution Press, Washington DC 1996) by Kenneth P. Werell documents the bombing of Japan.

For anyone who would seek to understand the sequence of events that led to the surrender of Japan in August of 1945, Richard B. Frank's definitive book, *DOWNFALL:The End of the Imperial Japanese Empire* (Random House, NY 1999) should be required reading. Frank worked with primary documents, reports, diaries, and newly declassified records to present the untold story of the final months of the war when American leaders discovered a massive buildup by the Japanese military on Kyushu, a buildup that was designed to turn the initial invasion of the Japanese home islands into a bloody shambles.

DOWNFALL replaces the myths that surround the end of the war and the use of the A-bomb with the stark realities of this great historical controversy. Frank establishes the undeniable fact that the use of the atomic bomb was the best of all existing alternatives and in fact saved many Japanese lives.

The Fall of Japan (Galahad Books, NY 1967) by Craig Williams is a concise account of the last days of the war.

John W. Dower's *Embracing Defeat: Japan in the Wake of World War II* (W.W.Norton and Co., NY 1999) is a thorough treatment of Japanese politics, society, and culture during the days and years of the occupation.

The Rise and Fall of the Great Powers—1500-2000 (Random House, NY 1987) by Paul Kennedy contains interesting observations and statistics regarding World War II as well as much food for thought for Americans and their leaders in today's world.